THE CRAFT OF STONE BREWING CO.

THE CRAFT OF STONE BREWING CO.

LIQUID LORE, EPIC RECIPES, AND UNABASHED ARROGANCE

GREG KOCH AND STEVE WAGNER WITH RANDY CLEMENS

PHOTOGRAPHY BY STUDIO SCHULZ

TEN SPEED PRESS
Berkeley

CONTENTS

INTRODUCTION

Howdy. Greg here, with a story to share. And as you'll note on the cover, right beside my name is that of my good friend and business partner for over fifteen years now, Mr. Steve Wagner. And, if you know anything about us other than the fact that we like (and make) great beer, it's that I'm sort of the loud (some might even say "outspoken") voice of the operation, while Steve has been the more quiet (some might even say "reserved") voice that is just as happy to let the beer speak for him. While this story is just as much his as it is mine, I guess I like the sound of my own voice more than Steve likes his. That being said, why don't I start?

So, we're a brewery. Why would we want to write a book? What makes our tale different or more interesting than the stories of mega breweries? Well, we're a *craft* brewery, and that unquestionably adds interest. I mean, we get to be creative and inventive, have fun, and make tasty beer without being brought down by some marketing department's focus group-driven ideas about what beer some random sampling of the populace thinks that perhaps they might think that others might think they might want. Wait, what? Hell, I barely understood what I just said there, so you can imagine my level of interest in any conclusions that might come out of interpreting the key matrices of the core objectives when overlaid with extrapolated bell curves and consumer acceptance coefficients. The truth is, I have no idea what I just said there, either. The closest I get to that whole world of data analysis world is reading *Dilbert*, which is plenty close enough. But I digress.

I was heading toward telling you why I thought a book about the Stone Brewing Co. story might be a good idea—worthwhile or, hopefully, at least not boring. And that reason is . . . drum roll, please . . . that I wanted to share the very simple idea that doing it our way is better. And by "our way" I really mean "your way." No, we don't do it *your* way—you do. *We* do it *our* way. Huh? Okay, maybe it's best to put it into the third person: What I mean is, I believe that things are almost universally better when people do something the way they think it should be done—the way they truly think is the best way.

The caveat is—and this is a pretty fundamental one—that you have to be good at what you want to do. For those of us at Stone Brewing Co., it's brewing tasty beer in our own particular style, and conducting our business in ways that have respected our personal and collective goals to do better—not John Q. Public's version of better, but our version of better. The beauty of this philosophy is that you don't have to agree. You can think that what we do is odd, too different, not good, or just plain awful. That's all okay, because if you don't like what we do, the reasons that we should pay attention to what you think are reduced, rather than increased. If you don't care for what we do and how we do it, then you're not our customer. And if you're not our customer, we don't need to fashion ourselves to your personal tastes. In fact, we shouldn't. If we did, it's questionable whether we'd make a loyal customer out of you, and we'd almost definitely alienate our customers that have been loyal.

I'll turn it around the other way. If you do something that you're quite good at and you're doing it your way (after all, it's always helpful to be unique AND good, rather than just unique or just good), then it's simply up to me, as your potential customer, to decide for myself whether or not I like what you do. If I do, then I've just discovered that finally someone is doing (insert whatever it is that you do or make) it in a way that gets me excited. I'm thrilled that you've learned to do what you do so well, and that you're doing it in a way that's unique and special. On the other hand, if I don't like what you do, then I can move on. Sure, I might decide that I'm so self-important that the best possible thing I could do for you is explain how much better it would be if you'd do what you do the way I think you should do it. But if you're smart, you'll file my comments along with those of all the other tens, hundreds, or thousands of people who have offered up their "invaluable" advice in that special filing system—you know, the round one that's under your desk or in the corner (hopefully with the word "Recycling" on it).

Now I'm not one to say that all advice or perspectives from others is bad. Far from it. So how do you separate the barley from the chaff? It's simple: Does the advice support your vision, or does it attempt to derail it? If the former, lean in. And that, in its own way, is what this book is about. Think about our story as providing a supporting context for your vision, whatever that may be—as long as it's good and you're good at it (or at least on your way to getting there).

The idea for this book has been fermenting for quite some time. I'm often invited to give talks at local universities or for a variety of business groups, and I enjoy the heck out of it. It's fun sharing the story of our unique brand of success, and I like advocating the "do it your way" philosophy. Folks love asking all kinds of questions about our business philosophy and why we've been such a fast-growing company for so long, and, of course, they love to ask all kinds of questions about beer.

I've also enjoyed keeping records of our journey over the years, in the form of photos, old notes, video blogs, beer bottles, other memorabilia, and so on. Gathering all of that stuff is sort of like scrapbooking, but for a business. But there's a challenge: while I love collecting all that stuff, I'm too damn busy to do anything other than . . . collect. Of course, if I truly wanted to spend time going through everything, I'd find the time. I can't stand it, though; I prefer to look forward. Every time I go looking for an old photo, it takes way too long and I get way too impatient.

So what's a would-be writer to do? Find a coauthor, of course. But that wasn't a natural inclination for me. I'm a do-it-yourselfer, especially when it's something I know I can do—or at least think I can do. No way am I going to farm it out. That seems like a form of cheating.

And then along comes this character by the name of Randy Clemens. I think I'd met him a time or two at some random beer event here or there, but it's hard to say. I've become an expert in not recognizing people at beer events. It's more the number of people than the beer, but the beer definitely plays an assist in the "sorry I don't recall" factor. But again, I digress.

So, Randy sent me an email and said (Randy, my searches on this computer won't go back far enough. Insert the relevant sentence you used in the original email you sent me.)

"Greg, I can't just distill it down to one relevant sentence; it was a string of . . . of . . . brilliant . . . yes, that's it, *brilliant* thoughts that I'd entitled 'A Modest Proposal.' And they were ever so carefully pieced together ~~at 3 a.m. one strange night~~ over the course of months, or maybe years! There's no way I could possibly compact all that genius into one paltry sentence for the purpose of this introduction. But I guess if you *really* need me to, I was basically saying I wanted to write an epic tome about Stone. I said it way cooler than that though, I promise. Anyway, Greg, you were saying?" —RANDY

Right. Thanks . . . I think. Well, at first I wasn't so sure about the idea. Yes, I wanted to write a book, but no, I didn't think I wanted a writing partner. However, Randy's timing was excellent. Plus, he had a winning combination of being a Stone fan, being an experienced writer, and, unlike me, having the patience to rehash all that Stone has done and accomplished over the last fifteen years. Randy was actually excited about the prospect of digging into our history and uncovering nuggets from the past—a perfect job for an impassioned outsider, who could look at everything from a fresh perspective, rather than filtered through my lens. (Take one look at any of my early video blogs, and you can see that I'm a lousy self-editor.) On top of all of that, I had more projects on my plate than ever before, and I knew this book, a sort-of fifteenth anniversary retrospective, probably wasn't going to happen if it sat solely on my shoulders. Thus, the idea of working with a coauthor went from "no thanks" to "the only possible way to get it done" to "sounds like a great idea to me!" Coauthor? Sign me up.

So, what do I want you to get from this book? It occurs to me that this book may just wind up as a badass coffee table decoration. And the truth is, that's quite fine with me. (It's a damn good-looking book, isn't it?) Heck, maybe we should have put a circle or two on the cover as suggested places to set your beer when you aren't actively using the book. But ultimately, I hope that you, dear reader, will actually read this book, and get a glimpse into the fun we've had over the years at Stone—and that the next time you enjoy a Stone beer, or any great craft beer for that matter, it will be tastier as a result. I hope that our story of doing it our way bolsters your confidence to do the things you're interested in *your* way. If you're great at what you do, the world is a better place as a result. And I thank you for it. So will others.

PART ONE

THE NATURE OF BEER

Before we get into the story behind Stone Brewing Co. and fun facts about all of our beers, let's take a look at beer as a whole: what it is, how it's made, and its history. Put on your safety glasses and lab coat. (Simple reading glasses or a proverbial thinking cap would be acceptable alternatives.) At times, this discussion is a bit technical and the tone is somewhat serious, but it's good information, damn it! And, in the interest of making this a complete guide to beer, we figured it best to start this epic tome, well, at the start with the simplest of questions: what is beer?

WHAT IS BEER? (*NOT* A STUPID QUESTION!)

Beer is an alcoholic beverage that is most typically made with four basic ingredients: malted barley, hops, water, and yeast. You may wonder how so many different beers can be made using just these four ingredients. Let's consult Stone's head brewer Mitch Steele and ask him to explain the role that each of these ingredients plays in the final brew.

Malted Barley

"As the brewing saying goes, 'Malt is the soul of beer.' It provides the color, the body, the sweetness, and, perhaps most importantly, balances the flavor of our hops. (Not to mention that without malt, there would be no sugar for the yeast to ferment!) A good-quality malt is crucial to brewing good beer. We talk a lot about the 'backbone' of our beer being the malt component. A good malt blend, with the right (balanced) amount of flavor, sweetness, and body, provides the foundation for every one of our beers." —MITCH

ALREADY AN EXPERT? Feel free to skim through this section or even jump ahead to **A Story Called Stone** on page 28 if you think you're so smart.

It's My Own Damn Malt

Hordeum vulgare, or barley to you and me, is the fourth most cultivated cereal grain in the world. It's used around the globe for making breads, soups, main courses, and salads, not to mention being a key ingredient in livestock feed. However, before it can be used to produce beer, it must undergo a simple process called malting, which involves soaking the grain until it begins to germinate, or sprout, releasing enzymes that begin to convert the starches in the barley into smaller-chain sugars—sugars that yeast can convert into alcohol and carbon dioxide.

VARIETY	PROFILE
Pale malt	As the name implies, pale malt is a light-colored variety. It's used primarily as a base malt for ales, providing body and sugars but not necessarily a heavy dosing of flavor. Varieties grown in North America, the United Kindgom, and Belgium have subtle differences and are typically used in each respective country's popular beer styles.
Pilsner malt	Pilsner malt is another base malt and is typically used in lagers, especially (you guessed it) pilsners.
Crystal malt	Also known as caramel malt, crystal malt is a style of pale malt rich with dextrins (sugars that are too complex to be broken down by the yeast during fermentation), which lends a fuller body and mouthfeel to the finished beer. Crystal malt can be roasted to many different darkness levels, denoted by its degree Lovibond (L), which can range from 2L to 500L (with higher numbers signifying a darker roast), each producing a different flavor profile.
Vienna malt	Vienna malt is a light golden or orange malt that imparts a full, rich body and a touch of grainy flavors to the finished brew.
Munich malt	Munich malt is a rich and complex malt that contributes a sweet malty flavor and an amber-red tinge.
Carapils	Carapils is brimming with dextrins, which add to the beer's body and help with head retention. Its name is a portmanteau of **cara**mel **pils**ner malt.
Caravienne	Caravienne, as you may have guessed, is a **cara**mel version of **Vienna** malt. Beyond the qualities imparted by the dextrins present in all caramel/crystal malts, caravienne contributes a nutty, slightly sweet flavor.
Caramunich	Yep, this is a **cara**mel version of **Munich** malt. Hey, you're catching on quickly! It imparts the same reddish color and sweet roasty flavors as Munich, but with the telltale dextrins of caramel malt.
Chocolate malt	This dark, roasty malt, which imparts a deep reddish brown hue to the brew, is used in porters and stouts, among others. Some malty sweetness is retained, in addition to notes of caramel and, yes, chocolate.
Black malt	Black malt (sometimes called black patent malt) contributes intense roasty, smoky flavors, often redolent of coffee. It's used sparingly and, as you may have guessed, lends a healthy dose of color to the pot.
Roasted barley	Roasted barley is actually unmalted barley that's subjected to high heat until nearly black. It produces telltale smoky chocolate and burnt coffee flavors in the beer.
Wheat malt	Wheat malt is similar to pale malt, barring the fact that they are made from different grains entirely. Wheat malt aids greatly with head retention and can add crisp, grainy flavor to the beer.
Rye malt	**Rye malt** is used to add a spicy, peppery, slightly fruity profile to beer. It is notoriously difficult to brew with, but it adds flavors that can't be replicated by anything else. **Flaked rye** hasn't been malted and isn't as potent.
Flaked oats	**Flaked oats** provide a creamy, almost buttery mouthfeel to beer. Not to be confused with **oat malt**, which yields a sweet, grainy profile.

You're Not the Only One Getting Toasted

Okay, so you've got a ton of barley soaking in water, with enzymatic reactions abounding, but you've got to put a stop to the fun eventually. Once the sprout, or acrospire, has grown to 75 to 100 percent of the length of the grain, the barley is said to be fully modified. At this point, it's quickly kiln-dried with hot air, which halts the starch-to-sugar conversions, stops the sprout from developing into a full-on seedling ready to plant in the ground, and produces dried kernels of malted barley.

Lighter and darker styles of malt are produced by variations in the temperature at which the malt is dried and the length of time it's heated. Lighter malts with higher levels of fermentable sugars and more enzymatic activity (pale malt and pilsner malt being two of the most common) are referred to as base malts and make up the majority of the grain bill called for in any given brew. Other varieties, called specialty malts, are used more for flavor than yeast fuel.

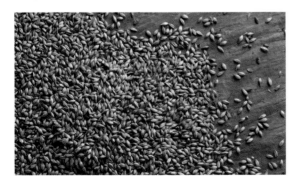

Lighter roasts in which the sugars in the kernel have begun to crystallize, such as crystal and Vienna malts, often impart notes of caramel, biscuits, toffee, and bread, among others. Further roasting at higher temperatures produces darker malts, such as chocolate malt or black malt, which, added sparingly, can contribute robust flavors similar to coffee and chocolate, adding complexity and a touch of roasty bitterness.

The brewer's selection of malts is the keystone for any quality beer, as it affects not just the flavor of the beer, but also the aroma, the color, and the all-so-important mouthfeel. The following table outlines some of the malt varieties most commonly used in craft brewing, along with all of the varieties called for in the homebrew recipes later in the book.

Let's Get Cereal

Other cereal grains can also be used to make beer, though barley typically makes up the majority of the base with other grains added in smaller amounts. Wheat, rye, and oats find their way into some brews to contribute flavor and mouthfeel. The megabrewers use a lot of corn and rice to create their fizzy yellow stuff, since neither grain contributes any real discernable flavor, *and* they cost a fraction of what barley does. Bonus! (Well, for them at least. What they gain in cost savings, we lose in taste.)

Hops

" Hops are often called the spice of beer, as they contribute bitterness, flavor, and aroma to beer. There are literally hundreds of different varieties of hops available to brewers, and each can contribute unique flavors, aromas, and bitterness. Several of our beers are identified with a particular variety of hops. For example, Stone IPA is most identified with Centennial hops, one of our favorites. A signature hop flavor is what craft beer lovers often seek when they try new beers.

I get really excited when we have the opportunity to use a variety of hops that we haven't used before. We've had some fun with one-time brewing projects using varieties such as Nelson Sauvin and Motueka (from New Zealand) and Sorachi Ace (from Japan). That said, I'm a huge fan of classic hop varieties, like Saaz and Hallertau, which we don't have much opportunity to brew with here at Stone, and also East Kent Goldings, which we've used a bit in our Stone Old Guardian Barley Wine. I tend to gravitate toward hop varieties that have unique flavor attributes, and we have fun trying to capture those flavors in our beers. " —MITCH

Hopping Mad

Hops are the cone-shaped flower of the perennial plant *Humulus lupulus*. They're very rich in resins, alpha acids, and oils that produce a veritable treasure chest of flavors and aromas familiar to anyone who has ever tasted an India pale ale or any type of "imperial" fill-in-the-blank. They can impart essences that are often redolent of citrus, spices, flowers, or grass, or they can exhibit piney, earthy, or woodsy notes.

Hops were probably originally added to beer for medicinal purposes, then later were found to extend shelf life, a very important factor historically speaking, since transoceanic voyages by boat lasted months and beer was a vital source of nutrition and clean drinking water, not to mention a way to unwind during a very long and possibly trying voyage. (It would have to be a pretty crazy ride for someone to confuse a manatee or dugong for a mermaid, wouldn't you think?)

As mentioned, hops add an element of bitterness to beer that balances the sweet profile of the malt. However, since a growing number of imbibers are gravitating toward bigger, bolder, and hoppier beers, the argument can certainly be made that the roles have changed and malt is being used to balance the hops. At least that tends to be how we view it at Stone Brewing.

MITCH: Dry hopping lends a much different character than simply adding the hops during the boil. It's a great technique for really getting the essence of hops into your beer. Fermentation can scrub out some of the delicate hop flavors that were obtained during the brewing process; dry hopping allows the brewer to recapture and enhance that flavor intensity.

Hour of Flower Power

Hops are traditionally added at three stages during the boiling process that all beers go through. (More on that later.) First added are the bittering hops, which, as their name implies, add the crisp bitterness and graceful bite found in many styles of beer, from pilsners to IPAs. Longer boiling time is critical for bittering hops—typically an hour to an hour and a half, although sometimes longer. During this time, certain otherwise insoluble compounds called alpha acids go through isomerization, a process that makes them soluble so they can lend their unique character to the final brew.

In contrast to the bittering components of hops, their aroma and flavor components are extremely volatile, so they evaporate during a long boil. For this reason, aroma hops and flavoring hops are typically added near the end of the boil: flavoring hops in the last ten to twenty minutes, and aroma hops in the final three minutes), to preserve their full sensory potential.

HOP MYTH DEBUNK DEPARTMENT: Perhaps you've heard the ridiculous slogans that mega-brewers came up with to try to sound "craft," for example, playing up that their beer is "triple hops brewed." It makes us want to slap a newly-minted marketing MBA's professor. To suggest that adding hops at two or three different times during the brewing process is unique to those beers makes them sound silly (if not uninformed).

Another popular method for boosting hop flavor and aroma is dry hopping, a simple procedure that allows the brewer to add hops to the beer after it has cooled and most, if not all, of the fermentation has completed. A nice long soak, ranging anywhere from a few days up to two weeks, allows the beer to draw essential oils from the flowers without fear of losing their amazing volatile aromas, since no heating is taking place.

Wet hopping may sound vaguely related, or reminiscent of some sort of bitter rivalry, but it actually refers to a completely different process. Sometimes called fresh hopping, it's simply the use of just-picked hop cones, directly from the vine rather than dried. These wet hops can be incorporated at any stage of the brew, including—believe it or not—for dry hopping. (What? Dry wet hopping? Wet dry hopping? Huh?)

What's in a Name?

You'll sometimes see the varieties of hops used in the craft beer you're drinking listed on the bottle, but what's the difference between them, and why should you care? The chart on pages 12 and 13 shows some of the varieties of hops most often used in craft brewing, along with a selection of the varieties called for in the homebrew recipes later in the book. Note that alpha acid content can vary from region to region and season to season; the values listed are approximations.

IBUs and You

So, how do you know how hoppy a beer is going to be? Well, beyond the clever names that sometimes warn (or entice) you about the palate wrecking you're about to receive, some brewers also alert you to the IBU count of their beers. IBUs—International Bittering Units, that is—are a measure of the bitterness in beer, with each IBU equating to 1 milligram of isomerized alpha acids per liter of beer. While IBUs can be used as a rough guide in gauging how bitter a beer will be, it does not take into account how much malt is used in the beer.

Case in point: Stone Imperial Russian Stout runs around 90 IBUs, while Stone IPA hangs out at 77. Even though the Stout has more IBUs, it also uses quite a bit more malt and alcohol to balance them, and thus the apparent bitterness will be less on your palate. Remember, IBUs are a measure of isomerized alpha acids *per liter* of beer. And the amount of malt you can use per liter ranges greatly between styles. So, while IBUs are accurate at quantifying bittering compounds in said liter of beer, it can't really predict how our tongues will perceive them.

MITCH: In many ways our beers are a showcase for American hops. Stone Levitation Ale is dry hopped with 100 percent Amarillo hops, and Stone Sublimely Self-Righteous Ale features a blend of Amarillo and Simcoe in the dry hop. We find exploring new and different hop varieties inspiring and look forward to trying many new varieties, primarily in our special release and collaboration beers. If I had to choose, I'd say my favorite is Centennial. I love the lemon zest flavor it adds to beer when used as a dry hop, and its bitterness quality is very pure.

VARIETY	ALPHA ACIDS	PROFILE
Ahtanum	5–7%	Ahtanum is a dual purpose hop used for its citrusy floral aroma as well as its moderate bittering properties.
Amarillo	7–10%	Amarillo, used primarily for flavor and aroma, is grown in Washington State. Its calling card is a telltale aroma of oranges and spice, making it a popular choice for dry hopping.
Brewer's Gold	7–11%	A British hop used primarily for bittering, it can also impart spicy notes and a hint of cassis.
Cascade	4–7%	This popular American cultivar has a distinctive grapefruit aroma and flavor. Cascade, Centennial, and Columbus are commonly referred to as the three Cs of American hop varieties.
Centennial	8–12%	Sometimes referred to as a Super Cascade, Centennial brings a similar citrus aroma but can be slightly less floral and have a touch more bitterness.
Challenger	6–9%	Challenger is an English hop variety similar in character to Northern Brewer that is used for bittering, and for its spicy tangerine character.
Chinook	11–14%	Although Chinook is primarily used for its bittering qualities, it can also contribute an herbal, spicy, and piney flavor and aroma profile.
Citra	10–13%	Citra is a newer variety on the market, and is a hybrid of many different German, American, and English hops. As its name implies, the flavor and aroma is very citrus-heavy, complemented by notes of tropical fruit.
Columbus	12–16%	Also marketed as Tomahawk, Columbus is an American dual-purpose hop. Often used for bittering because of its high alpha acid content, it can also be added later in the boil for a citrusy, slightly woody touch.
Fuggles	3–6%	Mildly earthy, spicy, and woody nuances give this English hop almost universal appeal. It has also been widely grown outside of England with great success.
Galena	11–14%	Galena is the most widely planted domestic bittering hop. Despite its high alpha acid content, it is relatively subdued and plays well with other varieties.

Water

" The claim can be made that water quality historically drove the development of different beer styles. These days, technically advanced analytical tools allow us to make adjustments to emulate any water profile, so we can brew any style of beer. However, there are two qualities any water used for brewing should have: it must be clean and potable, and it should have a neutral flavor. We taste our water every day to make sure it fits our requirements for brewing. " —MITCH

Chemistry?! But This Is a Beer Book!

Of the four basic beer ingredients (malt, hops, water, and yeast), it might seem like water would have the least impact on the flavor of the final product, but ask any brewer and you'll hear a very different story. Mineral content, pH levels, dissolved solids, and all sorts of other terminology come into play. So even though this is a beer book, we need to discuss some chemistry.

Did you dread high school chemistry class? Maybe you had a terrible teacher who was so deluded by overblown visions of his own self-importance that he didn't realize that his students just weren't getting it?

VARIETY	ALPHA ACIDS	PROFILE
Goldings	4–6%	A widely grown English aroma varietal with specific names depending on the area in which it's cultivated—East Kent Goldings were grown in East Kent, Petham Goldings in Petham, and so on. (However, Styrian Goldings is thought to be misnomer, instead being a variety of Fuggles.)
Hallertau	3–6%	Hallertau is actually a premier German hop-growing region. Hops labeled simply "Hallertau" are usually of the Hallertauer Mittelfrüh variety, classically associated with crisp German lagers.
Magnum	13–15%	Developed in Germany as a variation on Galena, Magnum adds a wollop of bitterness without introducing a lot of flavor.
Northern Brewer	7–10%	An English hop used mainly for bittering, it can also be added for fruity and earthy aromas and flavors.
Saaz	3–5%	Saaz is a classic Bohemian hop used widely in and around the Czech Republic (where it is called Zatec). Its subtle spicy flavors and earthy notes make it ideal for pale lagers and true pilsners.
Simcoe	12–14%	A domestic hop primarily used for bittering, Simcoe is also well regarded for its piney, woodsy bouquet.
Tettnang	3–5%	Tettnang is another German hop-growing region, but the name is also commonly used as a shorter version of the hops variety Tettnang Tettnanger. Used widely in lagers and wheat beers, it is prized for its floral, spicy characteristics.
Warrior	15–18%	An excellent domestic hop variety offering very high alpha acid levels and a clean, crisp bitterness.
Willamette	4–6%	Named for the Willamette Valley in the Pacific Northwest, this is an American version of the popular English Fuggles, with similar earthy notes but slightly more floral and grassy.

(Little did he know that one of those confused pupils would someday co-author a book and subliminally call him out on it.) But hey, I'm not bitter! (Except when it comes to beer, and then I'm very, very bitter!)

Anyway, fret not! We'll make it through this basic chemistry lesson together, and I promise to present the material in a clear, friendly, and interesting manner—the way we all should have learned it in the first place.

H₂O Yeah!

Pure H_2O, with a completely neutral pH of 7 and devoid of minerals, doesn't exist in nature. It can be manufactured, as in the case of distilled water, but it isn't of much use to the brewer. Water's properties in the brewing process are influenced by the amount of minerals the water has picked up as it travels through soil or rock. The mineral profile adds subtle flavor nuances and gives the great beers of the world much of their character.

Have you ever foolishly paid extra for bottled water from some exotic island because your tap water tastes chalky? Have you ever had trouble getting soap to lather, or had that darn white buildup on your showerhead? These problems can be explained by high levels of minerals in your water, which can easily be filtered out. (Get an under-the-counter filter or one of those pitcher systems for your fridge already and stop buying all those wasteful plastic bottles!)

ION	AKA	AND I CARE BECAUSE . . . ?
Ca^{+2}	Calcium	Increases acidity, aids enzyme activity, and strengthens yeast cell walls. Improves the clarity and flavor of the final beer.
Mg^{+2}	Magnesium	An essential nutrient for yeast and important cofactor for some enzymes. Causes a harsh and astringent flavor when excessive.
Na^{+1}	Sodium	Accents the flavor of beer in low concentrations, but in excess can impart a salty or sour taste and impede yeast growth.
HCO_3^{-1}	Bicarbonate	A strong alkaline buffer that hinders increases in acidity. Preferable in beers where darker, more acidic malts are used. Can be bitter or astringent in excess, and can leach harsh tannins from grain.
SO_4^{+2}	Sulfate	Promotes a drier, fuller finish and accents bitter compounds extracted from grain and hops.
Cl^{-1}	Chloride	Improves the clarity of the beer and lightly enhances flavor and fullness. Can contribute slight salty notes or, in maltier brews, increase the sensation of sweetness.

MITCH: Our water is from Rincon del Diablo Municipal Water District. It is basically Colorado River Water, and is somewhat hard. When it comes into the brewery, we run it through a carbon filter to remove the chlorine and any other off flavors. Next, we run a portion of the water through a reverse osmosis filtration system, and then blend the two streams back together, yielding a moderately soft water that's great for brewing a lot of different styles of beer with varying hop levels and virtually any type of malt.

I've Got My Ion You

Many minerals exist in water, but only six are of major concern to our friend at the brew kettle. They occur in the form of ions—atoms or molecules with a positive or negative charge—that form once the mineral is dissolved. Monitoring levels of these ions is crucial to a successful batch of beer. Water with a higher mineral content is referred to as hard water, whereas water with a lower mineral content is called soft water. Neither soft water nor hard water is universally advantageous for making beer; it is just another factor that brewers must take into account and adjust for depending on the style of beer being brewed.

Brewers must also filter or boil out the chlorine that's added by most municipal water facilities. Chlorine reacts with the grains to create off-flavors described as "medicinal" or bearing a strong resemblance to the smell of bandages.

Think Globally, Act Locally

Historically, long-established brewing cities have adapted to their water supplies, since, until the advent

YEAST OF BURDEN: At Stone, our yeast cells are the most dedicated and tireless of all our employees. Consider the fact that they do their work 24/7 until finished, with their only pay being a little malt sugar. So what do we do with them when they're done? Dump 'em unceremoniously down the drain? Heck no! We put 'em right back to work on a fresh batch of wort!

of reverse osmosis filtration, they really didn't have much of a choice. Plzen, birthplace of the Pilsner, is home to remarkably soft water, which naturally lends itself to the style.

Conversely, Dublin's water is quite high in bicarbonates, which are alkaline, so it takes a heavy hand with high-acid dark, roasted malts to balance them out, which explains Dubliners' affinity for making opaque dry stouts. Munich's darker dunkel and bock beers also owe a nod to the bicarbonate levels of their water. The sharply bitter India Pale Ale owes its success to the high-sulfate well water of Britain's Burton-on-Trent.

Modern brewers, empowered with this knowledge and special equipment, are able to filter out much of what they deem undesirable and add in minerals as they wish, making it possible to brew a very diverse range of styles of beer at the same location.

Yeast

" Yeast is the unsung hero of beer flavor. Yeast wasn't even identified as a living organism until 1857, but as early as the Middle Ages it was understood to be a necessary ingredient to ensure complete transformation from a syrupy sweet malty liquid called wort (pronounced *wert*) to beer. Before yeast was identified as a living organism, it was known by brewers as 'God is good.' They knew it was a something, but in absence of a firm scientific explanation, it was assumed to be a divine something. " —MITCH

While we now know that yeast is what gives beer both its alcohol and those beloved CO_2 bubbles, many people still don't understood the overwhelming influence yeast has on beer flavor. It's true that malt and hops tend to make up a large percentage of a beer's flavor profile, but the fact is, they also make up the flavor profile of the wort. Yeast is the wonderful (and maybe even divine) ingredient that plays such a huge role in making beer taste more like beer, and less like . . . wort.

STEVE: We got our yeast strain from a now-defunct Canadian microbrewery. A brewery in the Northwest U.S. (that shall remain nameless) was using it when I was living up that way and I really liked its properties—I thought it would be a great fit for the beers Greg and I had talked about making.

When we first moved down to San Diego, we brewed a few test batches with some yeast that Pizza Port let us have, but when it was time to get our own yeast strain going, I had my friend Jeff fly down with a batch of it from Oregon.

So, there he was at the airport with this huge keg filled with liquid yeast. He was checking it as luggage, and the attendant told him it was over the weight limit. So, he wheeled the keg into a stall in the men's bathroom, attached the fittings, and drained some of the yeast out. It wasn't a clean job though; the yeast had sprayed on the walls and around the seat and pretty much everywhere. I don't know if you've ever seen a liquid yeast culture, but it's not a pretty shade of brown. And, considering the fact that it was splattered over a large portion of a bathroom stall, I guarantee the poor janitor that discovered it didn't think it was yeast that made that Jackson Pollock.

So, unsung hero of the custodial arts, if you're out there reading this, please take it as our sincerest apology, and know that your work was not in vain! Our keg ended up under the weight limit and made it to San Diego safely, rolling down the baggage claim conveyor to scores of laughter and applause. Its contents have served us—not to mention countless fans—quite well ever since. We owe you a beer!

Blowing Bubbles

While water comprises upwards of 90 percent of a beer, yeast constitutes but a small percentage of the formula, and it's filtered out after fermentation in many styles of beer. But even though the amount of yeast added might not look like much, there are usually between 30 million and 100 million yeast cells slaving away for our benefit in each teaspoon of freshly spiked wort.

Yeasts are introduced to feed on the sugars present in the malty wort and convert them into alcohol and carbon dioxide. While there are several different yeast strains of interest to the brewer, the two most common are *Saccharomyces cerevisiae* (*Saccharomyces* is derived from the Latin for "sugar fungus," and *cerevisiae* from the Latin for "beer" or "brewer"), and *Saccharomyces carlsbergensis* (named after Denmark's Carlsberg brewery, where this strain was first successfully isolated and identified).

Besides producing alcohol and carbonation, yeasts also synthesize a variety of flavors and aromas, ranging from good to bad to ugly. Bottle-conditioned beers, in which the yeast remains in a layer at the bottom of the bottle, also provide a host of B vitamins, amino acids, and minerals to the lucky imbiber.

MITCH: We keep our master culture banked at White Labs here in San Diego, and they grow it up for us whenever we request it. We typically order a new culture of our house yeast when we hit the sixth generation in our fermentations. Our goal is to not exceed eleven or twelve generations before replacing the old culture with a new one, and at our current rate, that works out to a new culture about every ten weeks.

For our special releases, we do use some different yeast strains. We typically get those from commercial yeast suppliers or other breweries, and we like to do trial brews with them first before selecting just the right one for full-size batches.

Yeast Inflection

Most commercial brews are inoculated with carefully selected strains of yeast propagated in laboratories that specialize in yeast culture. Certain varieties produce specific flavors, tolerate higher alcohol levels, or exhibit qualities desirable for particular beer styles.

Saccharomyces cerevisiae is often referred to as ale yeast or top-fermenting yeast, and as the latter nickname implies, it does its bubbly work at the top of the wort. It thrives in warmer temperatures and tends to produce fuller flavors that are often fruity or spicy in character. More robust strains may also produce fusel alcohols, which in excess carry a heavy solvent taste, but in proportionate quantities can add complexity and a slight warming effect to the palate, as found in stronger Belgian ales and imperial Russian stouts.

Saccharomyces carlsbergensis, often referred to as lager yeast or bottom-fermenting yeast, tends to prefer cooler temperatures. Lager yeasts typically make a negligible contribution to the flavor profile of the beer, resulting in a more neutral beverage (or neutered beverage, in the case of industrial lagers) with cleaner, crisper flavors. Lager strains may also produce nitrogen and sulfur compounds, which in proportionate amounts can increase fullness and roundness of flavor. One example is dimethyl sulfide (DMS), which at moderate levels can be desirable in lagers, but in excess has a characteristic taste of creamed corn.

ALE/LAGER MYTH DEBUNK DEPARTMENT: No matter what some of our state and/or federal legislators may want to suggest (in what could best be described as a failed attempt to redefine science), lagers are beers and ales are beers. Nonetheless, some state laws mandate that once the alcohol percentage crosses a particular threshold, it's no longer a "beer" and must be labeled as "ale" or "lager". Another headscratcher involves certain states requiring beers over a certain (arbitrary) alcohol percentage to be labeled as "ale" even if it is in fact a lager style. C'mon elected officials, don't try extra hard to make yourselves seem like you don't understand the fundamental truths of science and nature!

We Want the Funk

Outside the world of controlled *Saccharomyces* and other single yeast strains, there exists a small but growing list of brewers willing to subject their brews to whatever Mother Nature throws at them. Spontaneous fermentation, in which the wort is exposed to the environment in large, shallow, open vessels known as coolships, allows whatever microorganisms are present in the air to "infect" the wort. Leaving the fermentation up to airborne yeast can be risky business, but in breweries with a long tradition of making such beers, the house yeast strains wafting about are actually fairly dominant and do a good job of keeping out rogue yeasts and bacteria that would otherwise spoil our fair beverage.

These spontaneously fermented brews rely on symbiotic fermentation involving both yeast and bacteria. Yeast strains such as *Brettanomyces bruxellensis* or *Brettanomyces lambicus* ("Brett" for short) are often implicated as spoilage or contaminants in most beers and wines, but for lambics, gueuzes, Flemish reds, and certain other styles, they add a sensory layer that is, if nothing else, polarizing: you either love it or hate it. These strains produce barnyard flavors, usually described as being goaty or like a wet horse's blanket.

To make things more interesting, varieties of *Lactobacillus* and *Pediococcus* bacteria often drop by the party to produce lactic acid, which adds a touch of sour pucker to the sudsy science experiment. Fear not these "infections." As many beer enthusiasts know, when a deft brewer's hand is at work, the results can be deliciously sublime. What's more, these bacteria are of the same genera as the suddenly in-fashion probiotics found in yogurt, kefir, and kombucha. See? Not only is beer good, it can be good for you!

But what of the brewer who isn't feeling spontaneous? Not a problem. With the help of yeast labs, breweries now have access to these curious cultures, allowing their use in controlled fermentation and removing the risks associated with spontaneous fermentation.

The World Is Your Oyster

In addition to these four seemingly basic ingredients—malt, hops, water, and yeast—just about anything else that's fit to eat or drink can be thrown into the mix. From açai berries to Zinfandel grapes, you name it, someone has probably tried it. Herbs, spices, honey, fruit, vegetables, coffee, tea, chile peppers, roots, tree bark, flowers, oysters, unicorn tears … the possibilities are nearly endless. The creativity of the brewer is the only real limiting factor when it comes to dreaming up a new brew. As to whether it's consumed, that relies first and foremost on a spirit of adventure on the part of the drinker.

HOW BEER IS MADE

Now that we've explored what four simple ingredients can do for us, it's time to take a look at how it all comes together. After all, you can't just throw barley, hops, water, and yeast into a bucket and wish for beer to materialize. (But wouldn't it be awesome if it worked that way!) It takes the illustrious and kinda quirky entity known as the brewing staff to transform these ingredients into the incredible beverage we all know and love so well.

At the Mill

A roller mill is employed to crack open the malted grains, making their sugars and starches much more accessible to the enzymes that will be working their magic once the grains take a swim in the brewing water. Though the grains' starches are of the greatest interest to the brewer, their fibrous husks aren't removed, since they're quite handy later in the brew, acting as a sort of natural filter during the sparge stage. (More on sparge shortly—and what is it with all these oddball brewing terms, anyway?)

It Was a Monster Mash!

Mashing is next in the lineup, in which brewers give the malt a little soak. The cracked grains (called the grist) are steeped in water that's been heated to a precise temperature, known as the strike temperature. All of this takes place in a large vessel called a mash tun, where the enzymes in the malt are activated and begin to convert the starches into sugars, which will later serve as food for the yeast and be converted into alcohol and carbon dioxide during fermentation.

Two Tuns of Fun

After a soak in the mash tun, the mash is transferred to a lauter tun, which essentially functions as a giant strainer. The husks from the grain settle at the base of the lauter tun, forming a natural filter bed that traps most of the solids while allowing the liquid to drain off. The liquid, rich with sugars developed during the mash, is the wort. The wort, which is relatively opaque and cloudy at first, is pumped back into the top of the lauter tun to further filter and clarify it.

The wort is then collected in a brew kettle, which is where, as the name implies, the brewing will ultimately take place. The layer of grain that remains at the bottom of the lauter tun is still holding on to a bit of sugar, which we certainly don't want to leave behind. That's future beer—we can't be wasting that!

So hot water is slowly drizzled over the grist, a process known as sparging, extracting any remaining sugars and maximizing the yield from the mash. What's left at this point is called spent grain, which can be used for mulch or compost, or sold to farmers for livestock feed. It can also be used in baking and soapmaking.

Fire Burn and Cauldron Bubble

Now that every possible bit of sugar has been extracted from the grain and into the wort, it's time for the boil. The wort is boiled vigorously in the brew kettle for an hour or more, which serves several purposes:

- Boiling sterilizes the wort to ensure that it's free of rogue yeasts or bacteria that could interfere with the flavor of the beer.
- It deactivates any remaining viable enzymes.
- Certain proteins that might otherwise cloud the final brew coagulate and precipitate out of the liquid, aiding in their removal prior to fermentation.
- Other proteins and amino acids undergo changes that allow for better head (foam) retention.
- As steam evaporates, the wort becomes more concentrated. Unsavory sulfur compounds that could lead to less than desirable flavors also evaporate out.
- Amino acids and sugars undergo the Maillard reaction, a complex chemical reaction that's only

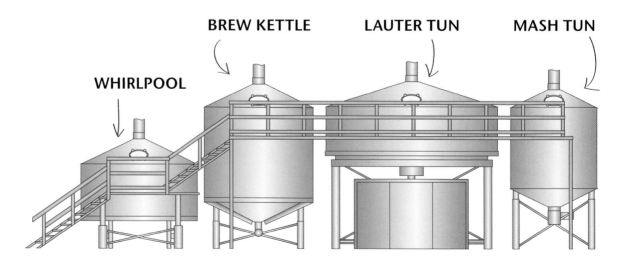

WHIRLPOOL　**BREW KETTLE**　**LAUTER TUN**　**MASH TUN**

BREWING STEP-BY-STEP	
Mashing	This is like a nice relaxing bath for your grains. The hot water activates enzymes, which convert the starches in the grain into sugars, which will later be digested by the yeast and turned into alcohol and carbon dioxide.
Lautering	Once the mash is complete, the liquid has to be drained off from the grain. This is done in a lauter tun, and the liquid that drains off is known as the wort.
Sparging	Hot water is sprinkled over the grain immediately after the lautering stage, extracting any sugars remaining in the grain that didn't drain off with the wort.
Boiling	Boiling the wort extracts bittering compounds from the hops, which also act as natural preservatives in the finished beer. Amino acids and sugars brown through Maillaird reactions (kind of like caramelization, but . . . different), contributing toasty flavors to the finished brew. Hops can also be added toward the end of the boil to capture their flavor and aroma without introducing much additional bitterness.
Cooling	The wort must be cooled quickly to minimize the chance of a rogue yeast or bacteria strain getting in and having a chance to propagate.
Pitching the Yeast	Once the wort has been chilled, the yeast is "pitched"—added in so it can begin multiplying and munching away at all the yummy sugars present.
Fermentation	Fermentation is vigorous as the yeast begin feasting on sugar, turning it into alcohol and carbon dioxide. Particulate also begins to drop out of suspension and sink to the bottom of the fermenter, helping to clarify the beer.
Bottling	Once fermentation is complete, the beer is bottled (or kegged) and left to carbonate before it can finally be enjoyed.

partially understood, leading to the development of roasty, toasty flavors.

- The hops are added at several stages during the boil: at the outset to contribute bittering components that double as a natural preservative, and near the end to impart their intoxicating aromas and flavors.

Hey, Cool It, Man!

After the long boil, the wort must be cooled fairly quickly. This helps reduce the chance that some random strain of yeast or bacteria will get into the brew and mess with its delicious formula. The hops are filtered out, and the wort is transferred from the brew kettle to a heat exchanger, where it is cooled from over 200°F to between 75 and 90°F as quickly as possible.

Batter Up

Once the wort is cooled, it's transferred to fermentation tanks. The yeast is pitched in and allowed to begin its work converting the sugars into alcohol and carbon dioxide (bless their little hearts!). Once the fermentation is complete (when the yeast has converted the available sugar into alcohol), usually after a few weeks, the fermentation tanks are chilled to near freezing, which causes the yeast cells to flocculate—in other words, cluster together and sink down to the bottom of the tank.

Then the beer is drained off, leaving the yeast behind. It's filtered and stored in bright tanks until it's ready to be bottled or kegged and—at long last—enjoyed.

BEER THROUGH THE AGES

Present-day breweries, Stone included, owe their existence to incremental knowledge based on countless prior successes and failures. Beer has been around for quite some time, and it's evolved dramatically over the centuries. (And quite dramatically over just the past few decades!) So let's journey back to learn what we can of the happy accident that came together as a sudsy, intoxicating drink that would eventually shape history, fuel industry, provide sustenance, quench thirst, and entice taste buds (not to mention provide a lifetime of inspiration and fascination for folks like us!).

EARLY BREWS

While it's difficult to pinpoint exactly when beer brewing began, it is generally thought that this craft got its start sometime between ten thousand and fifteen thousand years ago. Evidence of breweries in ancient Egypt and Mesopotamia has been discovered and studied extensively.

Many scholars believe the cultural shift from nomadic tribes of hunter-gatherers to agriculture-based civilizations can largely be attributed to the domestication of wild grains, including the forebears of barley and wheat. These grains could be widely planted and, once harvested, easily stored for year-round consumption. While such grains aren't particularly palatable in their raw form, early cultures found that simply germinating them or cooking them into a hot cereal made for a hearty and much tastier meal. Eventually, this lead to techniques for making bread, and this was likely the precursor to the brewing of beer.

Excavations of archaeological sites have unearthed buildings that were used as both bakeries and breweries, which makes perfect sense given that these two staples utilize strikingly similar ingredients.

One of the oldest surviving beer recipes in existence, dating back to around 1800 BCE, is from Sumer, in southern Mesopotamia (what is now part of modern-day Iraq). While older records exist showing quantities of ingredients that the Sumerians may have used to produce beer, this recipe is the earliest known to describe both the ingredients and the process by which early beer was made. Etched on a stone tablet, the recipe was scribed in the form of a poem known as "The Hymn to Ninkasi," Ninkasi being the Sumerian goddess of brewing.

The recipe calls for *bappir*, a dried loaf of bread that was stored as a reserve for periods of food shortage, with a simple soak in water bringing the bread back to life whenever it was needed. The rehydrated bappir would be mixed with malted barley and cooked, then spread onto reed mats that acted as a crude filter, separating many of the solids from the liquid. This liquid (the wort) would then be combined with ingredients that were originally translated to mean "honey and wine." Later research determined that the word thought to mean "honey" was more likely to mean "date juice," and the word thought to be "wine" should have been translated as "grapes" or "raisins." This makes perfect sense, as the skins of each are rich sources of yeast, which would help spark fermentation. The liquid was filtered again and then put in a collector vat for fermentation before being consumed by an assuredly enthusiastic Sumerian.

Although not as influential as the Sumerian contribution to modern brewing, in ancient China, a beverage known as *kiu* was brewed, typically from millet, rice, and/or sorghum. While it has been long thought that brewing didn't begin in China until about 2000 BCE, recent archaeological finds have unearthed drinking vessels used for beer dating back to around 7000 BCE.

The Egyptians were early adopters of brewing as well. There, beer was a drink of rich and poor alike and was often used not just for sustenance, but as wages of sorts for workers performing backbreaking labor to build the pyramids. Records and receipts show that in Giza, beer was given three times daily to the pyramid workforce. However, the records are mysteriously silent regarding naptimes. Heathens!

Wealthy ancient Egyptians were also quite fond of beer, and it was frequently given as an offering to the gods. And in a stroke of great foresight, beer was often buried in tombs with the deceased to carry them to the afterlife, a practice of other ancient cultures, as well. (Perhaps a precursor to the modern act of pouring some out for one's homies?) Hieroglyphics denoting beer and brewing can be found in ancient tombs throughout Egypt. The ubiquity of beer in ancient Egyptian culture is perhaps best illustrated by the fact that the hieroglyph depicting a beer jug makes an appearance in a variety of words, including those for wages, offerings, and possessions, in addition to breakfast, supper, meal, drink, and food.

Osiris, the Egyptian god of agriculture (as well as god of the dead, the underworld, and the afterlife), was also considered the god of beer. Ritual offerings were made both to the gods and to the deceased. One common "offering formula" found inscribed at many Egyptian tombs spoke of giving "bread, beer, ox, fowl, alabaster, linen—everything good and pure on which a god lives."

The Egyptians taught the art of brewing to the Greeks, who in turn passed this knowledge on to the Romans. Despite the fact that both the Greeks and the Romans are known for their affinity for wine, beer did enjoy some popularity in these ancient cultures, especially among gladiators and athletes, who relied upon it for strength.

THE SPREAD OF BEER ACROSS EUROPE

Like wine and spirits, beer has enjoyed a special reverence throughout its history. Before Louis Pasteur's time, the exact nature of yeast was unknown, and there was no understanding whatsoever of the science

"The appearance of beer has been regarded by some as an indicator of social complexity—the rather prosaic knowledge of brewing being regarded, in a sense following the Sumerian lead, as a sign of civilized behavior."
—Alexander Joffe, righteous archaeologist/historian

"Wherever a country did not permit the culture of the vine, there Osiris taught the people how to brew the beverage which is made of barley, and which is not greatly inferior to wine in odor and potency."

—Greek historian Diodorus Siculus

behind fermentation. Due to lack of sanitation, many water supplies weren't particularly clean or palatable. Disease was common, simply because drinking water was commonly contaminated with all sorts of bad news.

Beer, on the other hand, was free of waterborne pathogens—and offered calories (energy) to the lucky imbiber as an added bonus. Couple that with beer's intoxicating effects, and you had what people in those days considered to be a downright miracle. (Of course we think beer is a miraculous thing too, but in a different sense of the word.) They had no knowledge of bacteria, so how could they know that boiling the wort killed any pathogens in the water? Likewise, how were they to know that a unicellular microorganism called yeast was responsible for producing this miracle? They *didn't* know. They believed beer to be some sort of divine grace that not only helped them feel better about their lot in life, but also helped keep them from getting sick (other than possibly a slight headache the next morning).

This is a big part of the reason why monks became associated with brewing, as they were often charged with producing beers for their townsfolk, as well as for their own subsistence. It was no doubt a lucrative venture. Not only did it raise money for the church, but one might also presume that a religious message would be an easier sell if beer was involved. And when monks headed out on missionary campaigns, they took not only beer, but also the knowledge of how to make it.

BEER IN AMERICA

In America, beer's roots can be traced to Native American brews made with indigenous corn. British-style ales and stouts arrived with European settlers. In the late 1800s, millions of German immigrants crossed the Atlantic, bringing with them strains of Bavarian yeast that produced smooth, crisp lagers that were typical in Germany but hadn't been seen in America.

Because of the lack of transportation and refrigeration at the time, beers were produced locally and sold directly to taverns in barrels. Distribution beyond a certain radius was difficult because beer often spoiled due to the passage of time and fluctuations in temperature.

A major innovation in the 1870s not only helped solve this problem, it also completely revolutionized the beer industry (not to mention the food industry). Louis Pasteur's *Études sur la bière* introduced the idea of pasteurization, which didn't do any flavor favors for beer, but it did do wonders for the distribution side of the business. Pasteurization granted beer an extended shelf life and gave a fresh breath of life to a formerly less desirable vessel for beer: the bottle. Barrels had been the norm, and local watering holes were *the* place to get your drink on. Not. Any. More.

Why Things Went Terribly Wrong

The ability to package and distribute a particular brand of beer opened up a whole new ball game. Gaining access to a larger distribution scheme was key to the rise of captains of industry like Anheuser-Busch, Pabst, and Coors, because more sales meant greater cash flow—cash they could use to purchase existing breweries rather than construct new ones, simultaneously increasing production and decreasing competition. Out of the approximately 4,100 U.S. breweries in operation in the 1870s, less than 1,600 were still in existence in 1910.

Then disaster struck.

In 1920, Prohibition effectively halted all commercial brewing. Despite breweries and saloons crumbling under the long arm of the law, alcohol consumption actually *increased* during the thirteen-year so-called Noble Experiment. The breweries that survived did so by producing root beers and other sodas, ultra-low-alcohol cereal beverages (called near-beer) that were as close as most people could get to real beer. Larger brands like Pabst and Anheuser-Busch were able to stay in business by acquiring federal licenses that allowed them to produce malt syrup for "medicinal purposes" (malt syrup also being the base for most amateur homebrew beers). These sodas and syrups are what spurred breweries to begin bottling and canning on a large scale, and the few large brewing companies that survived Prohibition benefited immensely when it was finally repealed in 1933.

With the repeal of Prohibition and more widespread access to transportation and refrigeration, the beer market changed forever. Consumption of draft beer fell dramatically as cans and bottles gave consumers the chance to keep fresh, cold beer in their own homes. And the large breweries that stayed afloat during Prohibition had a huge advantage over local breweries, which had previously dominated the American landscape. During the long, dry years that put most of their competitors out of business, they maintained and improved their equipment, continued to train staff, and acquired bottling lines. These advantages allowed them to strike a fatal blow to most startups trying to establish new breweries. In this brave new world, marketing and labeling reigned.

Further promoting the rise of the megabrewer, many longtime brewers, soured by the results of Prohibition, jumped ship and sold their breweries to anyone willing to buy them. Unfortunately, these new owners often didn't know the slightest thing about brewing—or even drinking beer—since their generation had little access to anything other than bad homebrew of the "malt syrup flavored with hops" variety. Much of the beer introduced by newer brewers in post-Prohibition years was inconsistent, and if it was consistent, it often erred toward consistently bad. Roughly

200 breweries were in existence in the late 1950s, but that number dwindled to 125 or so by the late 1960s. A far cry from the 4,100 brewery heyday less than a century prior. The beer market was consolidating and consumption was down—understandably, given the typical quality of the products being churned out. My heart goes out the beer drinkers of that era.

Turning the Tide

One brewery that was whiling away the early 1960s making consistently bad beer was the Steam Beer Brewing Company, in San Francisco. Longtime makers of their flagship Anchor beer (not particularly tasty at the time), they were hovering on the verge of bankruptcy until they were ultimately rescued by young entrepreneur Fritz Maytag (pictured above), eponymous descendant of the washing machine lineage. While Maytag was eating at the Old Spaghetti Factory in San Francisco, the restaurant's owner tipped Maytag off that Steam was looking for a buyer. Despite the brand's deplorable reputation and the shop's outdated equipment, Maytag was a fan and eventually purchased the Steam Beer Brewing Company (partial ownership in 1965, full ownership in 1969), and proceeded to learn the craft of making beer the hard way.

One thing working in his favor was a shift in American palates and conscience. People began questioning the ingredients that went into what they ate and drank, and chemical additives started getting a well-deserved bad reputation. "Food elitism" was on the rise, and sourcing quality ingredients became a selling point. The early 1970s saw the establishment of Alice Waters's Chez Panisse, in Berkeley, touting local ingredients, and Seattle's Starbucks, originally a specialty coffee upstart, as well as publication of books like Frances Moore Lappé's *Diet For A Small Planet*. Pure was in, and people were willing to pay more for products considered to be clean. Beer wasn't immune, and those made with stabilizers, other additives, and untraditional ingredients like rice and corn syrups (used partly because they can cost about a third what barley does and partly because they largely elminate flavor and character) started coming under fire.

The 1970s also saw a resurgence in homebrewing, due in no small part to President Carter lifting the federal tax levied (though hardly enforced) on homemade beer. In the early 1980s, new legislation in many states allowed the reestablishment of brewpubs, whereby restaurants or taverns could operate their own brewery on premises and sell their beer directly to consumers. This offered several advantages that helped advance small-scale brewers. In terms of economics, profits weren't shared with distributors and retailers, and not bottling saved labor and cut costs. Just as importantly, it reintroduced the long-forgotten concept of regional breweries, and the smaller scale allowed brewmasters to experiment with new and exotic recipes or revive antiquated, nearly forgotten styles of beer.

So what did this mean for Fritz Maytag? In 1975, ten years after buying into Steam Beer—years filled with hard work, reformulation, and new equipment purchases—he finally turned a profit. Around that same time, Jack McAuliffe started up his influential New Albion Brewing Company. And while New Albion wasn't able to keep its doors open, closing in 1982, that same year saw the late Bert Grant establishing Yakima Brewing and Malting Co. and opening

Grant's Brewery Pub, the first brewpub in the United States since Prohibition. Sixty plus years without a brewpub? The horror!

Throughout, interest in homebrewing remained high. Specialty brewers like Maytag, and college professors like Dr. Michael Lewis, now professor emeritus of brewing science at UC Davis, were often inundated by phone calls and letters with questions about fermentation and associated arts. Charlie Papazian, originally just a humble homebrewer and amateur beer enthusiast, became a legend with the release of his authoritative *Complete Joy of Homebrewing*, which remains an invaluable resource to this day. Papazian (pictured below, circa 1983) has since become the driving force behind the American Homebrewers Association and the Brewers Association, as well as founding publisher

of *Zymurgy* and *New Brewer* magazines, and founder of the Great American Beer Festival.

These were all great signs, signaling a humble grassroots resurgence, and it couldn't have come at a better time. Just a few years prior, in 1978, the American beer market was at its most dismal. A mere 41 brewing companies existed, a far cry from the 4,100 or so that dotted our fine landscape back in the 1870s. This was undoubtedly rock bottom—the Dark Ages of brewing in the United States.

David and Goliath

So far, so good. People were starting to make smallbatch and craft beers, and people were interested in drinking them. Unfortunately, amidst all these great developments several new demons were taking the field. One was contract brewing, wherein a company has their beers produced for them at an existing facility. This avenue isn't renown for producing world-class beers, largely because it removes a lot of the individual touch that is so key to craft beer, and it often misleads the public as to the beer's true origins. But perhaps the greatest evil of these demons was the emergence of light beer. Then again, maybe it was a necessary evil, in the sense that the craft beer movement might not have been so bold were it not reacting to this low blow to beer's good name.

When light beer came on the market, it was an outrage to us, and it really should have been to everybody. Beer should be about flavors, not about calories. It's my (un)studied opinion that if someone is drinking such a great volume of beer that calories are a big problem, then the calories from each beer aren't really the problem— it's that maybe they're drinking too much. (Yep, I just said that.) It's always okay to drink less. (Yep, I just said that too.)

But, as ever, there was a shift in the prevailing dietary wisdom. As the food supply was pumped full of artificial this and trans fat that, waistlines increased, and Americans became obsessed with losing weight. The idea of moderation sank in, in regard to both food and alcohol. Some people turned to light beer, and we feel sorry for them . . . really, we do. Other, more *worthy* individuals responded by reducing the quantity of their intake rather than sacrificing quality, often compensating by splurging on a more expensive or exotic beer when they allowed themselves to indulge in their guilty pleasure. (If you only allow yourself one beer a week, do you really want to make it a watery flavorless fizzy yellow one?) As big beer manufacturers started seeing decreases in sales, microbrews and craft brews found new customers who were curious and adventurous.

"Big Beer" took notice and began striking deals to get in on the action. One of the first purchases was Wisconsin favorite Leinenkugel, snapped up by Miller Brewing in the early 1980s. Then Seattle-based Redhook sold a significant interest to Anheuser-Busch in exchange for space on Anheuser-Busch trucks and access to their massive distribution network. Widmer Brothers struck a similar deal not too long after. These are just a few instances of a story that has played out repeatedly over the years, with Anheuser-Busch eventually being consumed by international giant InBev. And the trend continues, with that combined force most recently buying out Chicago's Goose Island.

"The mouth of a perfectly contented man is filled with beer." —Egyptian proverb, circa 2200 BCE

"The mouth of a perfectly contented me is filled with a really hoppy beer." —Greg Koch proverb, circa 2011 CE

On the upside, as microbrews gained attention, and space on grocery store shelves, consumers and restaurants took notice. Seasonal beers, IPAs, smoked beers, bocks, porters, stouts, and other styles that had fallen into obscurity have experienced a renaissance. Sommeliers have developed beer pairing programs alongside tasting menus, and brewpubs enjoy the same reverence as the tasting rooms of Napa Valley vineyards. Years of focus and determination have revived the quality of American beers, and craft brews now make up about 5 percent of the American beer market, making a small but important dent in an industry that has been dominated by major players for far too long. It's about time they had their stronghold rattled. And despite the recent economic downturn, the craft beer segment has continued to see tremendous growth, while industrial brands have been challenged to hold on to their ground (hence all of the acquisitions).

We are happy and proud to be among the good guys in this battle, promoting quality, character, and good business practices above all else. We love the sense of camaraderie that the craft beer community promotes, and we're proud to have played a role in the resurgence of small, regional breweries dotting the American landscape after that long and unfortunate hiatus. There are now over 1,700 breweries in the United States, with representation in each and every state, and more opening every year. Now that's something we can all raise a glass to!

Okay, I hear what you're thinking: "That's all fascinating, but how did Stone get into this grand movement, anyway?" Excellent, excellent question. I thought you'd never ask.

A STORY CALLED STONE

THE BACKSTORY

Where did the story of Stone Brewing Co. start? I guess you'd have to go back to the mid to late '80s. I was living in Los Angeles, chasing a BA at the USC Marshall School of Business, and as college kids are wont to do, I often checked out the area haunts. There was this one bar I went to fairly often: Al's Bar—quite literally a dive in every way imaginable. It was hot, small, and sweaty. No sign. Often packed. It was great. The entire interior was completely covered with graffiti, and it seemed to change every week because Marc Kreisel, the owner, would let just about anybody come in and mess around with it. It was in the artist's district (or at least *an* artists' district—I doubt it was officially recognized as one) at the floor level of the American Hotel, near the intersection of Traction and Hewitt. You never knew what to expect when you went in, but you knew it was bound to be an experience.

Thursdays were "No Talent Night," and that was my favorite night to go. They'd let anybody off the street up on stage—I mean *anybody*. Marc called it "a kind of Gong Show of the avant-garde." There was one guy who played a trumpet into a guitar fairly close to an amplifier, which made for some really strange feedback. It wasn't good by any stretch of the imagination, but it was sonically very interesting. And it wasn't anything you'd see on a stage anywhere else but at Al's Bar.

It was a cool place to hang out, and they had about four beers on tap. This was how I'd come to have my first *real* "beer experience." (Let's not mention my first actual beer experience, which involved some awful beer that friends and I found in an abandoned parking lot when I was thirteen.) *This* beer—Anchor Steam—was inspiring. A little lightbulb went off in my head, like, "Wow, beer can taste like this?" I can't say it was a total epiphany and from then on I only drank craft beer; it was more of a singular experience in a wide range of beer-soaked college days.

After graduating, I toyed around with music production, band management, and allied arts. Although I played guitar and had written some songs, I'd come to the slow realization that I wasn't cut out to make it as a rock star. So I ended up opening Downtown Rehearsal, a rehearsal studio complex for bands, and that's where I met Steve Wagner, my future business partner (though I of course had no way of knowing that at the time). He was playing in a band at the time and renting a space there, but I really only met him in the strictest sense of the word; we never really chatted beyond a few cordial greetings here and there.

During those years, I'd hit a few of the little brewpubs in the area. There was Gorky's Cafe and Russian Brewery, a cafeteria-style spot downtown that was open twenty-four hours a day. It promised "Foodski, Funski, Brewski." One of those kinds of places. They'd started as an eatery and eventually added the brewery, which turned out a couple of interesting beers, including an imperial Russian stout. At the time, I still wasn't completely won over, and though I'm embarrassed to admit it now, I remember initially being ticked off when they started peddling their stuff exclusively and stopped serving the meager industrial brands of beer I was used to. Still, seeing the brewing system was a new experience, and it was fascinating to me. I'd never really given much thought to how beer was actually made and how cool the process really was.

I think the moment when I truly got it was while savoring a Boont Amber Ale from Anderson Valley Brewing Company. It was 1991, and a buddy had given me a bomber with a simple comment, "You're into beer, right? Here, I brought this for you." So, I stuck it in my fridge to enjoy later that night. That day actually turned into one of the worst days at work—I mean, seriously, just long and brutal, and frigging frustrating as all hell. All I could think about was that big bottle of Boont chilling, practically waiting for me to get home and have my way with it. I was counting down the minutes until I could.

Let me tell you, after the sixteen or however many hours I'd spent sorting through the mess that was my day . . . that beer just wiped it all away. But beyond that, it really hit home. I felt as if I could make it through just about anything if I had such a flavorful and well-made beer waiting for me in my fridge at all times. I think that's what really won me over—realizing that beer could be *that* good. This was the point of no return.

Aren't You That Guy?

Over the next few years, I got more and more into craft beer. My friend Mike Coker was a craft beer (well, "microbrew" as it was commonly known back then) enthusiast, and he took me around to some good

pubs but, let's just say that back then, the beer scene in Los Angeles was not one to inspire people. Luckily, I also spent a good amount of time in and around San Francisco during the early '90s, and the craft beer scene there was much more mature.

While loitering up in the Bay Area, I caught wind of a Saturday class called "A Sensory Evaluation of Beer," offered through the UC Davis extension program. I signed up, and when I got there, I saw this guy who looked so damn familiar. I knew him from somewhere, but I couldn't place him. Luckily, during a break, he came up to me and broke the ice—"Aren't you Greg from Downtown Rehearsal?"—and that sparked up a conversation. Yep, it was Steve!

Steve, say hello to the folks . . . tell 'em a little about yourself.

"Hmm, where to start? Well, I was born in Chicago but moved to Los Angeles with my family when I was ten. I went to UC Santa Cruz, and, of course, I drank a lot of beer in college. But that was back in the late '70s and early '80s, and I didn't come across anything that I'd qualify as particularly good beer. That is, until I was introduced to Anchor Steam. Like Greg, I had a bit of an epiphany. This was a beer that stood apart—it actually tasted like something! I was intrigued by it, and once I heard a bit of its story, how it was a regional beer and so on, I thought it was cool.

I was an English Lit major, which didn't really qualify me for much besides restaurant work. So I joined a band instead and worked as a professional musician for about fifteen years. I'd played piano my whole life—well, since I was six years old—but I mostly played bass in my bands, though we often switched around instrumentation. I also wrote some songs and did some singing. The cool thing was we got to tour around a lot. We went around the country, drinking beer along the way. We were finding all these little regional brews and I really started getting a taste for all of it.

I played in a few bands over the years: The Balancing Act, Squint, Walker Stories, Bedshredders... When I was in Bedshredders, one of my bandmates—Doug Freeman—was really into homebrewing. I asked him a lot of questions about it and kind of fell into doing it with him. It started casually enough, but like I tend to do with most things I'm interested in, I got obsessed with it. I started doing a lot of homebrewing, a lot of reading, and a lot of research. I was fascinated by it all.

Around the same time, I realized I wasn't getting any younger. I was in a serious relationship, and we were floating the idea of marriage. Constantly touring didn't have the appeal that it used to, and I started thinking about settling down and getting into the beer business. A lot of microbreweries were sprouting up, and it sounded like something right up my alley. So when I heard about this day class called, "A Sensory Evaluation of Beer," and I signed up immediately.

It was a cool class, with a surprising number of people in it, including this one guy who looked really familiar. I kept staring at him, wondering where the heck I knew him from, and it finally dawned on me that it was Greg, who I met back when Bedshredders rehearsed in his studios. As Greg likes to tell the story now, he didn't know me that well back then because we actually paid our rent on time. Well, we got to know each other a lot better during that class. I can't say for certain whether or not we came right out and specifically talked about opening a brewery together that day, but a seed was definitely planted. " —STEVE

DOUG FREEMAN: Steve and I shared many long car rides to and from the west side of L.A. to rehearse in Pasadena. During one of these lengthy trips, Steve brought up my past beermaking efforts, wondering if I still had my old brewing gear. And, if so, might I show him the ropes? I was game. Hadn't done it in almost ten years, but never really lost my interest in it.

Among Steve's other virtues, unexpected for someone of his artistic bent, was a good head for math and logic. As we ordered beermaking equipment and supplies, and measured them out while brewing, I was always impressed by his easy ability to estimate quantities and capacities. I suspect that's served him well in brewing, as the numbers obviously got logarithmically bigger. He was also adept at keeping track of the whole shebang on the computer (a Mac SE if I recall correctly; I want to say he researched and ordered supplies on it too, but I don't think the Internet was the Internet yet).

So we brewed several batches of ales, with varying degrees of sophistication. I think we were mostly doing extracts at the time, with the possible infusion of accent grains here and there. But one thing I recall for sure is dry hopping. I pushed us to try some over-the-top hopping, for which Steve quickly developed an affinity. If I have any tangible legacy in Stone Brewing Co., I like to think it's in the IPA that made Steve an icon.

Steve and I remain in regular-but-too-infrequent contact, meeting up a few times a year either here in L.A. or down in their neck of the woods. It's a thrill and honor every time I see the brewery and restaurant. I will say again now what I so often do: there is no greater or more honorable accomplishment in business than to create a product from the ground up that people are so happy to throw down their hard-earned money for. Steve and Greg have done this in spades, with the greatest of distinction. Deserve it or not, I take some little bit of pride in their operation, and am ever happy and assured that it couldn't have happened to a nicer or more deserving couple of guys.

Neither of us knew anybody else in the class, so it was nice to have that connection from the past and the thread of commonality with music. We sat next to each other for the remainder of the class, and our conversations quickly turned from music to another shared passion: beer. Steve actually had a homebrew with him and shared it with me. Believe it or not, it was a peach beer, which you'd never associate with Stone or Steve nowadays, but the bottom line was, it was fantastic. Rather than being sweet or syrupy, it was very rich, flavorful, and complex, and I was impressed. I'd done some homebrewing with friends and was pretty familiar with beer flavor profiles. Hell, I thought I understood beer pretty well, but apparently I still had a lot of education in front of me.

I'd already been thinking about going in to the beer industry—having ideas about starting my own brewery. But one thing I knew for sure was that I didn't want to do it alone. I wanted to find a suitable business partner. I felt I had a lot to bring to the table business-wise, but I was fairly green on the brewing side. So I found myself looking at Steve and wondering if I could maybe go into business with this guy. I think Steve started wondering the same thing, either then or shortly thereafter.

After the class was over and we'd parted ways, we got together from time to time, and it seemed like every time we got together, it had something to do with beer: beer research, visiting breweries, heading to his little bungalow in Santa Monica to homebrew . . . it was always beer. When it came to brewing, Steve took the lead. I called myself his assistant or lackey, which in the world of homebrew means I was washing and sanitizing, washing and sanitizing. (And did I mention sanitizing?) I also did the labels. I would spend hours upon hours at the computer, creating all kinds of crazy labels. Eventually, we stopped and said to ourselves, "Hey, let's talk about this. What are we up to?

What *Were* We Up To?

It took us a couple more years to buckle down. I was expanding my rehearsal studio business, building more, and wearing blinders to most everything else for months at a time because I was buried in blueprints and the like. During this time, Steve and his wife went up to Portland to house-sit for his brother, who was taking an extended sabbatical from his job to see the world. It wasn't long before Steve took a job with Pyramid Breweries up in Kalama, Washington, just north of Portland, giving him an opportunity to learn craft brewing from inside the industry.

"When Greg and I left that UC Davis class, the idea of starting a brewery sounded like a fun idea, naturally, but neither of us had any experience working in an actual brewery. Portland provided so much inspiration for me. Seeing the beer culture there and all the local breweries excited me and really helped to further ignite my passion. I'd taken up a job as a waiter at the now-defunct Heathman Pub, hoping to finagle my way into a brewing job, although the opportunity never presented itself.

One week, my good friend/former bandmate/homebrewing guru Doug Freeman came up to visit and we made the trek out to Pyramid. As luck would have it, right as we were leaving—literally, as I had maybe half of my right heel still inside their building—the tour guide mentioned that if we knew anybody looking for a brewing job, they were hiring. Before it could even register, Doug's wife Erika piped up, 'Steve's a brewer! Steve's an excellent brewer!' I got their information, went home, polished up my resume, and sent it off. They took the bait. I was in." —STEVE

Shortly after he'd started that job I was visiting and it happened to be right when he got to do his first solo brew. Boy, was he uptight! He did *not* want to be the one to mess up a big batch of beer. He was brewing on the overnight shift (being the new guy, he had to pay his dues), and he was incredibly nervous and practically wound himself up. He was just so damn focused, which I suppose was a good thing to see in a potential business partner, but man, he was no fun to be around that week.

"I was like a sponge. I wanted to learn absolutely everything I could about brewing and the industry. It was absolutely fascinating to me. And working at Pyramid afforded me a very intense education in production brewing. I fluctuated in and out of having doubts about opening my own brewery. It was nothing against Greg, I just wasn't 100 percent sure if it was for me. In fact, I was finding that I really enjoyed being a shift brewer. It made it harder when he started applying pressure; he was ready to get the wheels in motion. I was learning so much, and Laura and I absolutely loved Portland. Why would we leave?" —STEVE

With time, Steve got more comfortable with the big-boy equipment. He was actually becoming a bona fide brewer. We kept chatting and throwing ideas around. We were talking about opening a brewery in Southern California, but neither of us wanted to do that in Los Angeles. I was so over LA, and Steve didn't really want to move back there. One weekend, in March of 1995, I went down to Solana Beach to visit a friend. It was a spectacular weekend, the kind of stuff that SoCal dreams are made of. And in my short stay there, taking in as much of it as I possibly could, it dawned on me that I could absolutely see myself living there. Not to mention that I could totally see myself opening a business around there.

So I called up Steve and said, "Hey, how about North County San Diego?" Much to my surprise, he was all for it. His brothers had gone to college in San Diego, and Steve really liked the area. I knew this was it. I moved down a little over a month later and I started looking at sites. But there weren't a lot of warehouses to choose from. This was mid '95, and the real estate market had been heating up. Finding a place was obviously essential, but the right combination of what we thought we could afford, the right percentage of square footage for an office, a loading dock, proper ceiling height, et cetera, et cetera, eluded me.

Czech-ing Out

That summer, I took a trip to Europe to visit breweries, taste different beers, and just take it all in as a last hurrah before buckling down to start a new business venture in brewing. The last leg of the trip was a train ride from Brussels to Paris, where I'd catch my flight back home. On that train ride, I decided I'd had a humongous change of heart. I was ready to pack it all up and move to Prague. I'd fallen in love with Prague, and I'd done the math. I figured that, for just $24 a day, I could live like a prince—a *prince!*—in Prague. So I scripted and rehearsed, and rehearsed, and rehearsed an entire speech telling Steve that I was sorry, but I didn't want to open a brewery after all.

My rehearsal studio business had doubled. I'd been very successful with it, but I'd sacrificed my personal life—almost all of my spare time. A typical entrepreneurial scenario, sure, but I hadn't had much of a life for years. Now I had a general manager pretty much running the place, and if I wanted to, I could just pack up and go somewhere—anywhere I wanted! It was a classic vacation fantasy: "I'm gonna go back, quit my job, pack everything up, and live my dreams."

But as soon as I got back, reality started to sink in, and I never did deliver that speech. I'm not entirely sure why. I had become fully committed to *not* opening the brewery. And I had reasons beyond wanting to run off to Prague. For one, I thought maybe we were too late to make a splash in the world of craft brewing. The industry was getting pretty well established, some would even say saturated. And I just wasn't ready to work that hard. For years, I'd put in fourteen- to sixteen-hour days building up my other company, and I wasn't sure I wanted to do it all over again.

But after I'd sobered up from the travel experience (no pun intended), I started to think, "Maybe I will go forward with this—under certain conditions." So I told Steve straight up, "You know what? I'm only going to work four days a week, and only four to six hours each day. I mean, I want this brewing thing to be successful, but I really just want to have a little brewery and do our own thing."

STEVE: Reading over the manuscript for the book was the first I'd ever heard about this change of heart. It's a little surprising, really. Greg never seemed reluctant to move forward with this. He was always so confident and sure of everything, it seemed like he had no reservations whatsoever—like he just knew it would work, without a doubt. This was fascinating to read; he hadn't shared this story with me before.

Promises, Promises

So I'd made myself that promise: "Greg, you're only going to work four days a week, four to six hours a day, unless something . . . no! No more than six hours a day." I should have known right then I'd never be able to keep that promise. Maybe I did know, but I had to trick myself into believing it was at least possible. Even though it wasn't. . . .

Steve finally bit the bullet in October 1995 and moved down to San Diego. We eventually found a building, signed a lease, and moved in on February 2, 1996. A nondescript warehouse in a nondescript industrial park on Mata Way in San Marcos was our new home. We'd secured $500,000 in angel financing and purchased a 30-barrel brewing system and set out to change the world. (A barrel is 31 gallons, by the way, so 30 barrels works out to 930 gallons. And just to put that in context, in 1996 Miller sold 43.8 million barrels and Anheuser-Busch sold 91.1 million.) That was when my blinders went back on. Four- to six-hour workdays? Ha! I guess Steve had just been nodding his head during

my demands for a reasonable schedule because by now he undoubtedly knew as well as I did that I'm just not wired to work that little.

I ended up working fourteen- to sixteen-hour days again for the first year and a half but managed to cut back to the twelve- to fourteen-hour range the next year. But hey, it was only six and a half days a week! Ah, that glorious half day. Every Sunday I'd stroll the beach and look for these big stones that we ended up using for our tap handles. That was my time off. I wandered around alone, lonely as you could possibly get, because since I'd moved I hadn't had any time to make any local friends. My social calendar was dismally wide open—perhaps a moot issue since my professional calendar was overflowing.

"You know, Greg is lamenting these fourteen- to sixteen-hour work days. Don't get me wrong, he certainly had plenty of them. Some even longer. We both did. But I remember early on, I was slammed with all sorts of stuff: formulating beer recipes, researching brewing equipment, lining up suppliers, you name it. And Greg was obviously busy, but I remember he kept coming up with these other business ideas that he wanted to start once the brewery was up and running. (Ha!) It was funny, he always seemed to unknowingly pick the moments I was absolutely tired beyond belief to vocalize his next big plan. I wanted to shoot him sometimes, but that's just Greg. That's the way he is. He's always got another idea." —STEVE

The Name of the Game

Now that we had a site and some brewing equipment, what were we going to call this crazy venture? We'd been tossing names back and forth since we started talking about going into business, but it seemed that every name one of us came up with met a response from the other that was lukewarm at best, like "Hmmmmm...," "Ehhhhh...," or "Nooooooo."

Then, one night when Steve and I were having a planning session—doing spreadsheets, figuring out cash flow, that sort of stuff—I saw the word *stone* written on something and said, "Hey, how about Stone Brewing?"

... Silence. Sweet silence.

It felt perfect. After all, he didn't say no right away! But seriously, it stuck. It worked for our purposes. A stone is small. A stone is solid. A stone is natural. I think we liked it because it was so simple.

The Gargoyle

So we had the name, but we didn't have a logo. We'd decided we wanted a gargoyle. It seemed like a natural fit, as it had a very traditional European motif, and we'd initially planned on brewing traditional European beers. (Ha!) Beyond that, it was made of stone, and gargoyles were seen as protectors. I liked how much of our philosophy it expressed: the gargoyle warding off the modern-day evil spirits of chemical additives, cheap adjuncts, and pasteurization.

I thought it would be iconic, but I was underwhelmed by the designs I was getting back from graphic artists I'd found. Eventually, Tom Matthews came onto my radar. I'd seen some of his fantasy artwork—castles, maidens, dragons, knights—at a local T-shirt silk-screen shop, and it was incredibly intricate. I contacted him and he got to work.

The first gargoyle he sent us was way too aggressive; it looked like he was about to rip your head off, and for no apparent reason. The second gargoyle was great, but I thought it was still a little too aggressive. (Interestingly enough, about six years later when we developed our Stone Ruination IPA, I thought, "Now *this* is a beer that gargoyle would be perfect for," so I dug him out of the archives and finally gave him a home.) Tom's third submission was what we ended up going with. We worked on the facial expressions *a lot* though, getting that look just right, tweaking it again and again (and again) until it was perfect.

SOME NAMES THAT DIDN'T MAKE THE CUT:

Old Shoe Brewing, Midnight Brewing Co., 1516 Brewing Co., Rebellion Brewing Co., Miracle Brewing Co., KoochenVagner's Sublime and Beautiful Great California Paradox Ale Brewing and Trading Company Incorporated, Stōn Ales

STEVE: 1516 seemed good at the time (it's the year the German Beer Purity Law was enacted). We ended up using it for the alarm code. For Miracle, we'd joked, 'If it tastes great, it's a miracle!"

GREG: I was pushing pretty hard for KoochenVagner's until Stone came around. Then I pushed for Stōn for a couple weeks but eventually reverted back to Stone.

TOM MATTHEWS: Before meeting the Stone boys, I was a recently laid-off creative director for a company that designed and produced point-of-sale and point-of-purchase advertising for the liquor industry. I ran a staff of ten and worked with the likes of Coors, Anheuser-Busch, Jack Daniels, and Jim Beam. We worked with most of the big wine companies and a lot of breweries as well. Then, liability laws in regard to the liquor industry changed, and the need for our products dried up. I was at the curb and on my own. I started a small shop offering graphic design and illustration and found I didn't miss the corporate monster. I was my own boss and liked the freedom.

Greg had seen my work at a local silk-screen shop that I drew for and asked for my contact info. When I met Greg at the brewery in San Marcos, I saw a grain tower lying on a stack of cardboard in the parking lot and three guys brewing a small batch of beer and using a hand bottler. They met me at the door. Steve Wagner and "webmaster Mike" Palmer shook my hand and went back to work, and Greg and I had an hour-long meeting. By the end of it I thought they were out of their minds, but Greg's enthusiasm was contagious, so I took the advance and started sketching.

I could write a novel about what it was like to work with Stone Brewing Co. It was fun and grueling and tempting and many other things all rolled into one. It took about a hundred preliminary sketches to achieve the basic pose and attitude of the first gargoyle logo. Once we established that, we started the arduous journey of dialing in the face, the musculature and finally the wings. Yes, the wings were a long process as well. I'd say it took two months to dial in the first gargoyle and get everyone's approval.

Then it was time to lay out the first label. Greg often came by my studio in Vista, and we'd sit at my Mac and tweak and nudge and adjust for hours. Then he'd take the various concepts home, look them over, and call to say which one he'd chosen. Easy? No. We messed with font sizes, border widths, and details on the sheaves of barley over and over. But when we were finished, it was a thing of beauty.

About a year later, I was summoned over and introduced to the idea of Arrogant Bastard Ale, which I loved. When we got into the sketching part of the project, we realized the gargoyle needed to be humanized. We made him less stonelike and more anatomically correct. His face and posture and the position of the beer mug were done over and over. Because we had to fit the concept into a circular motif, the holding hand was tucked back and the head moved down to stay within the circle. Making the image work without looking cramped was tough, but eventually it worked out beautifully.

I'm sure Greg thought I got tired of the reworks, but I actually loved the process. During the entire creative journey we never fought and never really butted heads. Greg even loaned me his car once when mine broke down.

The Arrogant Bastard Ale gargoyle prompted us the revisit the original gargoyle, and we decided to carry the more organic, bodybuilding look into all the images. We airbrushed the gargoyle up for the case boxes and promotional uses, and I was often surprised to see him tattooed on people's bodies. The only gargoyle we created that was essentially approved with very little rework was the Ruination gargoyle. Something just clicked there. By the time we created the Levitation gargoyle, he had become as human as possible and easy

to reinvent, and was finalized in a very short time.

By this time, I'd been dabbling in writing and my first published book came out. I was doing less artwork and more writing. With the release of my second book, I was nearly out of the creative industry. So when Greg wanted to go another way with the tenth anniversary image, I was happy to step aside and let somebody else become the bearer of the Stone logo torch.

In the time I worked with Stone, I watched a small fledgling brewery grow and grow until they became what they are today. I'm extremely proud of the work we did together and what I helped create. Every artist has his swan song. Da Vinci has the Mona Lisa, Michelangelo has the Sistine Chapel, and I have the Stone Brewing Co. gargoyles. When I visit the brewery I'm treated like family and even get an employee discount. Greg and I see very little of each other these days, but the relationship continues through the images and the legacy we created.

OPENING UP

We opened for business on July 26, 1996, and Vince Marsaglia from Pizza Port bought our first keg of Stone Pale Ale. He even came and picked it up, which I appreciated at the time, but I almost wish he hadn't, because it gave me a completely unrealistic idea of what it was going to be like in this business. I just kind of thought, "Oh great, they'll come and pick up the kegs." I can count on both hands the number of times our accounts have come to pick up kegs over the past fifteen years. I quickly found out it was usually more like this:

"Where the eff are you? I'm out of your beer and I'm going to put something else on if you don't get your ass down here with another keg right now."

"Oh! Um (shuffling papers) . . . did you, uh, did you call us earlier and place an order?"

"No, I'm calling you now."

Let's just say our early accounts could be very . . . *demanding* at times. We still loved 'em though.

But that first night, still blissfully unaware of what was to come, I went down to Pizza Port. It was a Friday, and I started watching people order beer and trying to gauge why they chose particular beers. Some people were trying our beer, but it wasn't for any real reason; it was just like, "Stone? Yeah, sure, I'll try that one."

VINCE MARSAGLIA (CO-OWNER, PIZZA PORT): I remember Greg and Steve would come into Pizza Port Solana Beach a lot. In those days there were a lot of guys in who came through and talked about wanting to open a brewery, but they seemed much more serious about it.

When they started talking about numbers and the rest of the business side of it, not just about how much they loved beer, I told them to let me know when they were opening. They'd come in and tell me how things were going and show me pictures of everything being put in. It was all very exciting, even for me. I'd really gotten to like them, and their passion for great beer was very evident, even then.

When they finally opened, I drove out and picked up that legendary first keg of Stone Pale Ale. They wheeled it out and loaded it in my truck, and I took it back to Pizza Port. I didn't mean to give Greg a false impression that vendors were going to be coming to pick up beer from him—I just wanted the first keg!

Then a Japanese couple ordered a pitcher. They didn't know it, but they got the very first pitcher of Stone Pale Ale on the market. I went up to them and asked why they chose it. It turned out that they liked the name. I seem to recall that they had a friend with the last name Stone, or something like that. It was just a random thing, but I wanted so badly for it to be something more—that they'd heard Stone was a new brewery that had just opened up, or the bartender recommended it because they wanted to try something local. I wanted it to be one of the reasons why *I* wanted them to like our beer. It was only our first keg, but oh god did I want somebody to know about us already!

" Right about the time we opened was when Greg finally (thankfully) stopped dreaming up new business ideas. I had made all this beer that was sitting in the cold box, so a lot of the pressure was taken off of me. Now it was up to Greg to sell it. I quickly realized

that I now had a lot more time on my hands than he did. Invoices started piling up, and I knew we wouldn't be able to keep up as demand picked up, so I took a stab at the accounting.

They don't tell you that the other part of being a brewer is a lot of paperwork. But I liked knowing where we were spending money, and being able to keep an eye on it. I made a few mistakes here and there, but the State Board of Equalization was kind enough to let us know. (How was I supposed to know what a 'use tax' was? That one hurt. . . .) Audits aside, we were doing an alright job of navigating the maze. Most importantly, our beer was selling, and that in and of itself was no easy feat. *"* —STEVE

Just as the Bubble Burst

Turns out, our timing couldn't have been worse. We opened up just as the beer bubble burst, almost to the day. Just as we were gearing up to break ground, *20/20*, *Nightline*, or one of those other sensationalized news shows ran a program along the lines of "Is That Microbrew What You Think It Is?" It played like a total Anheuser-Busch advertorial, painting the perfect picture of their beers' consistency while "exposing" the contract brewing that was taking place in the microbrew world at the time. Seemingly overnight, it made people question whether they should trust these little breweries.

From the late 1980s to 1995, craft brewing sales growth had been impressive, ranging from 25 to 45 percent. In 1996 (when we opened), it plummeted to 7 percent, and in 1997 it nearly flattened out at a frighteningly underwhelming 2 percent. The brakes were on. The industry was being turned upside down. Wholesalers discontinued brands and retailers took them off the shelves, getting rid of them ASAP via steep discounts. The dynamic had shifted, and consumers definitely began looking at craft beer with a jaded eye.

It became the heyday of imports. The imported beer category began growing rapidly, essentially because these still offered something that many domestic big brands didn't (at least *some* flavor), along with the feeling of sophistication and distinction that people had gotten from drinking microbrews. We were opening up in crazy lean times, right in the eye of the storm. If we had opened for business just one year earlier, we would have been able to work with virtually any wholesaler we wanted. But now no one wanted us, so we had to do it the hard way.

The way we made it work was to solidify our own philosophies and buck all the existing trends. We had to say *NO*. No advertising. No free goods. No free glassware. No discounts. No illegal under-the-table stuff, which was so, so, so very common at the time (and still is, but to a lesser extent).

In San Diego County in the 1990s, if you wanted to get your beer in a bar with a decent amount of business, it was a pay-to-play situation, simple as that. But we *refused* to do it. Because of that, the majority of our early accounts were lower-volume places and our sales were a bit sluggish to take off. But we wouldn't play the game. It wasn't an easy choice to make because we were really struggling to get up to critical mass, but it was the right choice to make, and that's why we stuck with it.

Reason for the Season

With time, Stone Pale Ale started getting around. It was slow, but we were adding accounts here and there. In early December 1996, we released our second beer— Winter Stone. At the time, we thought we'd have a seasonal release program, like so many other breweries. We ended up making a few batches and it was doing well, so we didn't discontinue it until about April, which was much later than we'd originally planned.

We actually had a couple of accounts that said, "Hey! If you make that beer, I'll sell it. And if you don't make that beer, I'm not selling any of your beer." People told us they liked it, my mom *loved* it, and we loved it, so Steve and I sat down and talked about it. We felt it was a unique beer and deserved to be brewed year-round, so about a month and a half later we brought it back, but under a different name: Stone Smoked Porter.

We tried a few more seasonal releases. Stone Session Ale was supposed to be our spring seasonal (though as you can see, we were already breaking from our wobbly-established convention of putting the season in the name), and . . . well, it didn't catch on. It was pretty hoppy—not full-on hoppy like we do today, but for the time it was pretty hoppy, and for a session ale, definitely pretty hoppy. People didn't understand what a session ale was supposed to be about—plenty flavorful yet low enough in alcohol that you could enjoy a few in a session without getting tanked. So it came and faded away, all in about a three month period. Ho hum.

4.7% Alc.Vol.   Draft Wheat Ale
"Save the lemons and limes for your fish taco."

Believe it or not, we also tried our hand at a wheat beer. Stone Heat Seeking Wheat made it through two summer releases, but eventually went by the wayside. It was plenty tasty, but we ended up deciding it wasn't Stone. If we learned one thing from Heat Seeking Wheat, it was that we shouldn't try to brew what we

think people will like; we just need to brew what we like. Oh, and that we shouldn't let Steve come up with beer names. (Just kidding Steve!)

Beyond the Pale

We did alright our first year. We had a number of accounts, but few of them were turning big numbers, and by this time, we were hemorrhaging about $30,000 a month and *desperate* to reach a critical mass. We hadn't lost faith, but things were looking a little bleak at the time, *especially* on paper.

Getting volume was tough. In San Diego, infected, skanky beer from most microbreweries was the norm. Since then, the breweries in question have either cleaned up their acts or gone out of business, but at the time it was a major stigma for us to combat and it made our lives infinitely more difficult. Lots of buyers thought they shouldn't waste their time even talking to us.

On top of that, a lot of consumers were still finding Stone Pale Ale challenging. Even though it technically fit within the guidelines of a pale ale (that is, not dark, brown, or black), its deep copper color didn't fit into people's conception of what a pale ale *should* look like (that is, not deep copper). Plus, it was much more bitter than most people's palates were ready to appreciate at that time.

I can remember sampling Stone Pale Ale with bartenders and restaurant buyers, and having them react with this . . . shudder. They'd look at me as if it was a prank, like "Okay? Where's the hidden camera?" But when they saw the confident smile on my face, showing how much *I* enjoyed our beer, they quickly realized that they weren't on hidden camera. All too often, I got a quasi-quizzical look, as if they were still trying to figure out if I was serious, coupled with a polite-ish declination/explanation: "It's just . . . so . . . bitter."

Despite the initial resistance from a lot of bars and restaurants (partly because they mistakenly believed the beer to be too bitter, and partly because we've never been willing to pay for placement or give them free kegs), we knew that the end users—our faithful fans—were loving the hell out of our beer. And if the bars weren't going to get it to them, we were going to have to offer up an alternative solution.

So in June 1997, just a month shy of our first anniversary, we began offering Stone Pale Ale in 22-ounce bottles. Going to bottles was a big deal for us, in part because it takes a rather sizeable investment. As with every step our business had taken, we weren't sure how it was going to turn out. But that very day, some random guy just happened to wander in to the brewery and ask, "Hey! Do you have your beer available in bottles?"

It was equal parts eerie and serendipitous. I mean, we had literally just finished the bottling run. I don't think we'd even taped all the boxes shut yet. "Well, as a matter of fact we do."

It was a sign. And, with that, we instantly became the only brewery that was both brewing and bottling in San Diego County. Sure, there were some other San Diego breweries that had their brands in bottles, but, unbeknownst to most consumers, they were having their beer contract-brewed for them, in places as far away as Wisconsin and Minnesota. Personally, I found this to be a form of unacceptable deception. If we were going to put "San Diego County" on the label, then it was going to come from here, damn it!

Sticking to Our Guns

So, remember, like, four paragraphs ago, how I was talking about all the bar buyers telling us our Stone Pale Ale was way too bitter? Sure, we could have listened and scaled back on the hops, but we didn't want to. It wasn't our nature. We were brewing beers that *we* liked to drink, and if they didn't like it . . . well, we'd find other people who did. Maybe. Hopefully.

Instead of easing up, we went bolder. In August 1997, we released Stone IPA to celebrate our first anniversary. IPAs are almost de rigueur now for most breweries, but, at the time, drinking an IPA was a new experience for a lot of people's palates. Bitter, yes, but the fresh flavors and aromas that came from the hops— the citrusy, piney, grassy, floral bouquet—who knew beer could taste like this? Hopheads were being born, and Stone was certainly one of the delivery rooms. To quench this new thirst, we brewed ever-escalating IPAs for the subsequent four anniversary celebrations, going bigger and bolder each time, culminating with the now somewhat legendary Stone 5th Anniversary IPA.

This hunger for hops was a good thing, because we were gearing up to release another brew. It was (and still is) an aggressive beer. You probably won't like it.

STEVE: For what it's worth, I have to mention that we're still using the exact same recipe for our Stone Pale Ale today. We haven't changed it a bit, but people's palates have evolved so much. We've always kept it right around the 45 IBU mark, which at the time was pretty aggressive. After all, there were IPAs out there with less than 45 IBUs.

ARROGANT BASTARD ALE, OR: HOW I LEARNED TO STOP WORRYING AND LOVE THE BITTER

For the story behind Arrogant Bastard Ale, we've got to go back to the fall of 1995. Steve had purchased a new homebrewing system with bigger stainless steel pots and a couple of basic doodads that would help be more consistent with temperatures and such—luxuries we didn't have before. We got together to do the first brew at my place in Solana Beach, with the goal of triangulating the recipe for Stone Pale Ale. About two-thirds of the way through the brew, Steve groaned. Or, more precisely, he said, "Aw, hell!"

When I asked what was going on, he said (I'm paraphrasing, as I admit I don't recall the exact words), "I miscalculated and added the ingredients in the wrong percentages. And not just a little. There's *a lot* of extra malt and hops in there."

Being the soul of reason, I said, "Well, what do we do? Do we dump it out?"

He said, "I don't know. . . . Let's just finish it, ferment it, and see what it tastes like. But tomorrow or the next day we gotta make another batch with the right amounts." He was always so serious, that Steve.

I suspect that if it hadn't been so late in the day and so late into the brew, we probably would have dumped it out and just started over. Good thing we didn't.

A few weeks later, once it was ready, we tried it, and it was like, "Wow! . . . Yeah. Hmm. Oh! Oh . . . *hell* yeah!" But we wondered, "What are we going to do with a beer like this? Nobody's going to be able to handle it." I mean, we both loved it, but it was unlike *anything* else that was out there. We weren't sure what we were going to do with it, but we knew we had to do *something* with it somewhere down the road.

(Apparently, Steve's memory of how the discovery of Arrogant Bastard Ale unfolded is a touch different than my recollection. Similar, but different. He airs his side of it on page 70.)

Later that fall I named it—or rather, it *told* me what its name was. I think that Arrogant Bastard Ale (and this confuses some people) has always been named Arrogant Bastard Ale. I often see eyes glazing over when I say this, but I honestly believe that throughout the annals of time—*throughout the millennia!*—Arrogant Bastard Ale has always been there, and that it has always carried its righteous name. It just *is*. It patiently (or more likely impatiently) sat for eons, just waiting to be discovered. We did not create it. I did not name it. It was already there. We were just the first lowly mortals to have stumbled upon it. Steve was the first to learn how to brew the beer that already was, and I was the first to realize what its name already was.

One thing we knew for certain was that when we opened our brewery, this wouldn't be the first beer we came out with. We thought maybe two or three years down the road we'd revisit it and see what happened. Back then, there was almost no specialty end of the craft beer segment that went in this direction other than barleywines, massive flavor bombs jam-packed with tons of malt, tons of hops, and a sturdy alcohol backbone. Barleywine was the only "big beer" style that was really out there. Most people had no concept of a beer like this, so we essentially shelved it, but it was always on our minds. It wasn't that I doubted the beer (I didn't) or that we didn't love it ourselves (we did), it was that . . . well, dear readers, there's no gentle way to say this . . . it was that I doubted you.

You're Not Worthy

So, flash back to 1997, when, as I said, our sales volume wasn't that great. We were bleeding money—not like jugular status, but definitely scores of ultra-painful flesh-level wounds, where survival is a tenuous thing. The board of directors at our fledgling company heard me describe Arrogant Bastard Ale. They hadn't even tasted it—heck, we hadn't even brewed it again as there'd been no time in our 24/7 schedules—but they loved the name. A lot. They were convinced that this could be a very important beer for us and pushed us to release it, but Steve and I were convinced that the world still wasn't ready for it.

"The board wanted Arrogant Bastard Ale to be released. They thought it would help us have more of a billboard effect; with more Stone bottles next to each other on a retail shelf, they become that much more visible, and it sends a message that we're a respected, established brewery with a diverse range of beers. But we were reluctant, not only because we didn't think the world was ready, but because—to draw a music business analogy—we didn't want to curse ourselves into becoming a one-hit wonder. We didn't want someone buying it once as a novelty for their boss (or brother, or father, or . . .) and never trying it again." —STEVE

At the brewery, we had a little 10'x10' reception/gift shop area with a little cabinet in it. As an experiment, I made a small run of pint glasses that said Arrogant Bastard Ale on them. This was the summer of '96; we weren't even making the beer at this point, I was just curious how people responded to the name. We didn't have a logo yet, so we just used a sawtooth design that I'd come up with. (Needless to say, these are a super rare collector's item these days.) Well, we sold out of the glasses pretty quickly, and the board eventually convinced us to release the beer a little more than a year later. Still, I felt it was too soon, but I set about writing the label anyway.

I wrote the label from the perspective that most people really weren't going to like the beer. I was certain that would be the case. We were a nation made up primarily of fizzy yellow beer drinkers and fast food eaters, raised on soda pop and sugary cereal; the vast majority (99.9 percent?) were most certainly *not* worthy. I truly wanted to warn them away. I didn't want someone to buy it, taste it, think "Oh dear god!" only to pour it down the drain. Plus, we were only planning to do one batch and have that be the last of it. So when I wrote the label, I was thinking it was going to be a limited beer. I didn't want people wasting their money on it if they weren't prepared, and I didn't want them

ARROGANT BASTARD ALE

ar•ro•gance (ar'o gans) *n.*
The act or quality of being arrogant; haughty; undue assumption; overbearing conceit.

This is an aggressive ale. You probably won't like it. It is quite doubtful that you have the taste or sophistication to be able to appreciate an ale of this quality and depth. We would suggest that you stick to safer and more familiar territory—maybe something with a multi-million dollar ad campaign aimed at convincing you it's made in a little brewery, or one that implies that their tasteless fizzy yellow beverage will give you more sex appeal. Perhaps you think multi-million dollar ad campaigns make things taste better. Perhaps you're mouthing your words as you read this.

At Stone Brewing, we believe that pandering to the lowest common denominator represents the height of tyranny - a virtual form of keeping the consumer barefoot and stupid. Brought forth upon an unsuspecting public in 1997, Arrogant Bastard Ale openly challenged the tyrannical overlords who were brazenly attempting to keep Americans chained in the shackles of poor taste. As the progenitor of its style, Arrogant Bastard Ale has reveled in its unprecedented and uncompromising celebration of intensity. There have been many nods to Arrogant Bastard Ale...even outright attempts to copy it... but only one can ever embody the true nature of liquid Arrogance!

INGREDIENTS: Nothing but the finest barley, most aggressive hops, clearest water, our proprietary yeast strain and abundant arrogance.

www.arrogantbastard.com

QUESTIONS OR COMMENTS? If you don't like this, keep it to yourself—we don't want to hear from any sniveling yellow-swill-drinkin' wimps, 'cause Arrogant Bastard wasn't made for you.

keeping it from one of the rare souls who could appreciate it—someone who was worthy—so I did my best to warn the unworthy away.

Now, in hindsight, I can understand why so many people have taken it as a challenge. I've been told that it's a brilliant piece of reverse psychology, but it was never meant that way. I've seen so many write-ups calling it "a classic case of genius marketing" and so on. While the "genius" term was certainly complimentary (and appreciated!), it really didn't apply here. I was just writing what I felt, and intentionally sticking it to the fizzy yellow beer drinking masses in the process. They had it coming.

We had the release party for Arrogant Bastard Ale at Pizza Port Carlsbad on November 1, 1997. Saleswise, it was their busiest night second only to their own grand opening party. We were quickly finding out that we were on to something big.

Still, I stuck to my guns about warning people. When we did beer events, I never let people taste

Arrogant Bastard Ale first. Folks would come up to our booth or table, see the name, and want to try it. And I would tell them no: "You can try Stone Pale Ale, then Stone Smoked Porter, then Stone IPA, and then—and only then—if you're still interested in continuing, you can try Arrogant Bastard Ale. So! Would you like a Stone Pale Ale?"

I kept that up for several years at beer festivals, and some people got so riled up! The thing is, I knew a lot of people were just trying Arrogant Bastard Ale because of the name, and I wanted to convey that the beer wasn't just a name. It was a beer, and it was good, and, "Oh, by the way, we make three other effing fantastic beers that you will ignore and dismiss unless I *make* you try them."

Frankly, I think that was one of the major differences between our approach and that of other companies. We were willing to make you work for it. There's a barrier to entry: you have to do it our way. And that's not common, but it proved to be the right way to go because, at every festival, we got new fans of our other beers: "Wow, I would have never tried the Stone Smoked Porter, but this is awesome! Where can I get this?"

If I'd let most folks do what they thought they wanted to do—just to come up and try Arrogant Bastard Ale—they probably would have thought they'd tried the only interesting beer from Stone and

moved on, and I refused to let that happen. It was exhausting. I couldn't just take their glass and fill it with whatever they wanted, as I refused to allow our brewery to be viewed as a one-trick pony. I talked to *everybody* who came up. Every. Single. Person. But I contribute a lot of our popularity and success to the simple fact that I was willing to do that—that we were all willing to do that. We wanted to educate as well as entertain.

In the end, and in spite of my ardent warnings, Arrogant Bastard Ale took off. I think we made about 45 kegs and a hundred cases, and they sold out quickly. We made more. That sold out. We made even more. That sold out. Finally we realized that this wasn't going to be a one-off kind of thing. Despite my suspicions to the contrary, there were worthy people out there. And they were thirsty. The beer (and the name) was here to stay.

COMING OF AGE

Stone Pale Ale, Stone Smoked Porter, and Stone IPA were picking up. And with the advent of Arrogant Bastard Ale, people started taking notice of these crazy guys making "really bitter beers" down in San Diego. And as serious as we were about our business, we always had a bit of that "kid experimenting down in the basement" mentality—we might hit brilliance or we might blow up the neighborhood—but we loved risking it. So we just kept playing around with new beers whenever we had the time to spare.

I'm often asked how we came up with certain recipes or why we chose to make a particular style. I have something to confess. We've been making it up as we go along. It's true. Really. But within that freewheeling style, we do follow a few simple principles: 1) We determine if our fundamental philosophies are met, and 2) We have to like the idea. Oh, and I suppose a third criterion is implied: Do we think we can do it, and can we do it well—hopefully *extraordinarily* well?

That third criterion is easy to meet when you've got a guy like my partner Steve at the helm. He's never once let me down with his beers. We were (and still are) always brimming with ideas and new ways to reinvent the wheel. Part of making aggressive beers is putting them out aggressively. If you just follow marketing surveys and test groups and put out a new beer once every few years, you'll always be behind the curve. Who cares what the public thinks they think? Not us. We simply wanted to keep pushing the envelope.

We've made a business out of brewing the beer that we want to drink. If someone's got an idea they're visibly passionate about, and they can make a stellar pilot batch that I would want to drink, then there's only one way I'm going to get to drink more of it. . . . We obviously will just have to make more of it now, won't we?

We brought out another monster beer in February 1998: Stone Old Guardian Barley Wine. Steve and I had tasted some amazing barleywines in our beer travels (having attended the Toronado Barleywine festival in San Francisco for several years by this time), and we had always wanted to do our spin on one. With its massive malt character, high hop dosing, and ample alcohol level, a barleywine seemed a natural fit for our program. And it was cool to introduce the idea of aging beer— deliberately aging it, that is—to people unfamiliar with the concept. Even now, many people are surprised to hear that certain styles of beer not only can be aged, but actually develop more character in the process (see more on page 111). But back then, you may as well have been speaking a foreign language.

We continued our bigger beer brigade in November 1998, releasing Double Bastard Ale to commemorate

"Arrogant Bastard Ale: It's tempting to dismiss this as the brewing equivalent of a Weird Al Yankovic CD. The "You're Not Worthy" jeer emblazoned on the bottle and the high-attitude website ("This is not the belly-filling pap of the unwashed masses") are so over-the-top that you have to wonder if there's anything beyond the hype. There is. This big, bad beer is loaded with hops and malts and flavor."

—Peter Rowe, *San Diego Union-Tribune*, September 1999

the one-year anniversary of unleashing Arrogant Bastard Ale on an unsuspecting world. Once again, we weren't expecting such an aggressive beer to be widely embraced, but the demand was insane. This beer, perhaps more than any other in our early years, wreaked havoc when it was released. We put notes to retailers in the cases, asking them to limit customers to three bottles each, but . . . we got reports that customers were following our distribution trucks around town, just so they could get extra bottles. (This actually happened.)

Works Well with Others

One of the major challenges of making good beer, besides actually making it, is getting it to market. To that end, in April 1999, we rolled out our first case of six-packs. We felt it appropriate to lead with our first beer, Stone Pale Ale. As a bonus, it was the only six-pack brewed and bottled in San Diego County at the time.

But, as I've already lamented, in the David vs. Goliath world of distribution, when you're vying for retail shelf space in stores and keg placement in bars and restaurants, having a strong, eclectic portfolio of beers is paramount. Which is precisely why we wanted to do more than just take our beer to market: we wanted to take our beer *and* an incredible selection of some of the world's other great beers to market. So we did.

True, it may seem a little peculiar. You certainly wouldn't see a Toyota dealership sprinkled with Volkswagens and Chevys. But I figure all us "little guys" are in the craft beer business together, and I feel that creates a unique sense of community—maybe even a touch of responsibility. Plus, it helps satisfy my own desire to be able to purchase the selection of beers I want to drink!

It's symbiotic, really. Our distributorship (imaginatively named Stone Distributing) is undoubtedly helpful to the craft brewers who entrust us to sell their beer, getting them access to a list of established accounts with whom we do business. And as any small brewery can attest, the less they spend on a sales force, delivery

trucks, and so on, the more they can spend on equipment and ingredients. From a our standpoint as a distributor, having more brands on board is also helpful. As we can attest, stopping in at a brand new account and trying to build a new relationship with just one brewery in your arsenal (no matter how amazing) can be a challenge. Having beers from over thirty breweries to offer makes a world of difference.

GROWING PAINS

Between 1998 and 2002, Stone grew by 540 percent. We were named one of America's fastest-growing private companies, garnering a spot on the prestigious Inc. 500 list in 2002 and 2003. Our distribution business had also become the largest independent specialty beer wholesaler in Southern California.

Space kept getting tighter and tighter, even though we were using what we had as efficiently as is humanly possible. We kept knocking out walls and leasing more spaces in our industrial park. I'll always remember the first wall we knocked down. The adjacent suite had been occupied by a small business, and it was just perfect for them. Or so the owner thought. I'd approached him and asked if he'd consider moving and he gave me a straightforward answer: "No." And, with an installed brewery, it was pretty much impossible for us to move of course. That meant if we were going to expand (and oh, how we needed space!), one of us was going to have to move. So, I changed the question, and asked him what his *ideal* space would look like. Sure, he was happy with the spot he was in, but he agreed that there could possibly be better . . . but where? Armed with his parameters, I called up our real estate broker friend Dave Pinnegar and sent him out on the hunt. Dave found it, neighbor loved it, we kicked in a grand to help him with moving expenses, and *bam!* He became our former neighbor and we had our expansion space! Distant memories now, as the little 7,100-square-foot space we'd opened in had grown to become a 26,500-square-foot collection of adjacent suites, and yet it still felt like we were bursting at the seams.

"It's funny to think that when we were first looking for facilities back in 1995, we almost went for a spot in Vista that was stand-alone—with no way to expand. It would have made for a much different ballgame, that's for sure. Having the ability to expand into adjacent suites was, as we quickly realized, crucial for sustaining our growth. But even then, it was only a matter of time before we saw the inevitable on the horizon. Someday, we were going to have to move." —STEVE

"I do not care how much beer we make; I only care *how* we make it. If we end up leveling off, I don't mind . . . as long as we never compromise our standards."

—Greg Koch in the 2009 documentary *Beer Wars*

By the end of 2002, Steve and I had faced reality and started looking around for potential sites for our next home, and we wanted to make it a destination. There were a lot of details to consider, and I was doing it all over again; the blinders were going back on. We looked all around month after month after month, evaluating and re-evaluating a slew of potential sites before finally deciding on our little slice of heaven in Escondido.

Besides doubling in size to 55,000 square feet, we were upping our brewing game significantly. Our old 30-barrel system was a trooper, but it just wasn't going to be enough to sustain our projected growth, or any growth for that matter. We maxed it out, brewing 24/7 during our last year in San Marcos. So we had a 120-barrel system

STONE BREWING CO. ANNUAL PRODUCTION

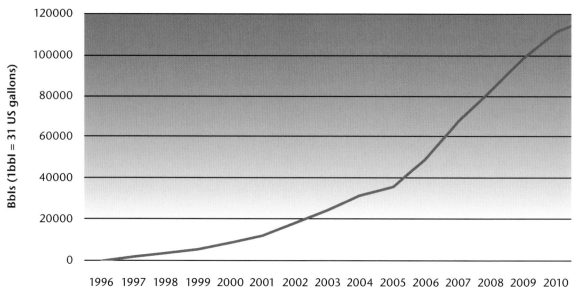

built for us by ROLEC in Germany, taking our per-batch capacity from 930 gallons to 3,720 gallons.

Once the details were squared away, we delivered the news to the world in late 2003. It was a very exciting moment, especially because we could share a preview of the space. The developers offered to let us use the fancy dirt lot at our brewery-to-be for the Stone 8th Anniversary Celebration & Invitational Beer Festival.

Not long after dropping our awesome news, we reached full capacity at our San Marcos facility. Even working around the clock, we literally couldn't make any more beer, yet we still weren't meeting demand. And as much as I loved our little brewery, I couldn't wait to get this new one underway.

> "It was a tough transition. We were lucky that we were still able to keep brewing at the old facility while the new brewhouse was installed. Fortunately for us, we weren't transferring tanks or big equipment, so production never had to shut down. As Greg said, we were brewing 24/7—nonstop, in a quest to somehow keep up. And once the new system was installed, we were operating both in tandem, moving beer from San Marcos to Escondido in dairy trucks.
>
> It was bittersweet bidding adieu to our first home. It had served us well for all those years, but it was definitely time to move on. There were dozens of mixed emotions associated with the whole transition, but if I really had to narrow it down to one, I suppose I'd have to choose 'exciting.' " —STEVE

We wanted to share in our excitement with the fans, because it was thanks to them—that is to say *you*—that we'd grown as much as we had (and still are!). I wanted to provide updates on the construction and everything Stone, so in January 2005 I decided to start a video blog, posting short, and sometimes not so short, videos that chronicled our transition—and anything else I felt like talking about. Interesting little note: You know that newfangled YouTube thing that all the kids are talking about these days? Yeah, we totally beat them to the game. They didn't even go live until about a month after

we posted our first video. So what if they got bought out for $1.65 billion a few years later?! We make *much* better beer than they do.

Squatters' Rights

Needless to say, there were a few hitches along the way . . . bumps in the proverbial road. It's bound to happen when you're dealing with contracts and legal jargon and millions of dollars. Even in the last weeks leading up to our move, we had a few hiccups with the developer of the property, none of which I care to go into here, but suffice to say it got a little tense toward the end. Not unexpectedly, our planned move-out date coincided with our move-in date at our new facility. And we had a *definite* move-out date because our good friends Gina, Vince, and Tomme from Pizza Port were taking over our old space. They'd been making and serving craft beers at their brewpub for years, and were wildly successful. Now they were branching out to establish the Port Brewing Company and Lost Abbey. They needed a production facility, and our San Marcos facility fit the bill perfectly.

But, as I said, there were a few bumps along the way. Not quite everything was ironed out with the puppet masters pulling the strings at our new building, and it really came down to the wire. I think we even technically passed the wire, if there is such a thing. We needed to move everything and everyone over and start making beer at our new brewery, like . . . *now*, even though there were still a few i's to be dotted and t's to be crossed before we could—or rather, *should*.

Ultimately, we just said screw it and moved in anyway. We ran a little covert operation (in typical Stone fashion—ha!): curtains drawn, keeping our heads low, parking behind the building, using the back entrance, the whole bit. We eventually worked out the kinks, made our occupancy legit, and all lived happily ever after (obviously). But if there's one thing you don't need during a humongous move like that, it's superfluous stress and anxiety. We already had enough of that to circle the globe a few times. Wondering if we were going to get shut down at any moment for essentially squatting was truly nerve-racking. It was less about wondering *if* it was going to happen. . . . It felt more like we were just waiting for it to happen. Luckily, it didn't, but it sure as hell had us biting our nails.

Changing of the Guard

By mid-December 2005, we were settled in. Although we hadn't known it, our friend and colleague head brewer Lee Chase, who'd been with us for nine and a half years, had been itching to go out on his own for a while. Being the noble chap he is, he hung around and saw us through the whirlwind transition, waiting until we were somewhat situated before announcing his imminent departure.

Mr. Chase, I don't believe we've properly introduced you. For those of us who might be unfamiliar with your story, would you be so kind as to sum up the world according to Lee?

"I grew up in the little town of Ramona, California. If you're from around there or have been through there, the name alone conjures up some interesting images. It's a weird mix of people in a fairly rural setting. It's certainly not known for its beer culture; in fact, there's plenty of bad beer there. Even when I was underage and alcohol in any shape or form is supposed to be liquid gold, I knew what we were drinking was crap.

I was involved in the local skateboard-punk-vegetarian scene there, and somebody had given me a copy of *Soy, Not 'Oi!'*—this counterculture vegan cookbook of sorts with 'Over 100 Recipes Designed to Destroy the Government.' And there was this section on brewing your own beer, 'because corporate beer sucks.'

I had never even given any thought to the fact that you could make your own beer, so that was real eye-opener. And given my age and the scene I was involved in, the whole 'Damn the man! Derail their agenda!' thing spoke to my sensibilities. So I started homebrewing (doubly awesome since I was still underage) and got really into it. Once I was out of high school, I started attending city college, but I was unsure of what I wanted to study. My brother suggested the brewing program at UC Davis. And when he offered to help with the tuition, I couldn't say no.

I interned at RJ's Riptide, a brewery in San Diego, and then started working at Brewer's Union, a now defunct brew-it-yourself facility that also made its own beers. I met Greg and Steve there and bumped into them fairly often at Pizza Port, and our philosophies about beer quality and character were strikingly similar. After talking with Greg and Steve more and more, I ended up becoming an unofficial 'cellar dweller,' either hanging out or helping out in their brewery once it was up and running. I had quit Brewer's Union, and I began working with Stone part-time . . . and Pizza Port . . . and White Labs, the yeast company. It was a little hectic, and seemingly all at once, all three were looking to hire somebody full-time. I ultimately went with Stone because I felt like it was the best fit for me.

Steve and I had a great brewing synergy. He brought a lot of experience to the table, and I brought a good deal of technical knowledge from UC Davis. We'd hammer out specifications for a beer we wanted to do, and then we'd each make a separate pilot batch and do a side-by-side tasting. We usually ended up going with a combination of the two, and it often seemed like Steve's malts with my hops would be the winner. Steve really knows how to build a great malt bill. They're almost deceptively simple, yet always delicious. He really lets a malt tell its story.

I came on when Stone was still in its infancy. They were only brewing the Stone Pale Ale and the Stone Smoked Porter, but the beer was catching on. Greg and Steve might have been complaining about the numbers, but there was never really a surplus or stockpile of beer. To be honest, even when the figures were 'dismal,' new equipment always seemed to be coming in. They were growing into their equipment quickly, but I never got the sense that quantity was the prime objective. Obviously, there was a critical mass they needed to achieve, but they really just wanted the beer to come out tasting good. It was never about tapping into a gold mine.

I really enjoyed working with them, and it exposed me to a lot of new experiences, great people, and, of course, amazing beer. The Stone 02.02.02 and 04.04.04 Vertical Epic Ales are still two of the best beers I've ever had. We were making beer that we could be very

proud of—beers that we would want to enjoy. And it was rewarding knowing that the beers we were making were going out to retail shelves and into people's homes. It was mostly unspoken, but we were motivated not to put out something subpar, because that would screw somebody who was buying an expensive six-pack of beer after a hard day at work. We knew what hard work was; we were frickin' doing it. And would we want to come home to a crappy beer after a day of hard work? Hell no. So we sure as hell weren't going to subject anybody else to such a fate.

Beyond that, I enjoyed the problem-solving aspect and figuring it all out: somehow squeezing in pilot brews and crazy one-offs, all while growing the core

beers at a phenomenal rate. Plus, I liked keeping busy, which was no problem at Stone. There was something new every day. But ultimately, after close to a decade, I decided my time there was up. Friends were telling me I was crazy to leave, and it was one of the hardest decisions I've ever had to make. I had become very close with a lot of people at Stone and it was a phenomenal place to work, but I just had this incurable itch to get out and do my own thing.

Greg and Steve put together a great going away party for me on my last day: March 10, 2006. They even issued a proclamation declaring March 10 to be Lee Chase Day. It was pretty cool. I took a couple weeks off to ponder and reflect, then did some consulting work and spent some more time with White Labs. Then, in January 2009, I opened up Blind Lady Ale House in the Normal Heights district of San Diego with my wife and two business partners. It's a great beer spot with an awesome kitchen, and we're getting our own brewing system underway: Automatic Brewing Co. Drop by and grab a pint sometime! " —LEE CHASE

" Seeing Lee go was tough in a lot of ways. I knew he wanted to do his own thing, which I can completely appreciate and relate to, but it was still hard after working so long with somebody, especially Lee, who worked every bit as hard as I did. Finding someone who is as passionate about your idea as you are is a rare find, and we had that in Lee. Without him, we'd be a different brewery to say the least. " —STEVE

We were definitely sad to see Lee go, but we were happy to have him as long as we did. Lee, you're a good man, and a beer genius. Best wishes in all your present and future undertakings!

As Lee set out to tread his own path, we put up a job posting for a new head brewer in the Brewers Association Beer Forum, an online industry message board. Funny enough, we got a bite from the place we least expected. Mitch, care to elaborate?

" Just prior to coming on board at Stone Brewing Co., I was working with the Specialty Brewing Group at . . . you ready for it? The Anheuser-Busch facility in Merrimack, New Hampshire. I took a fair share of ribbing about it from the guys here, but I worked with a very talented set of brewers at A-B, and it really shaped

my brewing career, which has now spanned a little over two decades. Say what you will about the fizzy yellow stuff, but the people physically making it are a savvy bunch, proficient in turning out a large volume of extremely consistent beer.

Besides Merrimack, I spent some time at the Fort Collins and St. Louis A-B factories. During my tenure, I was privileged to work in the Specialty Brewing Group, where I spent about three years as the new products brewmaster, which basically meant I got to play around with some of the not-quite-so-yellow fizzy stuff under their American Originals and Michelob Specialty product lines.

But my tawdry love affair with fermentation actually started with wine. I studied Fermentation Science at UC Davis, with an emphasis on winemaking. Even though I'd initially set out to study enology, I got a sudden itch to brew while I was there. Dr. Michael Lewis, the brewing professor at Davis, gave a guest lecture in a biology class I was taking. It was fascinating, and I still remember it so vividly. Beer was the new name of the game, and I changed my study focus to brewing science.

My interest only grew from there. Dr. Lewis would organize informal pub gatherings in the Davis area on Friday afternoons. One Friday we went to a place, aptly named the Pub, and I discovered Anchor Steam. I'd been drinking mostly imports and hadn't been introduced to craft beer, namely because there wasn't much of it around at the time. Somehow, Anchor Steam had stayed under my radar until that day. I remember thinking how malty and bitter it was, unlike anything else I'd ever tried.

Not long after that moment of beer Zen, our class took a tour of the Sierra Nevada brewery. Seeing it all in action, and seeing that it *could* be done, that people were making these flavorful beers, and that people were buying them—I really think it was right there, in that moment, when I decided I really, *really* wanted to be a brewer. But I heard about a job opening at Almaden Vineyards, applied for it, and stuck with wine for a bit.

When Almaden was bought by a big wine conglomerate, their focus shifted away from quality and leaned more toward quantity, and I quickly lost interest. Not long after that, as luck would have it, a gentleman by the name of Bill Millar hired me part-time to help set up shop at the (now-defunct) San Andreas Brewing Co. in Hollister. I was finally doing what I loved. I was makin' beer.

I took a few field trips while I was at San Andreas, and I remember being amazed when I went up to Portland for the Oregon Brewers Festival. It wasn't just beer; it was a beer community. The people there were so supportive and had fostered an amazing movement. Not that there was ever any doubt, but it really cemented in my mind what I knew all along: brewing beer was my calling. I was enjoying the hell out of it, and still am.

After about four years with San Andreas, I decided I was more interested in working at a production brewery than a brewpub. That's when I went to work at Anheuser-Busch. My fourteen years there gave me a firm grip on managing production, raw materials, brewing schedules, and, of course, volume. More than that, I was able to tune in my palate to very minute flavor inconsistencies. Consistency is king there, and you have to be able to pick up on the most infinitesimal of variance.

Being the new products brewmaster for the Specialty Brewing Group offered some opportunity to play around and try new ideas, but at times it was frustrating. For example, I made a pilot batch of an IPA that wasn't even that aggressive, maybe 70 IBUs. We poured it at the Great American Beer Festival that year, and people loved it! But the powers that be just wouldn't have it. So when I saw a job posting for the head brewer position at Stone, I sent in my résumé.

Once I got to talking with Greg and Steve, I felt like their portfolio and level of creativity meshed well with what I wanted to brew, and I think they knew that my experience and attention to detail was ideal for helping with their growth. It was a win-win situation, definitely. Still is . . . knock on wood. " —MITCH

" When Mitch applied for the position, I tried not to get too excited. I had met him a few times, but more than that, I saw him online all the time. He was the one guy from Anheuser-Busch who would come to the Craft Brewers Conference, or post on the Brewers Association forums. It was impressive: if somebody had a technical question, Mitch was always there to help. He seemed like the nicest, most knowledgeable guy, and, as anyone who has ever met him will tell you, that's exactly what he is. His touch and experience with managing larger brewing systems were icing on the cake. To say that I was thrilled to see him come on board would be an understatement. " —STEVE

With Mitch in place and the brewery up and running smoothly, it was time to hatch our next plan. Before even starting Stone, Steve and I had long contemplated operating a brewpub. And while we ultimately opted for a production brewery instead, we'd still wanted to have a restaurant. After all, what kind of dream house doesn't have a kitchen?

COOKING UP A STORY

In the interest of, well, being interesting, we'd wanted to do more than just have another brewery people could come visit. I mean, how many stainless steel vats, pallets of kegs and bottles, and stockpiles of grain bags can folks take pictures of before they all start to look the same? Anyway, run-of-the-mill just isn't how we operate.

For the better part of a decade, I'd sat in a little office in an industrial park in San Marcos longing for just a touch of scenery—direct sunlight, plants, trees, something green . . . some semblance of nature for inspiration. All too often, I'd find myself staring outside not quite admiring our parking lot, dreaming of some sort of garden where I could escape, if only for a few minutes, to clear my head. It felt like even if I never actually used it, just knowing it was there would be reassuring enough. As it was, the closest thing I'd had to an escape was taking my chair out onto the sidewalk and just basking in the glow of the sun, eyes closed, tilted back, shirt optional.

What I'd wanted, what I'd *always* wanted, was the Stone Brewing World Bistro & Gardens—a dramatic, stunning restaurant flanked by our new brewery on one side and a lush outdoor expanse on the other. I wanted a restaurant that eschewed the evils of the reigning culinary paradigm, just as our beers didn't fall victim to the evils of modern megabrewing.

But as you can probably guess by now, we weren't going to have any lowest-common-denominator crap on our menu. Just as we are surrounded by a world of generic sameness with commodity beer, we are surrounded by an overindustrialized food system that long ago traded quality and character for ease of production and the drive to make it ever cheaper, cheaper, cheaper. We decided that we should not, could not, and would not be part of that world. We wanted everything on our menu to be outstanding. You know how some restaurants feature a "signature" item—a unique dish that has become something folks go out of their way to get? As we worked on creating the menu for the bistro,

we thought, "Why not make everything on the menu a signature dish?" We wanted our food to be of the same caliber as the beers we'd be serving.

And speaking of the beers we'd be serving, we could have just lined up a bunch of Stone beers on tap and called it a day. But that's not how we roll. There was no question that we wanted to support other players in the craft beer biz, so we knew from the get-go that we would feature the best of the best from around the world, with a special emphasis on our San Diego brethren, of course, just as we were doing with the distribution side of our company.

Beer we knew. We could do beer. But with food, it was a new set of challenges. We had an idea of the food we were going to serve, but we needed a menu. We needed a chef.

Enter Carlton.

"I started working in restaurants at the age of nineteen as a dishwasher and worked my way up from there, mainly in San Francisco. After getting to the level of sous chef, I decided that I should have formal training, so I went to culinary school at the Art Institute of Seattle, graduating in 1998. I moved back to San Francisco for a year for my first chef post, and then down to San Diego, where my wife and I operated a small catering company and I began working at 150 Grand Cafe in Escondido. A year later I got the chef position at 150 Grand, a job I held for the next three years until the owners announced their retirement. My wife and I were already running the restaurant and bought it from them, owning for the next two years.

The guys from Stone were regular customers, and I was a huge Stone fan. Of the three tap handles in our restaurant, two were always Stone products. Greg showed us the plans for the Escondido brewery early in the process, and we were very excited about it. They asked us to cater the groundbreaking ceremony, which we did happily, even though it ended up being in the rain. When it came time to hire a chef, I think I was a natural choice for them, being local, experienced, and a big fan. I was thrilled when they offered me the job.

I had been a beer fan for a long time, both drinking and cooking with it, but never on the level of what Stone wanted to do. It was challenging to use the strong, hoppy beers to cook with—especially the Stone IPA, which has a tendency to get even more bitter through the cooking process. Some are easier to work with, like the Stone Smoked Porter, with that dark, chocolatey character that made it a natural choice for BBQ sauce. I was really into the whole beer scene, and it was a lot of fun to play around with the different brews.

What I enjoyed most about working at the bistro was the setup and testing process. Stone is very involved in tasting and testing their beers, and that process carried over to the food, as well. Although construction of the dining room and gardens was running behind schedule, the kitchen had been finished a little early, which gave us lots of time to perfect the recipes and make sure each was what everyone wanted. I also enjoyed working closely with Greg, whose ideas fly quickly, and I really liked the menu when we were done with it.

As far as favorite dishes, I got completely hooked on the Tempeh Fuego Burger. I'm not a vegetarian, and I routinely added bacon to my sandwich, but it was delicious. I think that's where my love of fresh chiles really developed. On the other hand, the Arrogant Bastard Ale Onion Rings were a complete bitch to prepare and keep up with. (You'll hear much, much more about that later.)

I worked as a consultant for about five months before the bistro opened, and then as executive chef for about three more months. Basically, I think of it as getting the top spinning, putting the right people in place, and then slowly letting go while the top keeps spinning. Two and a half years ago I moved back to Seattle, where I became the executive chef of the J&M Cafe in Pioneer Square, one of Seattle's oldest bars and restaurants. It's been going very well, and I'm happy to be helping get this Seattle landmark back on the map.*" — CARLTON GREENAWALT, opening chef at the Stone Brewing World Bistro & Gardens

Lookin' Good

So, for the bistro, good beer was a no-brainer. (I mean, c'mon, we're Stone!) And the food had to be good too, because if nothing else, I wanted to enjoy eating there. But I also wanted the bistro to look good—that's not the right word—I wanted it to *feel* good. I wanted someone to walk in, have no idea we even had a restaurant, take one peek in, and just know they had to come in and see what we were up to.

We worked in some cool architectural features and focused on incorporating a lot of natural elements. To let in lots of natural light and fresh air, we came up with the idea of large, 23-foot-tall slanted glass walls with 12-foot-tall panels that would slide up to open. That brought some of the outdoors to the indoors, but the outdoors was important too. Having been cooped up in a concrete jungle for so long in our old space, I wanted to have my own beer garden, my own little Shangri-la. I wanted to be surrounded by plant life, water features, and natural beauty. To boot, we've got the famously fantastic San Diego weather on our side, which you just can't beat most days of the year. Who wouldn't want to enjoy a beer or two outdoors here?!

Stone Wall Project

During the construction of the brewery, there were all these rocks—stones, if you will—that were scattered about the construction site or otherwise unearthed, and we wanted to think of a way to work those in to our design, rather than just having them hauled away. Enter the Stone Wall—a massive stone

"What's the best job you can possibly have? It's being the weatherman in San Diego, California. It does not get any better than that. You got a six-figure income; you're on TV for about thirty seconds. People go, 'What's the weather going to be like, Lew?'
    'Nice! . . . Back to you.'"   —Lewis Black, *Comedy Central Presents*

wall extending from inside the restaurant out into the beer garden. I checked out all types of stone veneer on the market. There's some beautiful veneer made from real stone, but we realized that using actual stones from the site, and from people's own backyards, would create a style and character far beyond any that could come from a veneer. What's more, we reached out to you to help build it. As in, actually, physically piece it together.

We decided that there would be no better way

to capture the look and feel we wanted than with the artistic touch of Stone fans and community supporters. Building on the community theme, we then hatched the idea to make it a charity project that would raise money for our favorite local charities. We called it the Stone Wall Project.

The stones varied in size based upon the amount of the donation, and to sweeten the deal for donors (beyond helping deserving local charities and having a little piece of history in our construction), each got a ration of StoneWall Ale, specially made just for this momentous occasion. Each bottle was emblazoned with the names of all the donors, and at 12.2% ABV, it remains the strongest beer we've ever brewed (at least as of printing time.... I don't want to rule anything out for the future). But unless you were one of the 472 philanthropists who chipped in, you didn't get any—well, at least not to take home with you.

So, this crazy wall. Lori Holt Pfeiler, the illustrious mayor of Escondido at the time, ceremoniously placed the first stone, and a small army of local dignitaries and extremely loyal Stone fans followed suit. After all the stones had been put in place, we filled in any holes, packed in dirt, threw some rebar in for strength, and poured cement over all of it. After the cement cured, cranes lifted the finished panels into place. The finished wall—fourteen feet tall at its highest point and over 100 feet long—really represents the strength of our community and the power of giving, having raised nearly $100,000 for our favorite local charities.

Open Sesame

We opened up Stone Brewing World Bistro & Gardens in November 2006, quite a bit later than we'd originally planned. It had been highly anticipated from the get-go, and the fact that the opening had been delayed added to the anticipation. We weren't sure exactly what

Stones were available in small, medium, large, and Arrogant Bastard sizes for a donation of $125, $250, $500, and $1,000, respectively. In the quest to come up with more Arrogant Bastard–sized stones, a behemoth was discovered and brought back to the brewery. It was dubbed "Double Bastard size"—the only one of its kind in the wall.

We knew this stone was special, and we knew it would command a special price. So, I did what plenty of other young(ish) people do when they want money: I called my mom. Although my folks had already pledged a cool grand for an Arrogant Bastard–sized stone, my own shameless arrogance managed to coerce another $1,000 donation out of them so they could lay claim to the biggest, baddest, and boldest boulder.

Stone Wall Cross-Section

to expect, but the launch went pretty well if you ask me. We did hit a few snags early on, which is to be expected. Funny enough, there were two unexpected hot-button issues that flooded my inbox daily, right from day one.

Issue #1: Arrogant Bastard Ale Onion Rings. They were the item that people loved to hate. (Check out the whole story behind them on page 126.)

Issue #2: No ketchup. We'd discussed it early on and didn't feel anything on our menu would be enhanced with a characterless condiment made of tomato concentrate, distilled vinegar, dehydrated onion, and possibly high-fructose corn syrup. Our Spud Buds and Arrogant Bastard Ale Onion Rings were better dunked in Stone Smoked Porter BBQ Sauce anyway. But people went ballistic over the fact that we didn't have it. After being inundated with unrelenting complaints for months, we reluctantly brought ketchup on board. But to show my disdain

and contempt for having to do so, I rolled it out with a tongue-in-cheek event dubbed The Night That Ketchup Attacked!—replete with a ketchup fountain, a blind ketchup tasting, a ketchup sandwich, and a slew of other jabs at the absurdity of it all.

Eventful

Other than the onion ring headache and ketchup whiners, we were getting lots of positive feedback, some of most enthusiastic about our special events: themed beer nights, pilot batch tastings with the brewers, "Beer U" classes, full-fledged brewmaster dinners, and more. We had beer and chocolate pairings, beer and cheese pairings, and other tasty educational events not only to have to fun with what we were doing, but also to show how versatile craft beer could be.

Because our events were so popular, we put on more and more of them. After a while, we really had to think about how to do something a new way or how to change things up so that we weren't just rehashing old ideas. (Not that they weren't awesome when we did them the first time!) Once we brought executive chef Alex Carballo on board, we had no problem putting together all sorts of exciting new events. Alex, this would be a great time to tell folks how you got lumped in with this craziness.

"Back in 2008, I was working at a seafood restaurant in Pacific Beach that it was very busy for its size. The restaurant sat about sixty-five, and it was strictly fish—no other meats on the menu. During my time there, I had the great pleasure of redesigning the whole restaurant. I was enjoying it quite a bit, but my contract was up for renegotiation, and just out of curiosity, I wanted to see what else was out there.

I looked around and responded to a few postings on Craigslist, one that just said some North County restaurant was looking for a chef, without the name of the restaurant or anything about it. I sent in my résumé, and a few days later I got a phone call from a recruiter saying she was calling from 'a restaurant and brewery in North County San Diego' and had a few questions for me. I kind of guessed what brewery it might be, but I didn't feel the need to press the issue with her.

After we talked for a few minutes, she asked if I was available to meet for an interview, so I must have done something right. I had a series of interviews and they all seemed to go well, but you can never really tell with Greg. He's a hard one to read.

Even though I still wasn't sure I'd get the position, I turned down a few other jobs that sort of looked better on paper in the hopes that Stone would bring me on board. Some of my friends told me that I was crazy for wanting to work at Stone and I knew that they'd struggled a bit finding their footing initially, but I really felt it was a good fit. The more I got to see what their program was about and what they stood for, the more I got this strong desire to work there. Something clicked. Something Greg said stuck with me throughout the whole interview process: 'We are not trying to find the best chef in the world. We're looking for the best chef for Stone.' I still remember that like it was yesterday.

I'd actually wanted to work for Stone when the bistro first opened, but it didn't pan out timing-wise. I was available early on in the developmental stages but had picked up my job in Pacific Beach before Stone started hiring. Needless to say, when I finally got the call, I took the job. It's been a great experience for me, and I've gotten to work on so many great events. Greg and Steve are always so supportive of my ideas and experiments. I love beer and was kind of hip to what was going on in the craft beer scene when I started here, but getting to work so closely with the brewers, and of course with our beverage supervisor, 'Dr.' Bill Sysak, my appreciation for beer has stepped up significantly.

And beyond the amazing beer and tasty food, knowing that we're putting out something wholesome makes me feel good. The bistro is the largest purchaser of locally grown organic produce in San Diego County, and we source from small-scale producers whenever possible. We support the tenets of the Slow Food movement and steer 100 percent clear

of junk like high-fructose corn syrup. That's important to me. 99 — CHEF ALEX CARBALLO

Alex runs a great kitchen and is stellar at putting on events. His farm-to-table FRESH! dinners have been wildly successful, which is kind of amazing because people buy their tickets with absolutely no idea what's going to be on the menu. The concept behind FRESH! is that everything is harvested, picked, butchered, and so on the morning of the dinner. Not even Alex knows what the menu will be before the day of the meal, which is pretty badass if I do say so myself.

Another solid fixture is our Master Pairings series, headed up by Alex in tandem with "Dr." Bill Sysak, our resident beer collector extraordinaire and bon vivant. Your turn, Bill. Who are you and how did you get transplanted here?

66 I'm a big lover and supporter of craft beer, along with being a serious beer collector. My love affair with beer started when I was pretty young. I had just turned fifteen, and my parents weren't home. I was hanging

out with two of my buddies in the backyard drinking Löwenbräu, and my dad came home early and busted us. Caught us red-handed. But instead of getting mad, he wanted to teach us about beer.

He'd been in the military and traveled through England and Germany, discovering beers along the way. Back when I was a teenager, there was a chain of stores called Liquor Barn, and they had what you could call an impressive selection of beers for that time. My dad offered to have a beer sampling every Friday with a handful of brews he'd pick up from Liquor Barn or get from friends. We'd taste anywhere from a couple of beers to a dozen or so, and there might anywhere from three to eight people around the table on any given Friday. The invitation was always open.

Later, I joined the military as well, serving as a medic in the Army and National Guard. Although I was strictly a medic, not a doctor, I somehow picked up the nickname 'Dr.' Bill, and it's stuck with me all these years. Anyway, I was stationed in Nuremburg

for a number of years, and I frequently found my way to all sorts of German breweries. I also made frequent pilgrimages to Belgium, picking up *lots* of beer along the way to squirrel away in my seemingly ever-expanding stash.

Once I came back to the States, I continued to add to my collection, and I also hosted parties where I'd break open these rare beers, maybe as some sort of an extension of what my dad used to do. He always shared his treasured finds, and I'd like to think I've stuck to that philosophy.

In the late '90s I was living in Southern California, working at the St. Joseph Hospital of Orange, and I took little trips down to San Diego pretty frequently. I got to know Greg and Steve sometime just after their first anniversary. I bumped into them at a lot of events and, of course, went to a lot of their events. For my birthday, I used to host what I called 'The Largest, Most Extreme Private Beer Party in the World,' where I'd open two rare beers every ten minutes for the better part of twelve hours. I'd have a bunch of kegs tapped, too, in case you got thirsty in the nine minutes between pours. And Greg actually made it up to a couple of those, and we developed a bit of rapport and mutual respect over the years.

When I decided I wanted to retire from the medical field in 2008, I mentioned to Greg that I'd be interested in a position at Stone. Coincidentally enough, a slot was just opening up in the bistro, and we made it official. It's been very cool, because it's allowed me to sort of feel like I have my own pub, but on Greg and Steve's dime. They've let me run with it and trusted me to continue to build an awesome beverage program, and I think I've done that.

The beer events we host, like the Sour Fest and Oakquinox, have been wildly successful, as have been the FRESH! dinners and Master Pairings. It's been a lot of fun, and I can't imagine ever wanting the fun to end.*"* —"DR." BILL SYSAK

ALWAYS RUNNING

Since we moved into our new brewery and opened the restaurant—hell, since we first opened in 1996—we've just been running the whole time. It's kind of weird, really . . . to not be running *from* something, or running *after* something. That's not to say we're tired

by any means. We just like to keep going. Full steam ahead. All or nothing.

During the past few years, most of our story comes down to the amazing beers we've continued to release, and what seems like never-ending expansion. I don't know how we keep finding room for more tanks, but we always seem to. We did move our cold-storage warehouse to a separate 57,000-square-foot facility, which definitely freed up a lot of floor space in the brewery. Our little bistro kitchen is now supported by a larger production facility to help with food preparation—a necessity for keeping everything running smoothly at the bistro, which has become a *very* popular destination. (If you're coming on the weekend, make reservations!)

What else? Oh, I got knighted! Yup, Sir Greg here. (Thank you, but no bowing, please. Seriously, stand up! Okay, okay . . . "You may rise.") I was made an honorary knight by the Belgian Knighthood of the Brewers' Mash Staff, which was a *humongous* honor. Best of all, I got to share the honor by getting knighted alongside my good friends Charlie Papazian and the Alström brothers from BeerAdvocate. I'd actually gotten an email the previous year telling me that they wanted to make me a knight, but it arrived something like a week before the actual ceremony, and I couldn't make it. Can you imagine being asked to become a knight and having to decline because you had prior commitments?

I had to email them back and express my honor, gratitude, and thankfulness for the amazing offer, but that I had to politely decline, and hoped that they would perhaps offer again in the future. Hitting send on that email was extremely difficult, but there was something scheduled that I just couldn't change. Luckily, they asked again the following year, and also gave a little more advance notice. Sweet! Sweet! Lemme put that in my calendar . . . oh. Oh crap. This time, it meant I would have to miss the wedding of one of my best friends. I was torn, so I just forwarded him the email from the Knighthood and asked,

"Dude, what should I do?!" He replied something like, "Dude. Go." Now *that's* a friend!

Other than that, the only real news is that we've just kept on running.

THE NEXT CHAPTER

So what's the ride been like? Fun! Okay, that's really the easiest answer, and I think I've gotten so used to saying it over the years that I may have started to believe it. While we have indeed had a lot of fun over the years, it's really not accurate to use that as a one-word descriptor for our fifteen-year venture. A better description would be fifteen years of rollercoaster! It started out with excitement—and panic. Excitement about starting off a new venture on a path I was very passionate about, but mostly panic as in, "What the hell am I thinking. . . . Well, I'd *better* make it happen." I had no choice, and I knew it. I would not, could not fail. Through sheer force of will we made it happen. In fact, a couple of years into it, I realized that I'd developed a reputation for being a rather large asshole—really. I was so high strung, with my force of will and "it *must* work" approach, that I made that impression on nearly everyone I worked with. I was uptight. Tense. Driven. I had no patience for things not being done the way I felt they should be . . . whatever that 'it' was. One day about three to four years into it I woke up and I said to myself, "I don't want to be 'that guy.'" And I set about changing how I interacted with other people. I didn't change overnight, and I still have (very bothersome) naturally uptight characteristics, but it's better. I manage to keep it mostly in remission.

Sure, it's been incredibly awesome to be in the middle of the swirling maelstrom that is Stone Brewing, but it's also felt quite natural. From the beginning, I was in this to be successful. No, not the typical vision of success—money, fast cars, and all the superficial stuff—just awesome beer done our way, with a foundation of undeniable integrity. In the early days, I used to jokingly comment, "Quality and integrity in this day and age . . . who would've thought it would work!" The

truth is, I did. I was certain of it. Dead certain. Willing to stake my life's ambitions on it. And it did. And I've been not surprised in the least.

I have to be the first to admit that, aside from having the vision that what we were doing would eventually lead to success, I had little idea of the shape it would take. It's been a work in progress.

Looking back, the beginning of Stone fifteen years ago seems like forever ago. So long ago, in fact, that the details are all quite fuzzy and indistinct—without the odd photo to remind me of long-forgotten details, I would recall even less. The time has definitely not flown by. . . . I like things to keep moving forward. Let's make a decision, and then move forward!

I'm often asked what I think of all the changes that Stone has gone through over the years. Whether I'd ever expected the brewery to grow as it has, as fast as it has. The answers are actually pretty simple because, to me, the company hasn't really changed that much. Sure, it's changed on the outside: we built an awesome new brewery in 2005, added the Stone Brewing World Bistro & Gardens in 2006, added distribution warehouses in Escondido and Carson, a catering kitchen and new offices in 2010, and the first off-site Stone Company Store in San Diego's South Park neighborhood in mid-2011. However, that's just set dressing. The core of Stone is based on a simple and straightforward philosophical and ethical foundation: doing things the way that we like and believe in. The ethics

of doing our best means to always do things the right way. We've built our company on that belief.

Hopstradamus

So, what about the next fifteen years? From the point where I stand right now, as I pen this in early 2011, I see interesting things on the horizon—not just for Stone Brewing, but for the craft brewing industry as a whole, nationally and internationally. I've long predicted an intensive regionalization of craft brewing, and in some regions, it's already here. As more and more craft breweries open up in the United States, and as they continue to get better and better, people in regions with a strong craft beer community will tend to choose local beers over similar brews from other areas. This makes sense, and our experience with Stone Pale Ale backs it up. We sell a lot of Stone Pale Ale locally in SoCal, but more Stone IPA and Arrogant Bastard Ale outside our region. Why? Chances are there are at least a few tasty pale ales made by local breweries in most regions. When we first started distributing Stone outside of SoCal, the San Francisco Bay Area was one of the areas where we tried sending our beer, but we didn't even bother to send Stone Pale Ale because Sierra Nevada Pale Ale already owned it up there. As people become increasingly interested in trying new beers, they don't want to try just

another pale ale from some other brewery. They want to try something in a different style. Fair enough.

I also foresee a fracturing of styles. I mean this in a positive way. It's like in music: First there was rock 'n' roll. Then there was blues rock, pop rock, and hard rock. Now there are subgenres of subgenres. Hell, there are at least seven different major subgenres of heavy metal alone. Sure, to a nonmetalhead they might all sound the same, but an enthusiast can wax poetically about the subtle and not-so-subtle differences (yes, I think you can wax poetically about metal music, especially with a good beer in hand). Likewise, a beer novice might not initially understand the differences between various sour beers, but enthusiasts want to know which strain of Brett was used and whether it was utilized in primary fermentation, or later for bottle conditioning. Is it a lambic, a Flanders red, or an American wild ale? And if it's a lambic, then which style: fresh whole fruit or (gasp!) syrups? You get my point. For an enthusiast, this conversation is a beautiful thing.

And just as in rock 'n' roll, a brewery can be authentic or go the poseur route. You can create a classic that will stand the test of time—Anchor Steam, for example—or you can create a throwaway Auto-Tuned pop song, a one-hit wonder. The analogies are too easy: Poseur gangsta rap? High ABV overcaffeinated malt liquor in flashy packaging. Megacorporate rock? Megacorporate craft beers. Sickly sweet teenage pap—I mean pop—song? Sickly sweet raspberry beer designed for adults with teenage-level palates. Milli Vanilli? Any number of brands that want you to think that they're brewing themselves, but instead work a "pay no attention to the man behind the curtain" sleight of hand and have some other company make it for them. Hey, either it's your voice singing the song, or it's not.

Manifest Destiny

What about the future of Stone specifically, you ask? Well, I can tell you one thing: it's full of hope, ideas, possibilities, excitement, and energy. In the Stone world, the crystal ball suggests a variety of new things, all following our core fundamentals, and all really, really cool.

It's our goal to continue to follow the direction of our hearts and imaginations. Constant change, constant growth. Whether in size—which looks like it will continue for awhile yet—or in scope. Breadth and depth. And fun. Sure, I get tempted to rest on our laurels, many times each week—usually before morning coffee, or after a too-big lunch when I'm feeling a bit sleepy. The rest of the time, I'm imagining the ways we're going to change the world. Or at least "move the needle," as I like to put it.

It might not seem like it from the outside (or to Steve!), but we turn down the vast majority of opportunities that come our way. To someone trying to engage us in a new idea, it must undoubtedly seem like dealing with a nearly impenetrable brick wall. It's not that we're dense, although perhaps I personally can be at times we're just inordinately selective—or at least that's how we like to think of ourselves. (If you think differently of us, please keep it to yourself so as not to shatter our idealized self-image.)

And yet we've never had so many exciting things in the "things we are planning" category, so I'll dive in. Keep up if you can!

We're creating Stone Farms, a little gem of an organic farm. Just fifteen minutes up the road from our brewery in Escondido sits an organic farm owned by a friend of a friend. For the last seven years it was run by a highly respected fellow who, due to a host of circumstances, decided to move on to things that had a little less in common with banging one's head against a brick wall. Not that he wasn't hardheaded— he was, in the most positive of ways—but the time to move on had come. When the property owner and I connected the dots between our mutual friends in the second half of 2010, it seemed almost serendipitous. They asked if Stone would consider stepping in and saving the farm, and after a bit of consideration, we gladly said yes. Is operating a small farm similar to running a small brewery? Yes and no. On the yes side, anyone who would consider getting into either business should have their head examined. Perfect for us, we figured! Also, the underlying philosophies of organic farming seemed like something worth protecting, and there was a chance the farm would go fallow if we didn't step up and step in.

We're also working on the expansion of Stone Distributing (which has already become Southern California's largest specialty craft beer wholesaler), a large new restaurant and brewery combination located at the historic Liberty Station complex near downtown San Diego (pictured below), a special line of beers called "Quingenti Millilitre," which will be sold in very limited quantities in cork-finished 500mL bottles, a new fermentation building for sour and specialty beer production just across the street from our Escondido brewery, an adjacent hotel—and opening a facility across the pond, which will make Stone the first American craft brewery to own and operate its own brewhouse in Europe (and that story will merit its own book some day!).

The only thing less realistic than jamming all that in one paragraph is that I'm actually serious about that list. Hell, the only thing I'm not currently contemplating is shooting a television show, at least not at this exact moment. Make an offer and I'll see.

Perhaps you think I'm full of myself. (I'd say I'm just full of ideas and am willing to at least attempt to chase many of them down.) Perhaps you think I'm crazy. (OK, you might have something there.) Perhaps you're as excited as we are. Perhaps you're ready for a beer. Perhaps you're mouthing your words as you read this.

PART TWO

THE BEERS OF

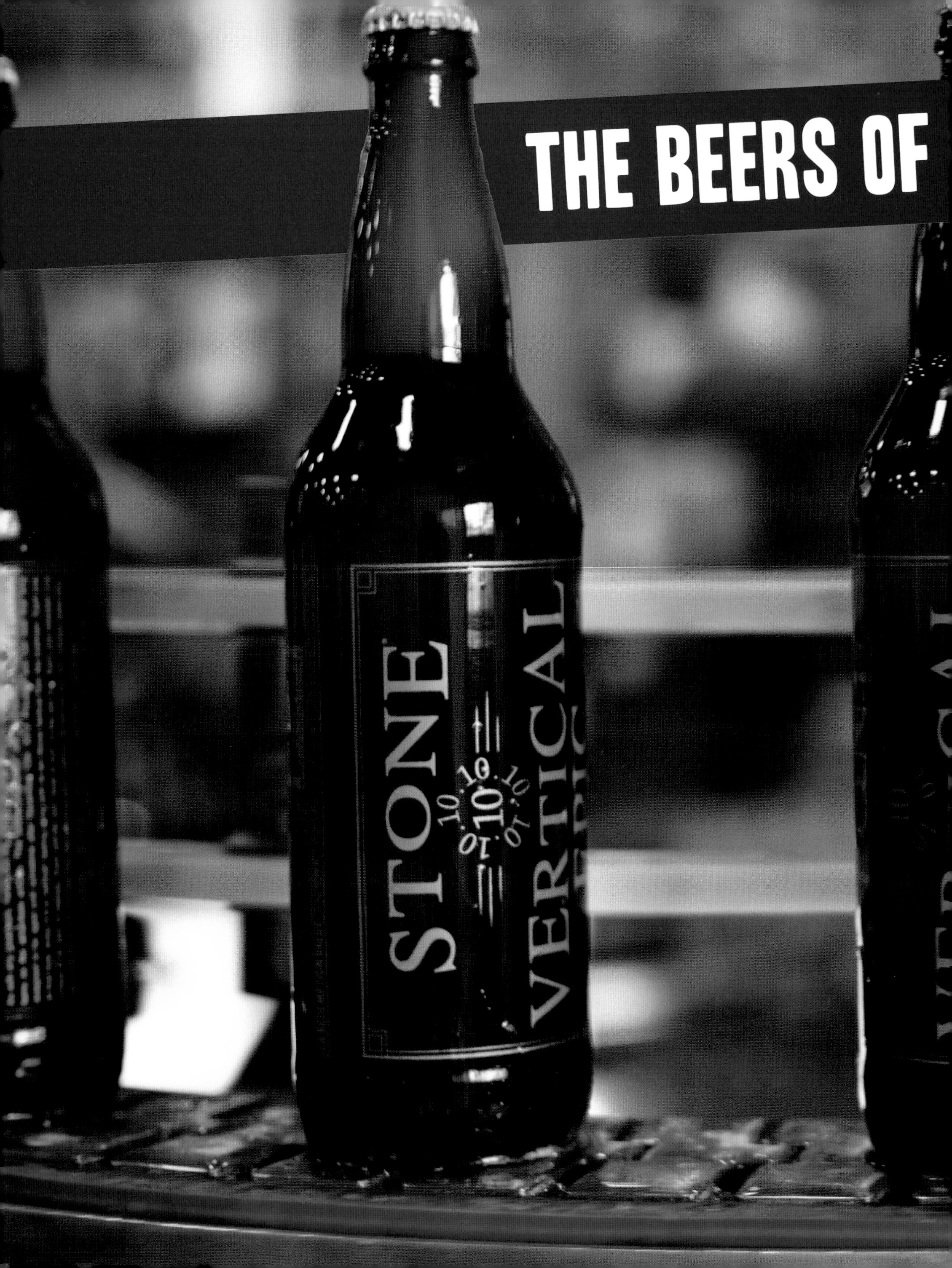

STONE BREWING CO.

Over the years, Stone's portfolio of craft beers has grown to encompass a wide variety of styles, flavors, and varying malt and hops profiles. We like to experiment with and celebrate the art of brewing, branching out and breaking convention. As such, we've developed quite an array of beers, and this section celebrates just about all of them. Some you may not have heard of. Some you may have forgotten about. Others, you might just learn a new factoid or two about.

We've included a good amount of information about each beer profiled here to try to paint a picture of how some of our favorite beers came together: the who, what, when, where, why—and the why the heck not?! We've also amassed some amusing anecdotes and reflective quotes to help give you the inside story of Stone.

YEAR-ROUND AND ANNUAL RELEASES

Behold our core lineup: nine year-round beers and three special releases. No, they're not seasonal, as they're not tied to any season, but they are definitely special. It's great to still be wowed year after year with them. I always have a pretty good memory of how each one tasted when I first sampled the previous release the year before, then I take a sip of the new batch and it always blows me away. Besides tasting great, the swig must trigger some sort of psychological comfort receptor or something, bringing with it a delicious end to the nearly yearlong absence-makes-the-heart-grow-fonder-anticipation/mild form of torture.

And it's been nothing short of amazing to watch our selection of year-round offerings grow the way they have. From day one with beer one, the evergreen Stone Pale Ale, to the nine beers we steadily brew now, we knew we loved them when we first made them, but I couldn't have predicted that so many others would embrace them as they have (and still do). It's incredibly humbling, and it's something I'm happy to be reminded of every time I have a pint.

STONE PALE ALE

Release Date: July 26, 1996
Availability: Year-round
Hop Profile: Columbus and Ahtanum
Style: American pale ale
IBUs: 41
ABV: 5.4%

"Greg and I made the decision early on to lead in with a pale ale. It was a solid style that a lot of other brewers were doing at the time, but we had a different take on it. In fact, a lot of people were making what they called a pale ale, but most were really just another fizzy yellow beer-like beverage. Some brewers were going for bigger pale ales, but they were often just trying to clone Sierra Nevada Pale Ale, getting that big, citrusy flavor from Cascade hops.

We wanted to do a pale ale without using Cascade hops, making it more of a hybrid pale ale and adding an American flair to a more English-style recipe. The recipe we used was one I had developed while in Oregon. I had been given some Ahtanum hops, a little-known cultivar at the time, and tried them out in a pale ale. I really liked the flavor they added and the way they balanced the malt. It was different from other varieties of hops I'd worked with, and it made a different pale ale than I'd tasted before. This was what we wanted to start with; this was how we would begin to carve our identity." —STEVE

DON'T CRY OVER SPILLED BEER

STEVE: When we started out, there was no shortage of long days and long nights. One such day (leaning heavily into night), I'd just finished filtering some Stone Pale Ale and was finally getting ready to close up shop. But heavy in a daze of sheer exhaustion, I made a costly mistake: I undid the wrong valve. Sooner than I could realize what I'd done, 30 barrels (aka 930 gallons) of pressurized, 34-degree beer came flooding out of the tank.

Between the onslaught of liquid and carbon dioxide, I was suffocating while trying to get the valve back in place. I managed to get a big enough breath of air to yell for Greg, who was in the office. He came running and immediately jumped into help. There was so much pressure, I wasn't sure we would ever get it closed back up, but we had to try. We *literally* could not afford to lose all of that beer. Fortunately, we managed to eventually secure the valve, but we still lost a pretty good amount of precious beer. And so much for being exhausted and ready to head home. . . . Now it was clean up time!

STONE SMOKED PORTER

Release Date: December 1996
Availability: Year-round
Hop Profile: Columbus and Mt. Hood
Style: American porter with smoked malt
IBUs: 53
ABV: 5.9%

"Wanting to brew a smoked porter came from my experiences in the Northwest. I'd tried versions from quite a few breweries, though it wasn't a particularly popular or available style then. Alaskan Smoked Porter was around though, and I vividly remember being blown away by my first taste of it. I loved how extremely smoky it was! It was unlike anything I'd ever had before. And while I really enjoyed it, I didn't know if I could drink it all the time, just because there was *so* much smoke flavor. Down the road, when we ultimately decided to brew Stone Smoked Porter, we wanted to take a different approach and have the smoke be an element of the beer, not *the* element of the beer." —STEVE

VARIATIONS ON A THEME

STEVE: We're always looking for fun little ways to tweak our beers, and two have been especially well received. We brew a version of Stone Smoked Porter with chipotle (which took a Silver Medal at the 2010 Great American Beer Festival, by the way) and another (courtesy of brewery trainer Laura Ulrich) made with vanilla beans. The flavor of each is so interesting; not only do the chipotle peppers and the vanilla beans bring their own profiles to their respective brews, each accentuates different flavors in the Stone Smoked Porter that are otherwise not as pronounced.

STONE IPA

Release Date: August 1997
Availability: Year-round
Hop Profile: Columbus, Chinook, and Centennial
Style: American IPA
IBUs: 77
ABV: 6.9%

I could wax poetic about Stone IPA—and IPAs in general—for quite some time. It's probably no secret that IPAs are my favorite style of beer. Back in 1997 when we decided to release Stone IPA for our first anniversary, IPAs were strictly in the realm of the extreme beer enthusiast. At the time, fans of craft beers tended to focus on pale ales, amber ales, amber lagers, ESBs (Extra Special Bitters), American-style hefeweizens, and (gasp! . . . shudder . . .) sweet, fruity beers and honey wheat beers.

It was the best of times, it was the worst of times.

Yet there was also a growing level of experimentation with hoppy styles among craft brewers. At Pizza Port Carlsbad, we'd found Swami's IPA, and that was hard to stray from, despite the long list of other fantastic beers they were putting out. It's hard to imagine now, but I can't recall any other big, hoppy IPAs being

brewed in San Diego County at the time. (Not to gloss over Blind Pig IPA, of course, which was being brewed nearby in adjacent Riverside County.) But San Diego County? Slim pickings back then, and many of them were IPAs in name only, not really living up to their hoppy potential. We wanted to change that.

"You know, we never did a pilot batch of Stone IPA. The only way that could have happened is if we'd essentially worked a double shift, and frankly, we were already stretched to our limit. So we just kept the recipe simple, brewed a full batch, crossed our fingers, and hoped to get it very right on the first try. I think at this point it's safe to say that we did."
—STEVE

ARROGANT BASTARD ALE

Release Date: November 7, 1997
Availability: Year-round
Hop Profile: Classified
Style: American strong ale
IBUs: Classified
ABV: 7.2%

"Greg's memory of how Arrogant Bastard Ale came to be (page 43) differs slightly from mine. Yes, I had messed up. Yes, I'd unknowingly added way too much malt and hops for a pale ale. Greg seems to think we realized the mistake mid brew, but I don't remember realizing it until we actually tasted the beer. I recall taking a sip and immediately going back to look through my notes to find my miscalculation. Sure enough, I'd scaled it all wrong for our new equipment. I was so disappointed that I'd messed it up that I wasn't letting myself be open to how great this beer really was. All I could think about was what it was supposed to be and how off the mark it was. It wasn't what I'd planned, and I chose to obsess over what wasn't in the glass rather than what was.

Greg finally got me to stop worrying about the calculations and actually taste the beer, without any expectations or preconceived notions of what it was supposed to taste like. After clearing my mind and taking another sip, I was able to smile about it. I really liked this beer. What was wrong with it? Why was I freaking out minutes before? Yeesh, what a worrywart! Well, my mind still wandered. It was great that we liked it, but I couldn't imagine anyone else liking it. It was much too good for the underdeveloped palates of most beer drinkers at the time. " —STEVE

TURBO BASTARD?

GREG: Every year, there's a Strong Ale Festival at Pizza Port, a tradition that started back in December, 1996. In 1997, after releasing Arrogant Bastard Ale, we had this crazy idea to make a freeze-distilled version, in which some of the water freezes, but the alcohol, of course, does not. Removing the frozen water (we call it ic') makes the beer more concentrated, both in flavor and alcohol content. Now, the legality of this is a sort of gray area, so of course we never would have made such a thing for said Strong Ale Festival. But if we had made it . . . *if* . . . I bet it would have tasted incredible, and just sooo big, like Arrogant Bastard Ale intensified, but quite different at the same time. And we would have called it Turbo Bastard. Too bad it never happened.

STONE OLD GUARDIAN BARLEY WINE

Release Date: February 1998
Availability: January/February
Hop Profile: Varies
Style: American barleywine
IBUs: Varies
ABV: Varies

"Greg and I knew we wanted to put out a barleywine pretty early on. We were big fans of other West Coast barleywines, especially Old Crustacean, Bigfoot, and Old Foghorn, and we wanted one to call our own. As an added bonus, our yeast happens to work exceptionally well with high-gravity fermentation, which is one of the defining features of barleywines, so we made it happen. Even though the flavor of the final beer is incredibly complex, the recipe is surprisingly simple.

We first made our barleywine in 1998, but we had trouble deciding on a name for it. With the first batch,

In 2010, we fermented some of the classic Old Guardian with our Belgian yeast strain (the same one we use for Stone Cali-Belgique IPA). We liked it so much that we brewed more to release for our Odd Beers in Odd Years program in 2011, dubbing it Stone Old Guardian BELGO Barley Wine. We'd planned on only releasing the "odd" version, forgoing the classic Old Guardian for a year, but people got a little up in arms about it (to say the least), so we decided to make both.

Stone Imperial Russian Stout got the same "odd beer" treatment that year, becoming Stone BELGO Anise Imperial Russian Stout. In addition to being tweaked by using our Belgian yeast strain, the bold stout was brewed with a bit of star anise and jazzed up with a brief soak in French and American oak. Who knows what oddities lie in store for 2013, 2015, 2017, and beyond . . .

the idea of calling it Y2K floated around, the idea being that you should age it until at least the year 2000, but we abandoned that idea pretty quickly. We decided to go with Lee's suggestion of Stone Old Guardian Barley Wine, but we didn't really intend to keep it. In fact, we printed the bottles with a note asking for name suggestions from anyone loyal and dedicated enough to read through Greg's typically lengthy musings.

But we weren't inspired by any suggestions that came in, and we had actually grown to like the name Old Guardian. Then, when Y2K came around (sans anarchy and apocalypse), the 2000 batch of Old Guardian took a silver medal out of a pool of sixty-five barleywine entries at the Great American Beer Festival.

Mind you, our stock of this brew was long gone, considering we'd only made a paltry 360 cases. But with the award, there was a lot of buzz, and everyone was clamoring for it. That sealed the deal: the name was going to stay.

The recipe changes slightly from year to year, but in 2001 we brewed the same recipe as in 2000 so more people could experience the greatness that got us our first Great American Beer Festival nod. " —STEVE

To continue sharing the wealth, the recipe for this award-winning version is also the one we chose to include in the book for your own homebrewing pleasure (page 186). You're welcome.

THE WRITING OF A LABEL

GREG: Steve made mention of my somewhat verbose label text, so I thought I'd write a note about my . . . notes. I like to write new text for our special release bottles each year, capturing the mood or moment, reflecting on the past year or forecasting the year to come, perhaps pontificating a touch (though some may argue it's flat-out filibustering). Each label I write has, over the years, developed a certain theme or style. Stone Old Guardian Barley Wine has, from the very beginning, been written in an in-the-moment stream of consciousness. When it comes time to pen it, I've always looked for an opportunity to sit down and write it all in one sitting. Random thoughts, conversations, and countless non sequiturs all exert their presence in what is, to the best of my knowledge, the wordiest beer label in the world. Not that it's a goal. It's not actually. Instead, it's more that I allow it to happen. Over the years, I've been fortunate enough to have the opportunity to write the label in a variety of countries, including India, Turkey, and Belgium, but always with a bottle of the previous edition at hand (open, of course!), and I've sought inspiration from my surroundings, and from the beer itself.

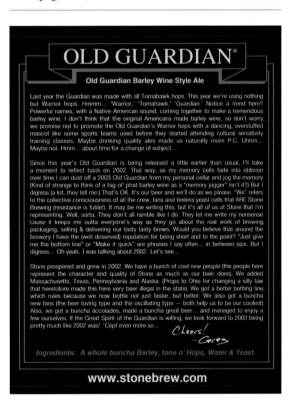

DOUBLE BASTARD ALE

Release Date: November 1998
Availability: November
Hop Profile: Classified
Style: American strong ale
IBUs: Classified
ABV: Varies

"As the one year anniversary of Arrogant Bastard Ale approached, the question of what to do about it arose rather quickly. Given that we'd just brewed the Stone 2nd Anniversary IPA, which was an amped up version of the Stone 1st Anniversary IPA, the idea to amp up Arrogant Bastard Ale was pretty universally lauded. Part of it was curiosity, sort of a question of "how hoppy can we get?" After all, we were incredibly leery of releasing Arrogant Bastard Ale just a year prior, when we honestly thought that very few people would like it simply because of its unapologetic strength and character. I think we can safely say now that there were a lot of people who liked it, and it took us a bit by surprise. And then there were those (albeit in the minority--remember, this was 1997-98) who really surprised us; they would take a sip and ask, "What's next? When are you making something even hoppier?!" Seriously? Alright!

And so, as the Bastard's first birthday came near, we decided to go all out and give him a special release big brother: Double Bastard Ale." — STEVE

STEVE: Double Bastard Ale was originally released to commemorate the one-year anniversary of its predecessor, Arrogant Bastard Ale. It was the same idea as what we were doing with our Anniversary IPAs: amping up our already amped-up beers. This also helped us stay away from 'holiday beers.' Everybody else was making them, and they quickly became a cliché.

STONE IMPERIAL RUSSIAN STOUT

Release Date: July 2000
Availability: Spring/early summer
Hop Profile: Warrior
Style: Imperial Russian stout
IBUs: Varies
ABV: Varies

"Coming home from a trip to Europe in 1995, Greg brought back a few small, 250 ml bottles of 1993 Courage Imperial Russian Stout that he'd picked up at a specialty beer store outside of Frankfurt. After settling back down stateside, he cracked one open with me. It was an epiphany, for both of us. Almost nobody was making beers like that at the time. We knew then and there that we wanted to put our own spin on this style at some point.

It's a fairly well-known style now, but in the 1990s imperial Russian stouts were practically unheard of—and largely misunderstood. In fact, our friends at the TTB (aka the Alcohol and Tobacco Tax and Trade Bureau, the federal agency to which all alcohol producers must submit their labels for approval) weren't quite sure how to deal with it. It took a couple of years (and large quantities of aspirin) to sort it out completely, but eventually it got resolved (obviously). And that was in no small part due to the diligence of Chris Cochran, Stone's community relations manager. I'll him let relive the entire ordeal for your reading pleasure. "
—STEVE

"Yes, we did run into some trouble years ago with labeling our beer as an imperial Russian stout. I think it started in late 2002, when the TTB, in reviewing our label application, claimed that the word Russian was misleading. They thought it would confuse customers into thinking that the beer was brewed in Russia, despite all of the text being in English, and the label clearly stating, 'Brewed and bottled by the Stone Brewing Co., San Marcos, San Diego, CA.'

We were given two options: either label it simply as Stone Imperial Stout or complicate matters by calling it Stone Imperial Russian-Style Stout. We explained that it wasn't actually a Russian style of beer, rather that it was an English style that had been brewed for the Russian court, but that seemed to fall on deaf ears. However, Greg is a stickler about words and accuracy, especially in regard to anything having to do with our beer, so he wasn't going to let this die.

And die it didn't. It actually dragged on for more than three years. Each time the TTB pushed back, I'd send them more information: photocopies of pages from books by Michael Jackson and Stephen Beaumont, printouts of information from BeerAdvocate .com and RateBeer.com—just huge stacks of supporting evidence. It became a shock-and-awe campaign, with some of my later packages containing hundreds of pages in defense of our claim that using the word

Russian was not misleading, but instead quite historically and stylistically accurate.

Sometimes we got by on a temporary permit, but the threat of having to change the name to just Stone Imperial Stout was very real, and it actually was labeled just that in 2003, much to our chagrin. Luckily though, Arlan Arnsten, our vice president of sales, happened to randomly meet somebody from the TTB at an industry event in Washington, DC. When Arlan mentioned Stone, our infamous reputation preceded us.

They apparently hit it off pretty well. The TTB guy knew all about our little naming battle, and he gave Arlan his business card and said he might be able to help get the issue resolved. I emailed him in short order, and he pointed me to the exact section of the code I needed to bring up: Title 27, Section 7.24(g), which states that using geographic names, such as Munich, Vienna, or Dortmund, is verboten, except in situations where the style and name had become prevalent enough so as to render the geographic significance, well, insignificant. If we could only prove this, victory would be ours.

Interestingly enough, we found out that the TTB didn't really know how to proceed with this any more than we did. The last time a change like this had come up was in the late 1930s, when the government ruled that India pale ale was a generally recognized style, as opposed to a mark of origin.

Unfortunately, though the style was being embraced by other brewers, most were brewpubs, so they typically weren't bottling their beers, and therefore weren't subject to labeling laws. While I wasn't trying to throw anybody under the bus, I had to name some names if we were going to win this thing. I ratted out North Coast Old Rasputin (sorry guys, but hey, it all worked out, right?) and the few others that were making the style at the time.

Eventually, in April 2005, we got a letter informing us that the TTB would formally review our request. And finally, after years of back-and-forth, we finally got the response we'd been waiting for. In a letter dated June 29, 2005 (I still have it framed somewhere), imperial Russian stout was recognized as a distinctive style, regardless of place of origin. Not only could we use the name, all American brewers could.

It was a day I'll never forget. Greg and Steve were ecstatic at having shaken up the status quo a bit. I was too, but more than anything, I was just glad to finally be done with it. I went home and popped open the oldest bottle of Stone Imperial Russian Stout I could find. I poured myself a glass out on my deck, sat with a copy of that approval letter, and watched the sunset. Victory was ours at last, with a little bit of righteousness mixed in for good measure. ” —CHRIS COCHRAN, community relations manager

final expression on the subject. At 8.5% ABV and well north of 100 IBUs, it was unlike anything else that existed. As much as we loved it (and we so very much did), we couldn't see it as part of our full-time lineup. Call it lack of vision, but back then we didn't think it was viable beyond a limited, special-release status. Well, that thought didn't last even a year. We soon found ourselves jonesing for a powerful hop smack, so in June 2002, Stone Ruination IPA was born. ”
—STEVE

STONE RUINATION IPA

Release Date: June 2002
Availability: Year-round
Hop Profile: Columbus and Centennial
Style: Double IPA
IBUs: 100+
ABV: 7.7%

“ Stone Ruination IPA was developed as a hybrid of the Stone 2nd through 5th Anniversary IPAs. We'd been steadily bumping up the hop levels of the anniversary releases every year, but after the massively hoppy Stone 5th Anniversary IPA, adding any more would have been impractical . . . verging on impossible. We thought it fitting to bring out a year-round release that would be an homage to our first five years and the IPAs that celebrated them. Stone Ruination IPA was the first bottled double IPA to be brewed year-round (in the entire world!). No, Stone Ruination IPA wasn't the first double IPA ever (it's our belief that the honor belongs to Blind Pig's Anniversary Ale first, Rogue's I²PA second, and our own Stone 4th Anniversary IPA perhaps third), but it quickly became the most widely available example of the style.

It's funny, because up to that point our intention had been for the Stone 5th Anniversary IPA to be our

GREG: Interestingly, the label text I wrote for Stone Ruination IPA almost seems a bit dated today, and it amazes me how fast that happened. You see, in 2002, a beer like this was an anomaly—a shock to the palate, with a bitterness profile and intensity theretofore almost unknown to the beer-drinking world. I carried on and on in the label text (as I'm known to do) about the ruinous effect of such an intense beer. I'd thought perhaps 0.0001 percent of the world's population would be prepared for such a punch.

Fast-forward a few scant years later, and that small percentage blossomed dramatically to—and I'm hazarding wild-ass guesses here, mind you—0.001 percent, a disproportionate number of whom can be found posting their musings on beer enthusiast websites, pooh-poohing the bold text on the bottle as being dramatically overstated (lacking, as they do, the advantage of historical context that you, dear reader, now have in your beer trivia data bank).

Fair enough. By today's standards of hoppy extremes, the label copy might be a touch overstated. So be it. But at Stone we were eating hops for breakfast before 99.9999 percent of those young punks even knew what an IBU was! Now get off my lawn!

STONE LEVITATION ALE

Release Date: September 2002
Availability: Year-round
Hop Profile: Columbus, Amarillo, Simcoe, and Crystal; dry hopped with Amarillo
Style: American amber ale
IBUs: 45
ABV: 4.4%

" With Stone Levitation Ale, we wanted to create something with the same flavor impact you'd expect from a Stone beer, but with a lower alcohol content. We wanted to keep it below 5% ABV, but finding that balance of flavor, mouthfeel, and alcohol proved difficult. Originally we joked that this would be like a 'Junior Bastard Ale,' but it ended up being so much more than that. It commands its own respect—and requires a deft hand at the kettle. Lower-alcohol beers can be a bit harder to brew correctly. Without that big wall of alcohol to support them, the flavors are so transparent that there's a much smaller margin of error. It took a lot of different malt trials and tweaking of the recipe to get this one right, but I couldn't be more pleased with it. " —STEVE

OAKED ARROGANT BASTARD ALE

Release Date: November 2004
Availability: Year-round
Hop Profile: Classified
Style: American strong ale
IBUs: Classified
ABV: 7.2%

" We experimented with Arrogant Bastard Ale, tossing in American oak chips to see how it might play with the brazen flavor. The oak chips (check them out above) contributed some subtle notes of vanilla and gave the normally angry beer a more sophisticated feel. We really liked it and decided to put it out as a special release in November 2004 in 3-liter bottles, and finally in 12-ounce six-packs in November 2006. " —STEVE

STONE CALI-BELGIQUE IPA

Release Date: August 2008
Availability: Year-round
Hop Profile: Columbus and
    Centennial; dry hopped with
    Chinook
Style: Belgian IPA
IBUs: 77
ABV: 6.9%

"Brewing up a Belgian-style beer requires us to culture a big batch of our Belgian yeast strain. We usually do that in a small amount of Stone Pale Ale wort, then separate and transfer it to a large fermentation tank to do its work. When we set out to make the Stone 08.08.08 Vertical Epic Ale (see page 86), we wanted it to have a very light color—so light that we thought the residual Stone Pale Ale mixed in with the yeast would darken the brew too much. So we opted to grow the yeast in Stone IPA wort. After separating out the yeast and transferring it to the tanks for the Vertical Epic Ale, we tasted the resulting Belgian-ized Stone IPA and were inspired to dry hop it with Chinook hops, as opposed to the Centennial we use for Stone IPA. The result? Stone Cali-Belgique IPA." —MITCH

STONE SUBLIMELY SELF-RIGHTEOUS ALE

Release Date: January 2009
Availability: Year-round
Hop Profile: Chinook, Simcoe, and
    Amarillo; dry hopped with Simcoe
    and Amarillo
Style: Black IPA
IBUs: 90
ABV: 8.7%

"Mitch wanted to call this beer San Diego Negro, but as you can see there's a little problem there . . . a bit of lexical ambiguity, if you will. The Spanish word negro translates to 'dark' or 'black,' referring, of course, to the color of the beer. And with its Spanish pronunciation (nay-gro), negro sort of rhymes with San Diego, so the name sounded kinda cool. But without that Spanish inflection, it's . . . we just decided against it, okay? Personally, I thought being afraid of the name was an overreaction, but there were some folks concerned that the chance of misinterpretation was too great. Eventually, I had to agree that there just wasn't sufficient reason to use a Spanish word that people might mispronounce, no matter how close we are to Mexico or how great it sounded. Mitch understood. Plus, Stone Sublimely Self-Righteous Ale flows off the tongue much more easily, doesn't it?" —GREG

STEVE: We've loved all of our anniversary releases, but we knew we had to bring the 11th Anniversary Ale back. It was just too awesome. Everyone around the brewery had sequestered their own personal stash, but these were dwindling pretty quickly. We finally discussed it at a meeting and almost unanimously decided to bring it back on an ongoing basis. And thus was born Stone Sublimely Self-Righteous Ale.

Check out the discussion of Stone 11th Anniversary Ale (page 82) for more on the story behind this liquid masterpiece!

STONE ANNIVERSARY ALES

We love any excuse to brew another great beer, and our Stone Anniversary Celebration and Invitational Beer Festival provides a great opportunity to do just that. It's always a good time, with many of our fans making the pilgrimage to enjoy great food and, of course, great beer. It grows every year, with well over one hundred beers from more than forty of our favorite breweries available for sampling at our fifteenth anniversary in 2011. We also view our Anniversary Celebrations as a great opportunity to raise funds, and awareness, for worthy causes. Over the years, we—or, rather, our fans, through your ticket purchases—have contributed over $1,000,000 to some of our favorite charities, like the Boys and Girls Club of San Marcos, Surfrider Foundation, Palomar Family YMCA, and Fight ALD. We love a good time, and it's incredible to think how much you support us, the charities we support, and the craft beer movement. So, thank you!

STEVE: We got a lot of inspiration for our anniversary IPAs from Vinnie Cilurzo when he was running Blind Pig Brewing Company. That is to say, we borrowed a lot of ideas from him. He was playing around with his hops and getting some incredible-tasting beers, and I found myself picking his brain, figuring out how he was getting those complex flavors and aromas. He was very open about sharing information and techniques, and due in part to his influence, I couldn't help but want to make bigger IPAs each year, both as a gift to ourselves and our fans, and as an homage to the envelope that Vinnie had been pushing.

1ST THROUGH 5TH ANNIVERSARY IPAS

Release Dates: August 1997, 1998, 1999, 2000, and 2001
Hop Profile: Varied
Style: India pale ale
ABV: Varies

"We commemorated our first anniversary with a pretty bold IPA (which you now know and love as the aptly named Stone IPA). Then, in our eternal quest to outdo ourselves, we brewed our Stone 2nd Anniversary IPA with twice as much hops. And while the Stone 3rd Anniversary IPA didn't have quite three times as much as the first, it was pretty darn close. When it came time to brew the Stone 4th Anniversary IPA, we couldn't really use four times as much hops, though we got as close as we could. So we did the next best thing: upped the alcohol from 6.9% to 8.5% ABV. With the Stone 5th Anniversary IPA, we literally amped the hops up as much as humanly possible and went with 8.5% ABV again." —STEVE

STONE 6TH ANNIVERSARY PORTER

Release Date: August 2002
Hop Profile: Tomahawk
Style: Imperial Porter
ABV: 8%

"After the 5th Anniversary IPA, we'd reached a point where we couldn't realistically add any more hops. Plus, we wanted to broaden our horizons and enjoy the fun of branching out again as brewers. It had been a great run and we certainly ended it on a high note, but we wanted to change things up for our sixth anniversary.

Since our 2nd through 5th Anniversary IPAs were amped up versions of our 1st Anniversary IPA, we thought we'd extend the concept and start making intensified versions of our existing lineup. The Stone 6th Anniversary Porter was a version of Stone Smoked Porter that we cranked up a notch or three, adding more malt and more hops, and conditioning it on French and American oak. It was a beauty." —STEVE

MIKE PALMER, CREATIVE DIRECTOR (AKA "WEBMASTER MIKE" AKA "'MIKE'S BEER CHEESE' MIKE"): The truth is, there was a catastrophe with the Stone 6th Anniversary Porter. It was the first time we'd played with oak chips in our big tanks. We'd filled big nylon mesh bags with oak chips and set them in the fermenters. I don't remember exactly what went wrong, but the bags weren't anchored correctly and they settled to the bottom. So when Lee Chase went to turn the valve to transfer the beer, nothing happened. It was clogged, and we didn't know what to do. So Lee and former lead brewer John Egan came up with this wild scheme to freeze the pipe at the base of the tank, break it off, and somehow make a new connection, but it didn't pan out. We ended up with a stream of Stone 6th Anniversary Porter shooting out like a fire hose. It required quite a cleanup.

STONE 7TH ANNIVERSARY ALE

Release Date: August 2003
Hop Profile: Magnum, Ahtanum
Style: "Super special pale ale"
ABV: 7.7%

"Just as we'd crafted larger versions of existing beers for prior anniversaries, the brewers set their focus on Stone Pale Ale for our next incarnation of the series. The resulting Stone 7th Anniversary Ale was a 77 IBU, 7.7% ABV, deep amber masterpiece, quite hoppy and with a fruity aroma and a toasty malt flavor that came through in the finish. It was no ordinary pale ale. Nay, this was a super special pale ale! Admittedly, a fictional style name that we coined for the heck of it, but the flavor of the beer certainly backed it up." —STEVE

STONE 8TH ANNIVERSARY ALE

Release Date: August 2004
Hop Profile: Amarillo
Style: Imperial mild
ABV: 7.8%

" The Stone 8th Anniversary Ale was, like all previous Stone anniversary releases, an adaptation of a previous release—in this case an "anniversary-ized" version of Lee's Mild, a limited-release beer from 1999 (see page 89). For the anniversary version we used some of the same malts as in Lee's Mild, added more hops, used less water (to bring the alcohol content up), and found a tasty balance of toasty roastiness from the malt and a subtle (by Stone standards) hop presence. To add further complexity, we used oak chips to round out the character and give the beer a bit of vanilla/bourbon influence from the wood. " —STEVE

STONE 9TH ANNIVERSARY ALE

Release Date: August 2005
Hop Profile: Amarillo and Crystal
Style: Imperial Wheat
ABV: 7.8%

" For our ninth anniversary we decided to look back at a wheat beer we released in the summers of 1997 and 1998: Stone Heat Seeking Wheat (see page 88). While it was a plenty tasty beer, we ultimately decided that it didn't really reflect what Stone was all about, so we unceremoniously dropped it from our lineup. Ho hum. Yet we weren't above revisiting it for Stone 9th Anniversary Ale. We carried forward some of the characteristics from the Stone Heat Seeking Wheat: clear, not hazy; hoppy, not yeasty; combining a delicious balance between hop bitterness and wheat tartness. But the similarities ended there; the bumped-up malt bill, elevated alcohol, and the more-than-generous amount of intensely piney hops took it to another level entirely. " —STEVE

Stone 10th Anniversary India Pale Ale was released in ten different bottles, with ten different notes written by the Stone team members who had been with us the longest. In addition to co-founders Steve Wagner and Greg Koch, others who got to put pen to paper, or rather, glass, were creative director Mike Palmer, vice president of sales Arlan Arnsten, sales rep Dave Dyer, accounting manager Connie Green, transportation manager Jake Ratzke, driver Mike Lopez, executive assistant Karen Westfall, and brewing facilities manager Bill Sherwood.

STONE 10TH ANNIVERSARY IPA

Release Date: August 2006
Hop Profile: Summit, Chinook, Crystal, and Simcoe
Style: American IPA
ABV: 10.0%

"Stone 10th Anniversary IPA harkened back to our earlier anniversary ales, with abundant hopping at many stages of the brewing process. Appropriately, the aroma was over-the-top, with pronounced piney and resiny hop flavors combined with tropical fruit esters and more subtle notes of toasted malts and alcohol. It weighed in at 10% alcohol by volume (perfect for our tenth-anniversary beer, and not entirely circumstantial) and had a little more color and malt character than our other IPAs. In addition to using Summit hops to provide the powerful bitterness, we went back through our records and found some of our favorite hops over the years and used them to flavor this brew, including Chinook, Crystal, and large doses of Simcoe in the dry hop to provide a huge, complex, piney, fruity, and floral hop character. This was a colossal beer, big in every sense: hoppy, malty, rich, and strong—right up our alley!" —STEVE

STONE 11TH ANNIVERSARY ALE

Release Date: September 2007
Hop Profile: Chinook, Simcoe, and Amarillo
Style: Black IPA
ABV: 8.7%

"As soon as we wrapped up the brewing of the Stone 10th Anniversary IPA, we started brainstorming ideas for the Stone 11th Anniversary Ale. Not long before joining Stone, I had the chance to try a black IPA called Darkside. It was made at The Shed, a little brewpub in Vermont, where Shaun Hill was brewing at the time. He'd gotten the inspiration from the late Greg Noonan, who had been brewing a black IPA at the Vermont Pub and Brewery since the late 1980s.

I was really taken with the style and wanted to brew one myself. Greg was a little hesitant, but he came around quickly after tasting the pilot. It was a challenging brew to formulate in terms of achieving what we considered the ideal flavor balance between intense up-front hops and balanced roasted malt flavors. When we finished tinkering with the recipe and brewed that first batch, though, we found we'd nailed the perfect combination of deep, rich flavor, and a hearty bitterness. We absolutely loved it." —MITCH

STONE 12TH ANNIVERSARY BITTER CHOCOLATE OATMEAL STOUT

Release Date: July 2008
Hop Profile: Ahtanum, Summit, Willamette, and Galena
Style: Imperial oatmeal stout
ABV: 9.2%

"We wanted to go with a dark beer for our twelfth anniversary for several reasons, one being the hop shortage the industry faced at the time. We weren't terribly affected by it on the whole, but we did have to make a few substitutions and trades with other breweries here and there, which really spoke to the level of camaraderie that exists in the craft beer world. Anyway, given the situation, even if we had been sitting on a surplus of hops it wouldn't have been terribly couth to come out with a hop bomb while we had friends struggling to meet target production on their core beers. Plus, we had been ruminating on some really cool dark beer ideas, especially after tasting lead brewer Jeremy Moynier's pilot batch of oatmeal stout and transportation manager Jake Ratzke's home-brewed Imperial stout with Oaxacan chocolate. Stone 12th Anniversary Bitter Chocolate Oatmeal Stout was born by combining these two ideas." —STEVE

STONE 13TH ANNIVERSARY ALE

Release Date: June 2009
Hop Profile: Chinook; double dry hopped with Simcoe and Centennial
Style: Imperial Red
ABV: 9.5%

"In 2009, we wanted to make up for the hop shortage that had befallen the industry the year before. While we've tried not to pigeonhole our anniversary releases into just being big hop monsters (balanced, mind you), the fact is, our first five and our tenth anniversary ales were big, hoppy IPAs, and really, all of our anniversary ales have been pretty aggressively hopped except the Stone 12th Anniversary Bitter Chocolate Oatmeal Stout and the Stone 6th Anniversary Porter.

For anyone who thought that we'd somehow lost our love of hops (as though that were actually possible), we came back with the hoppiest beer we had brewed to date. The Stone 13th Anniversary Ale used an impressive four and a half pounds of hops per barrel. When you take into consideration the fact that our 10th Anniversary IPA incorporated about two and a half pounds per barrel, and you can see that we meant business with this brew." —STEVE

STONE 14TH ANNIVERSARY EMPERIAL IPA

Release Date: June 2010
Hop Profile: Target, East Kent
Goldings, and Boadicea
Style: Imperial IPA
ABV: 8.9%

"In 2009, Mitch and I went to England to learn more about IPAs. We wanted to get a better taste of their history, since many accounts of it can be confusing or downright contradictory. (Shameless plug: Mitch and I are actually writing a book on IPAs as we speak. It helps set the record straight on their history, includes lots of amazing recipes, and is a definitive guide to all things IPA.) Needless to say, looking through 150-year-old handwritten brewer's logs and tasting some stellar beers on our adventure inspired us, and we came home with a resolve to brew a decidedly British IPA!

We used all British malt, hops, and yeast. Even our water was given the royal treatment, as we adjusted with water salts to more accurately reflect the waters of Burton-on-Trent. But as always, we got pretty aggressive with the hops, giving the beer our signature San Diego touch." —STEVE

STONE 15TH ANNIVERSARY ALE

Ah, if only I had a time machine to go into the future and tell you what we were going to make. You see, the world of publishing doesn't move quite as quickly as the world of brewing, and as of the time of this writing, we had no idea what we had up our sleeves for this one. But by the time you get to this point in the book, the beer will already have been released. Just get a pen and write some notes in here after you taste it and pretend they're from me.

STONE VERTICAL EPIC ALES

As with any good epic, within the tale of Stone Vertical Epic Ales lies the promise of larger-than-life experiences, heroics, and twists and turns as the adventure unfolds. These bottle-conditioned ales are specifically designed to be aged until sometime after December 12, 2012—provided you can hold on to them for that long. Every iteration of this Epic is unique to its year of release. There's no master plan, no vision of what the next beer might be. It's whatever inspiration strikes us.

These beers have been fashioned to be enjoyed together in a vertical tasting that promises to provide the beer connoisseur with the flavor equivalent of a Mozart symphony (or perhaps a Wagner opera?) with multiple movements—eleven, when all is said and done. In fact, the Stone Vertical Epic Ales are undoubtedly destined to be the magnum opus of the Stone brewing team . . . until we figure out something more ambitious and grand once this comes to an end.

As you begin reading the descriptions below, you will assuredly wonder, "What about Stone Vertical Epic Ale 01.01.01?" Well, we didn't think of the idea for Stone Vertical Epic Ale until the fall of 2001—obviously too late for an 01.01.01 release, but perfect for 02.02.02.

ARLAN ARNSTEN, (VICE PRESIDENT OF SALES): Greg called me in late 2001 with this idea for a vertical lineup of beers, and after hearing his entire, extravagant explanation, I said, 'Man, it's like a vertical . . . epic.' Greg might not remember it that way, but I came up with the name, without even meaning to.

As you now know, we ended up running with the idea, and when the first round was released, the Stone 02.02.02 Vertical Epic Ale, the most important thing I needed to do, and Greg couldn't have stressed it enough, was set aside seven cases in the cold box. That's all. He wanted to make sure we had stock of it to taste down the road to see how it was progressing. Sounds simple enough, right? Well, I forgot.

Our trucks took out all the stock to our local accounts. We'd held back five cases for Sun Devil Liquors in Mesa, Arizona, and five cases for Belmont Station up in Portland, Oregon, and I guess that's why I got confused: I saw those in the cold box and thought they were the cases we were holding back. And then those went out and I realized I'd messed up royally. I called the sales guys to see if we could get any of it back from our accounts, but it had already sold out just about everywhere.

Even Sun Devil had already blown through their five cases; I think they'd allocated it to customers before even receiving it. I made a frantic call up to our Oregon sales rep to see if there was any left at Belmont Station. Luckily, the truck had arrived not long before I called, and he rushed to the store. Even so, three cases had already sold.

continued

He made it just in time to buy the other two cases back from the shop.

The next day, the UPS guy rolled in and I heard him before I saw him, with what sounded like the heart-breaking sound of broken glass. I looked up and saw him wheeling in a dolly with those two cases of beer, not protected or bubble wrapped or anything, just wrapped in brown mailing paper. I was shocked, mortified, and overcome with this feeling of utter anxiety. But when we opened the boxes, much to my relief, somehow, there were twenty-four pristine bottles of Stone 02.02.02 Vertical Epic Ale, undamaged.

I don't know how they made it. There must have been guardian angels looking over that beer. That's all I can figure. And those very same boxes have been in our cold box ever since. I can't help but laugh every time we pull a bottle to sample and think back on what a nightmare I accidentally put myself through.

STONE 02.02.02 VERTICAL EPIC ALE

Hop Profile: Centennial
ABV: 7.5%

"Greg came to me with this great idea for Vertical Epic Ales. It was very last-minute, but it was a great idea and I wanted to run with it. We had no real plan, no path to follow. Our only criterion was that the beers for this series should have some sort of Belgian influence. And how serendipitous that Lee had recently returned from a trip to Belgium. The Stone 02.02.02 Vertical Epic Ale was the first beer where I gave Lee free rein, and he didn't let me down. He crafted a bumped-up version of a Belgian witbier—a style of beer often made with wheat, coriander, and orange peel—and threw in a sprinkling of black pepper and a healthy dose of Centennial hops for good measure.

I actually let the brewers run with a lot of the Vertical Epic Ale series. I never wanted it to be just about me. This series and the Anniversary Ales provided us with a great channel for creativity, and it was important to pass that around. In general, we were so busy just trying to keep up with production of the year-round beers that we didn't have much time to entertain new ideas or explore new brews as much as we would like to. This forced us to make time to play around, which was good." —STEVE

STONE 03.03.03 VERTICAL EPIC ALE

Hop Profile: Warrior, Centennial
ABV: 8.2%

"The demand for the Stone 02.02.02 Vertical Epic Ale was way beyond what we had expected. And given our already strained brewing schedule, squeezing in an extra beer at short notice that first year allowed us to make only 300 cases. So when it came time to brew the Stone 03.03.03 Vertical Epic Ale, we planned ahead and upped our production to a much friendlier 2,500 cases. That year's release took a different turn, using witbier loosely as an inspiration, but incorporating a dark-roasted wheat malt, Warrior and Centennial hops, and a blend of Belgian yeast and our house yeast strain.

While this beer was in process, we also came up with a fun way to give some of our loyal fans an extra chance to get their hands on some of the elusive Stone 02.02.02 Vertical Epic Ale. We initiated a 'Liquid Lottery,' in which everyone who came into Stone and bought a growler fill received a green ticket to fill out and drop in a box. On 02.02.03, my boys, Walter and Henry, drew twenty-five lucky tickets from the box. If your name was on it, you got to come down and purchase a growler full of Stone 02.02.02 Vertical Epic Ale—practically liquid gold!" —STEVE

STONE 04.04.04 VERTICAL EPIC ALE

Hop Profile: Sterling
ABV: 8.5%

"Lee had an idea to brew a kind of Thai spin on a Belgian-style farmhouse ale this time around. The yeast strain we used contributed some of the fruity esters typical to the style, but also some notes of tropical fruit and banana that are typically found in a German hefeweizen. The Thai twist came in the form of aromatic kaffir lime leaves; they gave a unique flavor that balanced so well with the malt and yeast. It really started melding together nicely after six months. I loved it, and I know Lee did too. To this day, the 04.04.04 is one of his favorite beers that he made while he was here." —STEVE

STONE 05.05.05 VERTICAL EPIC ALE

Hop Profile: Amarillo
ABV: 8.5%

"We shot for a darker Belgian style beer this time, using a chocolate wheat malt and dark crystal malt to end up with a mahogany tone. The beer was redolent of spices, though we didn't use any this year—flavors of anise, molasses, and dried fruit came entirely from the yeast strain, and mixed nicely with cocoa notes from the darker malts. That spice character was surprisingly strong, but mellowed and blended over time. Still, it was amusing how many people refused to believe that we didn't actually add any spices to it!" —STEVE

STONE 06.06.06 VERTICAL EPIC ALE

Hop Profile: Magnum, Mt. Hood
ABV: 8.66%

"The 06.06.06 Vertical Epic Ale was bittersweet since it was Lee's last formulation for us before he moved on to pave his own path. What a high note to leave on, though! This was a definite winner. Very dark, and fermented with Belgian Trappist yeast, this beer was deep and complex. The toasty, dark malt flavors combine nicely with hints of cloves, anise, and dried cherries. It will be interesting to see how this beer ages, and how the interplay of the smooth roasted malt character and spicy Belgian yeast evolves over time." —STEVE

STONE 07.07.07 VERTICAL EPIC ALE

Hop Profile: Glacier, Crystal
ABV: 8.4%

❝ The 07.07.07 Vertical Epic Ale was crafted to represent a Southern California summer with a little Belgian twist. Since it was released in July, we were looking for something refreshing, so we took inspiration from Belgian farmhouse-style saisons, and heavier (though not darker!) tripels. As such, the Stone 07.07.07 Vertical Epic has a deep golden hue with a flavor that's spicy, fruity, complex, and refreshing. For complexity we added exotic spices, including ginger, cardamom, grapefruit peel, lemon peel, and orange peel (that's what you see in the image below), the latter three paying homage to sunny SoCal. ❞ —STEVE

STONE 08.08.08 VERTICAL EPIC ALE

Hop Profile: Simcoe, Amarillo, Ahtanum
ABV: 8.6%

❝ The 08.08.08 Vertical Epic has its roots in a trip to Belgium taken by Mitch and I in early 2008. While there, we found Duvel Tripel Hop, which as the name implies, is a Belgian tripel dosed up with American hops. When we returned home, we opened the bottle and became delightfully inspired to brew our own take on it. We tried a few other Belgian IPAs, namely Houblon Chouffe Dobbelen IPA Tripel and Urthel Hop-It, and made the Stone 08.08.08 Vertical Epic Ale a variation on this theme. Spicy and fruity, is has a crisp bitterness that combines San Diego attitude with Belgian sophistication.

As it turned out, brewing this beer led to the creation of Stone Cali-Belgique IPA (page 77) around the same time. We also brewed the AleSmith / Mikkeller / Stone Belgian Style Triple Ale (page 92) and another batch of Sawyer's Triple (page 89), leading Mitch to declare Summer 2008 as 'Summer of the Triple.' ❞ —STEVE

STONE 09.09.09 VERTICAL EPIC ALE

Hop Profile: Magnum, Perle
ABV: 8.6%

❝ We brewed a Belgian-style imperial porter of sorts for the 09.09.09 Vertical Epic. I'd always wanted to brew a chocolatey beer with some orange in it, so during the brewing process we added tangerine peel, Belgian dark candi sugar, and vanilla bean to complement a porter. The vanilla bean enhances the chocolate character from the roasted malts. French oak chips added during fermentation contributed more vanilla character, and the candi sugar added a nice hint of molasses to the finish. ❞ —MITCH

STONE 10.10.10 VERTICAL EPIC ALE

Hop Profile: Perle
ABV: 9.5%

❝The opportunity to sync a brew with the grape harvest sounded like fun to me, especially since I spent some of my formative years as a vintner—not to mention having studied enology at UC Davis. Working with our neighbors at South Coast Winery, about thirty miles north of the brewery, we were able to score some fresh grape juice that we used to provide a unique backbone to this beer.

The aroma is very fruity, redolent of banana and berries and with hints of clove. Though the flavor imparted by the grapes is relatively delicate, their presence is known thanks to their acidity, which leaves the beer a little tart and extremely dry. We also brewed with a touch of chamomile and a grain called triticale, which is a hybrid of wheat and rye that has a unique spicy quality to it. I'm especially interested in tasting this as it ages. ❞ —MITCH

STONE 11.11.11 VERTICAL EPIC ALE AND STONE 12.12.12 VERTICAL EPIC ALE

Here's a good reason why you'll want to pick up an updated edition of the book once we publish it. Yep, you've stumbled upon another section that will be outdated not long after the book hits shelves. As of the time we're writing this, we have no idea whatsoever regarding what we're pursuing for these two beers. Okay, I can give you one small insider clue: they will be absolutely delicious!

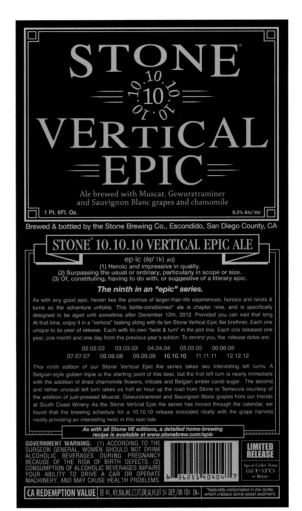

SPECIAL RELEASES AND RETIRED BEERS

We've had some beers come and go through the years. A few early recipes were yanked from the line-up; others have been made for a special purpose or for charity, or simply as a planned one-off, brewed more or less for fun.

STONE SESSION ALE

Release Date: Spring 1997
ABV: 4.5%

"When we first started out, we thought we were going to have a line of seasonal beers. After the success of our winter seasonal, Stone Smoked Porter, we thought we'd for sure have a winner with our spring offering: Stone Session Ale. Tasty? Of course. A raging success? Mmm, not so much.

Light-bodied and refreshing, Stone Session Ale had a complex malt character balanced by a crisp hop flavor. And at a moderate 4.5% ABV, it embodied all that a great session ale should: plentiful flavor but smooth enough to be enjoyed during a relaxing and extended 'session' with friends." —STEVE

HEAT SEEKING WHEAT

Release Date: Summer 1997
ABV: 4.7%

"Not long after the original seasonal beer experiment with Stone Smoked Porter, we came out with a summer seasonal, Heat Seeking Wheat. I'd been inspired by the Pyramid Wheaten Ale that was brewed when I worked with Pyramid. Greg didn't want it from the get-go, but I somehow persuaded him to let me run with it. And while it never did take off, it did serve as the inspiration for the wildly popular and delicious Stone 9th Anniversary Ale (page 79)!" —STEVE

LEE'S MILD

Release Date: October 1999
ABV: 3.8%

"Lee's Mild was brewed in 1999, and only three hundred cases were produced. Lee Chase, our head brewer at the time, had taken a pilot batch to the local Real Ale Festival, and it ended up taking the brewer's choice award. We'd planned to call it Stone Hock Ale (hock being an obscure style of dark, mild beer, deriving its name from an Old English word for harvest), but we were using Lee's Mild as a placeholder. When Peter Rowe, beer columnist at the *San Diego Union-Tribune*, printed up a story on the winning beer—Lee's Mild—we ran with it. The flavor profile was heavily roasted and toasty, with little to no hop presence. It was bottle conditioned and weighed in at a mere 3.8% ABV." —STEVE

GREG: I still have a couple bottles of Lee's Mild in my fridge, and it's never tasted better. True, you're not supposed to cellar a mild ale, but because Lee's Mild was artfully crafted and bottle conditioned, it's not only held up beautifully, it's actually improved over time. I opened one in 2010 when the gang from the web-based series *New Brew Thursday* came by to shoot an episode with me and James Watt from BrewDog, who was visiting for a few days. We all agreed it was fantastic.

LEE CHASE: I was fascinated with the idea of making a dark mild. I played with some different approaches and eventually came up with something I was quite taken with. When it won the brewer's choice award, I was pretty stoked. We made a batch for distribution, but I think it was difficult for a lot of people to wrap their head around. A mild, dark Stone brew? It was delicious, but I think it was the worst-selling beer ever offered by Stone.

STONE SAWYER'S TRIPLE

Release Dates: October 2003 and
November 2008
Availability: For sale in the Stone
Company Store and at the Stone
Brewing World Bistro & Gardens
Style: Belgian-style tripel
ABV: 7.6%

"It's hard to describe what Sawyer's
Triple means to me personally; obviously
the beer, and the motivation behind it, is very close to
my heart. Greg and Steve came up with the idea of
brewing a special-release beer as a fund-raiser to help
pay for the expenses of a bone marrow transplant, Sawyer's only hope for survival. Unfortunately, ALD is an
extremely aggressive disease, and Sawyer passed away
just days before the beer was released, only six months
after his diagnosis.

The day of the release was unbelievable. Janis and
I came to the brewery midmorning that Saturday and
there was a line out the door, leading into the parking
lot. People came from as far away as Northern California to purchase their maximum limit of six bottles in
support of the cause. It was very touching. The entire
batch sold out that day.

If Sawyer hadn't been misdiagnosed repeatedly, if
even one doctor had known the early onset symptoms
of ALD in children, and had ordered the simple and
inexpensive blood test that could confirm the diagnosis, Sawyer would still be alive today. Knowing that,
Janis decided to use the proceeds from the sale of the
beer to start a foundation with a mission to educate
medical professionals about the early onset symptoms.
She created educational materials and started going to
medical continuing education conferences, setting up
a booth and handing out this material.

After several years, she decided that this approach
just wasn't cutting it; word wasn't getting out effectively enough. She made up her mind to go on the road
and hand deliver the information directly to all of the

children's hospitals across the country—more than two
hundred of them. I told her, "Yes dear, that's a nice idea,"
thinking there was no way in hell she could pull that off.

Sawyer's TRIPLE

cour•age (kûr'ĭj) *n.*

**The state or quality of mind or spirit that enables one to face
danger or fear, with self-possession and resolution; bravery.**

Inspiration comes from many sources. The inspiration for Sawyer's Triple came
from namesake Sawyer Benjamin Sherwood, the 8 year-old son of Stone brewer
Bill Sherwood and his wife Janis. Over a period of four years, we had the distinct
pleasure of getting to know Sawyer via his visits to the brewery or at the occasional
backyard BBQ. An engaging and athletic kid if you ever knew one! In early
2003 Sawyer was diagnosed with Adrenoleukodystrophy — also known as ALD
— a rare neuro-degenerative disease. At the time of the original creation of this
beer and writing of this label in August 2003, Sawyer was in a fight for his life.

It felt like a crushing blow when we lost Sawyer in September 2003, only days
before the initial release of Sawyer's Triple. The outpouring of support from
family, the community, and fans of Stone Brewing brought comfort and solace to
such a great degree that it simply cannot be expressed in words. When you
enjoy this brew, we encourage you to lift a glass to the noble fight in all of us.
When your own fight is overwhelming, remember to seek help. And when you
are able to, offer help to others. On Sawyer's behalf, and for all who need
assistance with their own fight, we thank you for yours.

This beer has been dedicated to Sawyer and to the courage in all of us.
To not giving up, even when it may appear impossible to win. For those
like Sawyer, who possess an indomitable spirit, giving up is never an option.
Such people inspire others, and so have we been inspired to help fight
for awareness, research, understanding, and ultimately, a cure for ALD. As with
any important battle, this fight is invaluably aided by help from our friends.
Pulling together for a common cause is as elemental to the human spirit as the
search for knowledge and betterment.

We at Stone and the Sherwood family would like to honor and thank all those who
have generously donated their resources towards the creation of this brew. To view
the full list of benefactors, in addition to information about ALD, visit
www.stonebrew.com/sawyerstriple. 100% of the proceeds from the sale of this beer
originally went towards ALD causes and charities, and it is no different today.
Attendees at our fundraising Stone Anniversary Celebrations have become
accustomed to seeing the "Fight ALD" booth. Created by Sawyer's mother Janis
Sherwood, Fight ALD is a non-profit organization whose mission is to spread
awareness for the all-important early detection of the disease and search for its cure.

Well, it's amazing what can happen when a person
truly commits to a cause. Between the funds generated
from the second edition of Sawyer's Triple in 2008, an
RV donated by a close friend, and the growing support of the ALD community, Janis started on the road
in spring of 2009. She generally hits the road for four
weeks at a time, going to every children's hospital,
pediatric clinic, family practice, and so on, and taking
a couple of weeks off between trips.

She usually hits between eight and twenty places
a day. Sometimes she gets brushed off, but more often
than not she gets warm welcomes, hugs, tears, and a
promise to get the information to all of the doctors and
nurses. Best of all is when teaching hospitals agree to
add the information into their curriculum. I believe

that this is where she gets the biggest return for her efforts. I don't know the exact number, but I know for sure Janis has distributed information to over a thousand medical facilities. We think the project is only about half done, and that it will probably take until 2013 to cover the whole country.

Long range, the best possible scenario is to have newborns tested for ALD. After that, we have to focus on the adult onset of the disease which is a whole other story.

It's a challenge to our family that Janis is gone over half the year, but the cause feels so urgent to us that it's a small sacrifice to make when boys' lives are in such jeopardy. Sawyer's Triple has been a great avenue for helping save other boys' lives, and has been a catalyst to turn crushing grief into a constructive mission."
— **BILL SHERWOOD, brewing facilities manager**

For information about ALD, and to learn how you can help our mission, please visit www.fightald.org.

STONEWALL ALE

Release Date: 2005
Style: American Barleywine
ABV: 12.2%

StoneWall Ale was brewed in 2005 as a tribute to all who participated in the Stone Wall Project, which raised over $85,000 for local charities. (Check out page 57 for more info on the project and the beer.) The names of all 472 donors involved in the fund-raising event were printed on the bottle, and bottles were doled out to the donors based on the size of their donation. This beer was not made available to the public, except at some special events, and then only for consumption at the event. And, of course, any money raised from the sale of StoneWall Ale at these special occasions still goes to charity.

STONE CALIFORNIA DOUBLE IPA

Release Date: 2008
Hop Profile: Admiral, Centennial, Simcoe
Style: Double IPA
ABV: 7.8%

"Never heard of this one, eh? Well, it was a one-time batch that we brewed back in early 2008. Great Britain's JD Wetherspoons pub group was holding the world's largest real ale festival and they invited Steve and me out to brew a San Diego-style IPA for them at the oldest operating brewery in the United Kingdom: Shepherd Neame, in Kent.

We were supposed to have a keg of this put aside to bring back with us to Stone, but somewhere along the way, somebody goofed and they sold it instead. So after getting back stateside, I took the recipe up to 21st Amendment Brewery and brewed it there as part of their Brewer Outreach Program. I worked with brewmaster Shaun O'Sullivan and head brewer Jesse Houck to put it together that August, renaming it the 21st Amendment/Stone Transcontinental IPA." —MITCH

LUKCY BASARTD ALE

Release Date: November 2010

Availability: One time special release, unless we decide to make it again

Hop Profile: Classified

Style: American strong ale

ABV: 8.5%

❝We created Lukcy Basartd Ale because we wanted to celebrate arrogance, and because we wanted people to understand where Arrogant Bastard Ale ranks in the history of American craft brewing. We decided to blend all of our bastards—Arrogant Bastard Ale, Double Bastard Ale, and OAKED Arrogant Bastard Ale—in the fermenter, dry hop it, and unleash it to commemorate the 13th anniversary of Arrogant Bastard Ale.

So what does that have to do with all the fkuny wirtnig? Arrogant Bastard Ale was originally based on challenging convention and shaking up people's perceptions of what beer can and should be. I wanted the Lukcy Basartd Ale to continue in that vein. I wanted to force people to think. The bottom line is, those who are worthy will read it; those who aren't will give up. What's interesting is that the more you relax and just let it flow, the easier it is to read. ❞ —GREG

COLLABORATION BEERS

Working together with other brewers to craft interesting new beers has been one of the most rewarding endeavors the Stone brewing team has undertaken. It's an interesting phenomenon that we enjoy in this industry, being able to call up somebody who technically, I suppose, is one of our "competitors" and ask if they want to come over and brew some beer with us. It's almost like a grown-up version of inviting friends over to a tree fort. We have a ton of fun with it, and the experience is quite different every time—as are the beers. And that's one of the huge benefits of these collaborations: we always push ourselves to make something we've never made before, and something none of use would have been likely to come up with on our own. Sometimes we work with an old friend we don't get to see that often. Other times we might invite one of the rising stars in the industry or an international underdog that we've become friends with and whose work we admire. And sometimes we invite passionate homebrewers and give them a chance to play on the big-boy equipment.

Whatever the case, we always come away with a feeling of accomplishment and a newfound respect for each other (and sometimes even for ourselves). The exchange of knowledge and ideas never ceases to amaze me, and neither do the beers that we collectively produce.

GARRETT MARRERO, MAUI BREWING CO.: Collaborating with Stone was awesome. Some people outside of our industry think it's weird that we work so closely with what they perceive as our competitors. I just tell them that some of our biggest competitors are our best friends and that we're all in it together. There's a mantra that the beer industry is a 99 percent asshole-free industry, and it's pretty much true. At the end of the day, whether you think we're competitors or collaborators, for us it's just all about brewing great beer.

SYMPOSIUM ALE

Release Date: April 2004
Hop Profile: Saaz
Style: Belgian strong golden ale
ABV: 7.48%

" This ale was brewed for the 2004 AOB (Association of Brewers, now the Brewers Association) Craft Brewers Conference, held in San Diego. It's the result of a collaborative effort between three San Diego County brewers and breweries: Peter Zien of AleSmith Brewing, Tomme Arthur of Pizza Port Solana Beach and Port Brewing (nowadays of Lost Abbey and Port Brewing), and our Lee Chase (nowadays of Blind Lady Ale House). They gathered together at Stone Brewing Co. to brew this Belgian-style strong golden ale that incorporates multiple yeast strains, a substantial amount of Czech Saaz hops, and a touch of lemongrass. While this was not an official start of our collaboration series, as it was brewed specifically for the Craft Brewers Conference, it was our first collaboration. " —STEVE

2004 SYMPOSIUM ALE

Symposium \ sim pō′zē əm \ n.

A convivial meeting for drinking, music and intellectual discussions where ideas are freely exchanged. (Latin from Greek: symposium—drinking party, syn, together, posis, drinking).

This ale is the result of a collaborative effort between three San Diego County brewers and breweries. It's just one small example of how fun it is to be in the Craft Brewing industry. Peter Zien of AleSmith Brewing, Tomme Arthur of Pizza Port Solana Beach /Port Brewing, and Lee Chase of Stone Brewing all gathered together and brewed this celebratory ale up at the Stone Brewing Co.

The brewing community in San Diego --- and Southern California --- is thrilled to be hosting the Association of Brewers' Craft Brewers Conference in San Diego this year. We're honored to have so many leaders, innovators, enthusiasts, supporters, and respected members of craft brewing in town. We'd like to wish everyone a terrific conference and another year of healthy, sustained growth for our industry.

This Belgian-style strong golden ale was brewed with multiple yeast strains for those great Belgian-style esters, a pretty substantial amount of Czech Saaz hops for their wonderful aroma, and a touch of lemon grass for, well… just because!

**Craft Brewers Conference and BrewExpo America®
are presented by the Association of Brewers
www.beertown.org®**

This ale was co-sponsored by: Cargill Malt, HopUnion & White Labs.

AleSmith / Mikkeller / Stone
BELGIAN STYLE TRIPLE ALE

Release Date: September 2008
Hop Profile: Perle, Amarillo, Centennial
Style: Belgian Tripel
ABV: 9.5%

Ever since we brewed the Symposium Ale for the Craft Brewers Conference in 2004, Steve and I had the idea of further collaborations in the back of our minds. Working with Tomme Arthur and Peter Zien on that beer was a great experience, but it was only made for attendees of the CBC, not the public. Four years later, when Mikkel Bjergsø (of Mikkeller fame) got in touch wanting to do a collaboration beer, we jumped at the chance. He wanted to brew a traditional Belgian-style tripel to honor the famed beer writer, Michael Jackson, who had just passed away.

I wanted to include a third brewer to really cement the idea of collaboration, so we again tapped our good friend Peter Zien who was more than happy to sign on. I don't want to rub it in about how cool our jobs are, but it's so nice to be able to hang out with some of our friends to brew a beer. (Does it get much better?)

Jolly Pumpkin / Nøgne-Ø / Stone
SPECIAL HOLIDAY ALE

Release Date: November 2008
Hop Profile: German Perle, Columbus
Style: Winter warmer
ABV: 9.0%

The beginnings of this beer lie in Tokyo of all places, where I had a chance encounter with Kjetil Jikiun, of the Norwegian craft brewery Nøgne-Ø, at a cool little craft beer bar called Bar Sal's. We met again at the Craft Brewers Conference in San Diego, and I scheduled a trip out to Norway to check out Kjetil's brewery. One of the beers I tried was the Nøgne-Ø Underlig Jul, a spiced seasonal ale based on a Norwegian Christmas drink called glogg. I was so taken with it that I wanted to create a collaboration beer that could also serve as Stone's first-ever holiday beer. Bringing Ron Jefferies from Jolly Pumpkin on board completed the trifecta.

In the interest of collaboration, we wanted to source one indigenous ingredient from each of our brewing regions. We decided to represent SoCal with white sage. Kjetil suggested juniper berries for Norway (although we couldn't get Norwegian juniper berries, unfortunately, so we went with Italian). He also wanted to use some rye malt for added spice. Ron brought Michigan chestnuts into the mix and contributed some caraway seeds to complement the rye.

JOLLY PUMPKIN ARTISAN ALES • NØGNE Ø • STONE BREWING CO.

Special Holiday Ale

One of the best things about craft brewing is the people involved in it. There is openness, friendship and camaraderie in craft brewing that you probably would not find in other crafts or trades. Craft brewers share experiences and learn from each other constantly. I find this quite remarkable, especially given the fact that craft brewers span from being experienced and educated brewers to homebrewers doing their best to come up with something they can launch commercially.

When Greg from Stone visited Nøgne Ø in Norway in the summer of 2008, we at Nøgne Ø were delighted to meet him and his family. We were extremely flattered and happy when he later suggested that we should team up with Ron Jeffries from Jolly Pumpkin and brew together. It is hard to think of anyone more different in background and flavour profile than Stone, Nøgne Ø and Jolly Pumpkin. And that is a great thing. Sharing ideas and experiences in spite of great differences.

Ever since my homebrewing days, I have always looked at the US craft beer scene with awe and envy. Reading publications and newsletters about successful brewers in the US was always very inspirational, but also a grim reminder of how lonely it is to brew in a country with no understanding and appreciation of craft beer. Brewing with Stone and Jolly Pumpkin is to me very significant. This is about coming in from the cold or brushing shoulders with the stars.

Hopefully this beer is able to tell a story: the story about three different brewers putting their heads together to share and create. If we have been successful, you will be able taste the influence from Stone, Jolly Pumpkin and Nøgne Ø.

Kjetil Jikiun, Head Brewer/Owner
Nøgne Ø, Norway
October 21, 2008

Ingredients: Barley, Hops, Water, Yeast, Chestnuts, Juniper Berry, White Sage & Caraway Seed

BrewDog • Cambridge Brewing Co. • Stone Brewing Co.

Juxtaposition Black Pilsner

While at Stone Brewing Company this week I thought a lot about frames, foundations, and skeletons. Not in a macabre way, but in the sense of structural integrity, which is often demonstrated in our small industry by a profound sense of camaraderie. It is upon this strong frame of brother and sisterhood that our industry's muscles grow, strengthening our creativity and desire to share with one another, and bolstering our willingness to push each other beyond our personal limits of comfort.

This beer was not created with the intention of fitting within your comfort levels, nor the parameters of your expectations. It was brewed as a challenge to Stone, BrewDog and Cambridge to make a beer we might never have come up with on our own, with ingredients we'd never used before. And to You, to challenge your own notions of style parameters and definitions, and to test your ability to bravely accept a big hoppy punch in the face–and like it. Winston Churchill put it this way: "When you have an important point to make, don't try to be subtle or clever. Use a pile driver. Hit the point once. Then come back and hit it again. Then hit it a third time - a tremendous whack." I think that sums it up nicely.

Will Meyers, *Brewmaster*
Cambridge Brewing Co.

brewdog.com • cambrew.com • stonebrew.com

BREWED AND BOTTLED BY THE STONE BREWING CO., ESCONDIDO, SAN DIEGO COUNTY, CA

BrewDog / Cambridge / Stone
JUXTAPOSITION BLACK PILSNER

Release Date: July 2009
Hop Profile: Sorachi Ace, Moteuka, Hallertau Saphir
Style: Black Pilsner
ABV: 10%

"For the BrewDog / Cambridge / Stone Juxtaposition Black Pilsner, we really wanted to throw everybody a curve ball. One of the reasons that I enjoy doing collaboration beers—and I think I speak for a lot of brewers here—is that you get to brew something different, something out of your comfort zone. And we've definitely done some collaborations that were out of our realm of expertise, but a big 10 percent ABV Black Pilsner wasn't just out of the ordinary for us, it's kind of an entirely new concept for everybody.

It was so bizarre that we released a blog post and some videos featuring fellow brewers James Watt and Will Meyers on April 1 . . . and sure enough, we got some fans calling it out as an April Fools prank. But the joke was on them, this April Fools Day beer release was very real—and very delicious." — MITCH

STEVE: Collaborations are one of the greatest things to come out of the craft brewing scene, in my opinion. It's unique to this industry, and it's a somewhat new development. But I'm glad to see that it has become so accepted . . . expected, even!

The BrewDog / Cambridge / Stone Juxtaposition Black Pilsner also gave birth to an additional one-time beer that was available only at the brewery. When the brewers were propagating the pilsner yeast for the collaboration beer, they fed it with wort from batches of Stone Pale Ale, Stone IPA, and Stone Imperial Russian Stout.

When the yeast was pumped out to the fermentation tanks to work its magic on the Juxtaposition, former lead brewer John Egan saw potential in the hodgepodge beer remaining in the propagation tank. So he added coriander, French oak chips, and a handful of chopped vanilla beans and then let the eclectic mix sit and mingle for about a week before kegging it.

Its name? Stone Bombastic Lager.

According to John, "As far as style goes, I have no idea. It was kind of a 'suicide,' like we did with sodas as kids: just a mix of whatever's available. It tasted like an ale to me, but it was a lager—and a weird lager at that!"

BASHAH

GREG: Bashah was a beer that Mitch, Steve, and I brewed with the BrewDog boys during our visit to Scotland in 2009. James, Martin, and the entire team at BrewDog, the largest independent brewery in Scotland, really put a lot of energy into showing us a great time. During our few days of drinking and working with them, we created bashah, the world's first black Belgian-style double India pale ale.

But if you're wondering what bashah really meant, it was an acronym for Black As Sin, Hoppy As Hell. But the truth is, it really didn't turn out to be crazy hoppy. It's just nicely hoppy, but that would spell basnh, and that's not what we named it. In any case, it was nicely hoppy, and plenty tasty.

KEN SCHMIDT / MAUI / STONE
KONA COFFEE, MACADAMIA, COCONUT PORTER

Release Date: September 2009
Style: American Porter
ABV: 8.5%

❝Back in March 2009 we held a rally for the American Homebrewers Association at the Stone Brewing World Bistro & Gardens. Alongside it, we hosted our March Madness Homebrew Competition, with the winning brewer getting the chance to brew their beer at Stone and have it served at Stone. Taking inspiration from Maui Brewing Co. CoCoNut PorTeR, homebrewer Ken Schmidt entered his Aloha Plenty, which incorporated Kona coffee, macadamia nuts, and toasted coconut. We had a winner.

In fact, we liked it so much that we buzzed our buddy Garrett Marrero from Maui Brewing Co. to see if he wanted to jump in and make it an official collaboration. He did, and Ken was thrilled. And so Aloha Plenty became the Ken Schmidt / Maui / Stone Kona Coffee, Macadamia, Coconut Porter. (Rolls right off the tongue, doesn't it?)

In scaling up the recipe, it became apparent that we were in for some serious labor. And these ingredients were not cheap. We needed about a thousand pounds of coconut, three hundred pounds of macadamia nuts, and two hundred pounds of Kona coffee. And that coconut had to be hand toasted to get the flavor just

KEN SCHMIDT • MAUI BREWING CO. • STONE BREWING CO.

Kona Coffee, Macadamia, Coconut Porter

Aloha is the Hawaiian greeting meaning love, affection, friendship and compassion. It also means joyfully sharing life and treating others with love and respect. It is the "breath of life" and something that everyone should experience.

My love for Hawaii is deeply rooted within me, and I wanted to capture its tantalizing scents, the peace of the islands, and the essence of the spirit of Aloha. "Aloha" whisks me off to beautiful beaches and inviting waters. I can even feel the warm sand and the gentle trade winds bringing the fragrance of exotic flowers and heightening my senses.

I am extremely honored that my award-winning homebrew, "Aloha Plenty," was chosen for this collaboration. It has been brewed with deep loving care and respect for you to enjoy. This is a robust porter using 100% Kona coffee, toasted coconut, and macadamia nuts. Enjoy the bountiful flavors and aromas of the Islands and their abundance of Aloha.

Aloha 'Oe, may you be loved.

Ken Schmidt

Ken Schmidt, *Homebrewer & Creator of Aloha Plenty*

alohaplenty.net • mauibrewingco.com • stonebrew.com

right. With our small oven setup in the Bistro, the kitchen staff worked overtime, bless their hearts. All told, it took about four eight-hour shifts to toast it all up. But, in the end, it was worth it. *"* —MITCH

21st Amendment / Firestone Walker / Stone
EL CAMINO (UN)REAL BLACK ALE

Release Date: March 2010
Hop Profile: Challenger, East Kent Goldings, Styrian Goldings
Style: American strong ale
ABV: 9.5%

" This beer is an homage to California and the road that unites us. El Camino Real (the Royal Road, or the King's Highway) is a historic landmark that stretches from San Diego up to San Francisco. It originally connected the region's Spanish missions and settlements and ultimately became one of the first highways in the state, helping connect NorCal with SoCal and everything in between. We chose to work with Matt Brynildson of Firestone Walker Brewing Company and Shaun O'Sullivan of 21st Amendment Brewery, since the ol' el Camino Real ties all of us together.

Furthering our Cali love, we brewed with several strange indigenous California ingredients: chia seeds, pink peppercorns, fennel seeds, and some Mission figs that Shaun brought from a friend's farm. Matt also brought down some oak barrels so we could mimic the Union barrel-fermenting system that Firestone Walker employs. *"* —MITCH

Dogfish Head / Victory / Stone
SAISON DU BUFF

Release Date: May 2010
Hop Profile: Centennial, Amarillo, Citra
Style: Saison
ABV: 6.8%

A long time ago, in a galaxy far, far away . . . alright, so it was only in 2003, and it was just in Boston. But still, it was important, okay? Or at least we thought so. A bold new partnership had been formed: Brewers United For Freedom of Flavor (BUFFF). Dogfish Head's Sam Calagione, Victory's Bill Covaleski, and I staged a press conference the day before Boston's Art of Beer Festival as a call to arms for mass rejection of fizzy yellow beer-like beverages. And while the press conference was not heavily attended (thanks for coming, Jamie!), we remained steadfast in our mission.

Fast-forward to 2010, drop an F (who capitalizes *for* anyway?), and strike up the band! BUFF is on the prowl. A conversation was sparked about making a collaboration beer, and as with previous collaborations, we were looking to broaden our horizons and try our hands at something new. The idea of a peppery, citrusy saison sounded especially appealing. In fact, I'd been wanting to brew a saison with sage, so I threw it out to Sam and Bill. They were game, and we riffed from there. How about rosemary? Sure! Thyme and parsley? Why the hell not?

Saison du BUFF

Dogfish Head • Victory Brewing Co. • Stone Brewing Co.

It's a saison of sorts; hellaciously herbaceous and hopefully contagious. This was not a ready made ale. But it is a ready made collaboration. Meaning Stone & Victory are 2 breweries that are exactly like DogFish in that they do/brew exactly what they love and they do/brew it exactly like no other brewery out there. (♥ lots of it in this bottle)

Sam C. Cly 11

dogfish.com • victorybeer.com • stonebrew.com

BALLAST POINT / KELSEY McNAIR / STONE SAN DIEGO COUNTY SESSION ALE

Release Date: August 2010
Hop Profile: Warrior, Columbus, Citra, Simcoe, Amarillo, Chinook
Style: American pale ale
ABV: 4.2%

"Just as Ken Schmidt had won our 2009 March Madness Homebrew Competition with his Aloha Plenty, Kelsey took home the 2010 honor with an intensely hoppy session beer he had named West Coast Bitter. This brew was citrusy, spicy, piney, bitter, and strikingly complex. We loved it. After winning the chance to brew his beer here at Stone, he was also given the opportunity to name the third collaborator in the series. His choice? Colby Chandler of Ballast Point Brewing and Spirits. *"* —MITCH

GREEN FLASH / PIZZA PORT CARLSBAD / STONE HIGHWAY 78 SCOTCH ALE

Release Date: February 2011
Hop Profile: East Kent Goldings, Target
Style: Scotch ale
ABV: 8.8%

"With our collaboration beers, we really strive to do something different—something we're not known for or something we otherwise wouldn't be able to try. For some time, I'd been talking with Chuck Silva and Jeff Bagby, of Green Flash Brewing Co. and Pizza Port, respectively, about doing a brew together. We got together one night at Pizza Port and Jeff threw out the idea of doing a Scotch ale.

We thought it would be great, so we set about formulating a recipe. We used three different crystal malts: chocolate malt, English pale malt, a touch of Sucanat (a type of raw sugar), and just enough East Kent Goldings and Target hops to provide a peppery backbone. *"* —MITCH

APRIL FOOL'S DAY "RELEASES"

We've had a great deal of ironic fun over the years with our periodic April Fool's beer release announcements (the originals are reprinted in gray below). We've used the opportunity to poke a little fun (or, more accurately, seriously lampoon) different trends in the industry. The first victim of our sarcasm was the sugary-sweet aberrations known at the time as "malternatives," now referred to as flavored malt beverages, or FMBs. We've also targeted very-high-alcohol beers, low-carb beers, and the burgeoning energy drink industry. And as you'll see, we also aren't above poking some fun at our own sector: extreme beer enthusiasts. To complete your education in all things Stone, and to provide a little extra entertainment, we thought we'd share those press releases, in all their glory.

EXTREME LEMONYLIME

On April 1, 2002, Stone "introduced" Extreme LemonyLime, thus entering the fast-growing "malternative" market. The malt-based product featured a light citrusy flavor and 5.5% ABV.

Like other category leaders in the malternative segment, Stone has made the flavor profile of the new Extreme LemonyLime no more complicated than a typical soft drink. Sure, we could continue just brewing beers that appeal to the educated and sophisticated beer lover, but we decided we should be able to go after the lemming consumer too.

Industry reports suggest that legal-drinking-age consumers with the undeveloped palates of teenagers are demanding more and more light, fruity, and fizzy alcoholic drinks. The company expects that the core consumer for Extreme LemonyLime will be in the very influential 21 to 21-and-a-half age group. Consumers who buy these soda-pop flavored malternatives are clearly newbies to alcohol and don't like the taste of alcohol—they just want the effect. Our research has shown that our existing lineup of full-flavored beers does not appeal to this type of consumer, and thus came the idea for Extreme LemonyLime.

The word Extreme is hot right now, and we are especially pleased with our melding of the words *lemon* and *lime*, thereby creating the entirely new word *LemonyLime*. This word tested very well with our target audience when we interviewed them at the shopping malls and the Family Fun Center. The word *ice* was also considered as a strong candidate to be in the name, but it was felt that target consumers for the brand might have trouble remembering a name as long as "Extreme LemonyLime Ice."

MONOLITH

"Debuted" on April 1, 2003, Monolith was a fabled ale boasting 27.3% ABV, which at the time would have set a new world record for the strongest ale. (Our friends at BrewDog have since shattered that record, by the way.)

Monolith is the result of a secret project that has been seventeen months in the making at Stone Brewing. This rare ale was produced by brewing 17 small batches on the brewery's pilot brewing system, fermenting with 17 different yeast strains over the 17-month period. In fact, our code name for the beer was "17."

In keeping with the "17" theme, the brewery is releasing 17 cases at $1,700 each (retail). Yes, we realize that few people will be able to pony up the $142 per 17-ounce bottle price and that fewer still will even be able to find it. However, we still think it's a good way to help some real hard-core beer enthusiasts part with their cash and get some free media attention to boot. Let's be real here, this is not about taste or quality or value. It's about collectability.

STONE JUSTIFICATION ALE

Remember that whole stupid low-carb diet that swept the nation a few years back? Good, we don't either. But believe it or not, there was a time when people actually thought they could lose weight and be healthy by eating a ridiculous amount of protein and fat, as long as they didn't eat any of them there evil, good-for-nothin' carbohydrates. ("Double-bacon cheeseburger, please, hold the bun.") Light beers jumped on the bandwagon, touting their strikingly low amounts of carbs (despite being a beverage that is made from . . . carbs).

Some consumers drink light and lo-carb beers because they prefer the light flavor and texture. They like the fact that it doesn't taste like real beer, while being accompanied by marketing that says it does. We want to send the message to the consumer that Stone Justification Ale can be that beer. We can talk in tried-and-true terms of the beer not making you feel full, of it not slowing you down, of it being satisfying but not heavy. Stone knows that some consumers would be delighted if we could figure out how to liquefy air and add a little alcohol to it. We're working diligently on that, but in the meantime: Stone Justification Ale is your beer.

In Stone Justification Ale, we have created a beer with an extraordinary depth of flavor lightness. One might think that the near nonexistence of carbs in the beer would lead to a similar nonexistence of flavor. However, we're going to tell people different. In

fact, much of the deep, rich, satisfying flavor of Stone Justification Ale comes from the way we describe it, which adds no carbs at all! In our promotional materials we describe it as having significantly more character than it actually has—which is nearly none. The preponderance of the American public will perceive the beer in the way we tell them to perceive it. The brewery justifies this because it is the standard that has long been established in the light and lo-carb beer arena.

People are going to choose fat, calorie, and carbohydrate-laden foods no matter what. Stone Justification Ale helps them to feel better about those choices, and better about themselves as a result. Holding a Stone Justification Ale sends the message that you are taking care of yourself and that you are on your way to shedding those unsightly pounds. You can fake that you are enjoying the beer, but you can't fake how others see you. They have to do that themselves. Stone Justification Ale is a valuable piece of armor in that battle. The fact of the matter is that it is much easier for us to fool ourselves than it is to fool others. Stone Justification Ale is your partner in doing both. Don't want to go to the gym today? Have a Stone Justification Ale! Overdid it at lunch? Have a Stone Justification Ale! Don't want to do anything other than sit on the couch, munch on empty-calorie snacks and watch games on TV all day? Have a sixer, or more, of Stone Justification Ale!

BASTARD OXIDE

We shocked the world (or at least a few people) when we announced we were branching out and entering the burgeoning energy drink market with Bastard Oxide on April 1, 2006.

Most energy drinks out there contain caffeine, taurine, guarana, ginseng, B vitamins, and the like. Although Bastard Oxide does load up on those ingredients to their fullest potential, it also contains many, many more complex ingredients. People need more metal in their diets: both internally and externally. Thus, contained in the large 22oz, 7.14% ABV bottle of Bastard Oxide is a special compound called X-Metal Complex(r) that contains Vitamin A, Vitamin K, Boron, Chromium, Copper, Iodine, Iron, Manganese, Molybdenum, Nickel, Silicon, Vanadium, and Zinc.

Geared toward metal-heads, it was even endorsed by some hardcore followers. Burton C. Bell, lead singer of Fear Factory, said, "Nothing gets you amped like Bastard Oxide . . . and buzzed . . . the perfect combination if you're in one of our mosh pits!"

(Warning: Though effective, Bastard Oxide is not recommended to be utilized for its side effect of sterility. The surgeon general has determined some of the contents in this product may not be suitable for mammals.)

BREWDOG / STONE
LUCIFERIN GOLDEN IMPERIAL STOUT

The year 2010 brought new technology to the April Fool's Day prank. James Watt, managing director of BrewDog, and I made a video in which we did a blindfolded tasting, analyzing the notes of "dark, rich chocolate . . . coffee . . . vanilla . . . a little licorice" and so on, all whilst holding a goblet of golden ale.

"Is this Dark Lord?" I ask.

"Speedway Stout?" counters James.

"This isn't Stone Imperial Russian Stout, is it?"

After removing our blindfolds, James and I let the viewing audience know what we were actually trying: BrewDog / Stone Luciferin Golden Imperial Stout, so named because Lucifer means "light bearing" or "bringer of light" in Latin. It's a style-bending brew flavored with cacao nibs and coffee to mimic a true imperial stout (and with an 11.8% ABV to back it up), but brewed with pale and extra pale malt to keep its color light.

Oats were added to increase the rich mouthfeel, and it was aged in whiskey casks. There was only a limited run of two thousand bottles, each packaged with a blindfold so drinkers can challenge their perception of what an imperial stout really is, and how an imperial stout should really look.

The final word from James and me? "A really unique combination of ingredients coming together to make a beer that has all the classic imperial stout flavors but is, well, golden."

BASTARDSHOTZ

BastardSHOTZ Gel Pakz were a stroke of genius in the Art/Media department, enticing the Bastard on-the-go crowd, by condensing an entire 22-ounce bottle of Arrogant Bastard Ale into a 3-ounce pouch (concentrating it to a mighty impressive 52.8 percent ABV in the process). Although some people called it out as April Fool's right away, we also got a healthy share of emails from people complaining that they were disappointed in us for stooping so low (one guy cc'd a bunch of his friends, who in turn replied and told him to look at his calendar). But the biggest surprise was how many people actually wanted us to make BastardSHOTZ. Sorry folks, not in this lifetime!

PART THREE

“DR.” BILL PRESENTS:

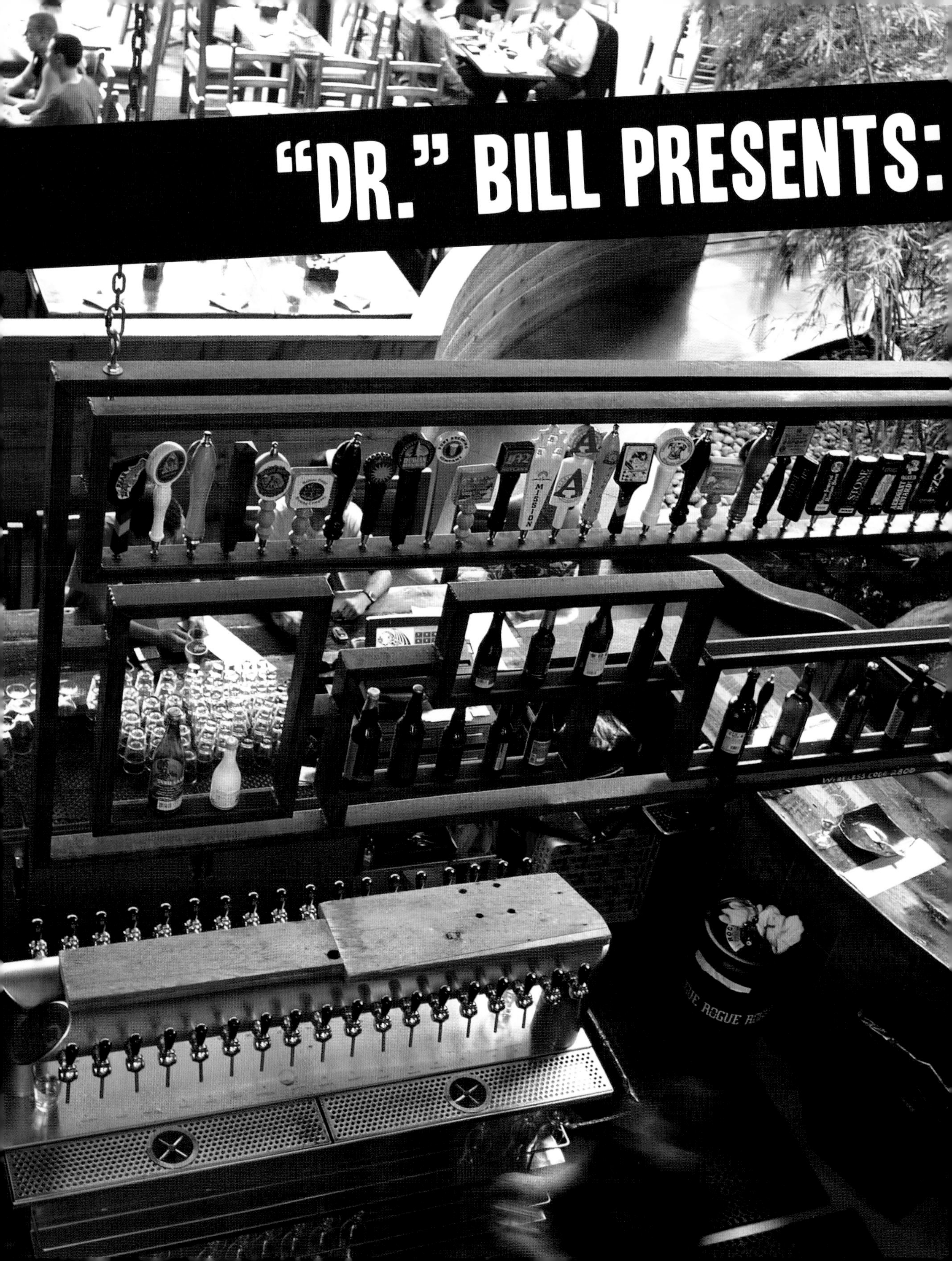

Our beverage supervisor, "Dr." Bill Sysak, has been around the beer block a few times (check out his story on page 60), and he's no stranger to treating craft beers with the care, respect, and reverence they truly deserve. Read on to get his tips on serving, tasting, cellaring, and food pairings.

"DR." BILL'S GUIDE TO SERVING CRAFT BEER

Sure, you *can* pull a beer out of the old icebox, crack it open, and drink it straight out of the bottle. But you'd be missing out on much of the experience of enjoying and savoring a properly served beer. Here, let me help you with that.

Selecting the Proper Glass

Beer is just like wine, aperitifs, and a host of specialty libations, in that selecting the right type of glassware for your drink has a large effect on how it tastes. Just as you wouldn't want to drink red wine from a champagne flute, specific beer styles have corresponding glasses that enhance flavor and aroma characteristics.

Pint glasses or tumblers can be used without ill effect for most English and American styles of beer, but if your beer is highly aromatic, do yourself a favor and get a few tulip glasses. If the pint glass is just more to your style, try to find an imperial (also called nonic) pint glass. It holds 20 fluid ounces versus the typical 16 and has a slight bulge toward the top. This not only helps with gripping your beer, it also aids in forming a full, frothy head.

Everyone has their favorite, but if I had to choose just one universal style, I would prefer to use a stemmed tulip glass. The glass curves inward, with the rim turning out, which helps retain the volatile aromas. Weizen and pilsner glasses are great for their respective eponymous styles, but you aren't going to find many of those coming out of the Stone doors. I'm not ruling it out, but given our history . . .

All of that said, any glass will work in a pinch, as long as it's clean. Cleanliness is key, as even the most infinitesimal amount of soap, dust, lipstick, or other contaminant can sour an otherwise perfect pour. For best results, hand wash your glasses with a mild dish soap solution, rinse well, and allow them to air-dry.

BEER	GLASS TYPE	
Stone Pale Ale	Pint/Imperial Pint	
Stone Smoked Porter	Pint/Imperial Pint	
Stone IPA	Pint/Imperial Pint	
Stone Ruination IPA	Pint/Imperial Pint	
Stone Levitation Ale	Pint/Imperial Pint	
Stone Cali-Belgique IPA	Stemmed Tulip	
Stone Sublimely Self-Righteous Ale	Stemmed Tulip	
Stone Sawyer's Triple Ale	Stemmed Tulip	
Arrogant Bastard Ale	Goblet	
OAKED Arrogant Bastard Ale	Goblet	
Lukcy Basartd Ale	Goblet	
Stone Old Guardian Barley Wine	Snifter	
Double Bastard Ale	Snifter	
Stone Imperial Russian Stout	Snifter	

Just as important as properly washing glasses is how you store them. It's best to keep them upright in a clean cupboard, but if you like to store them with the mouth down, make sure the glass is completely dry to avoid trapped moisture. What about keeping them frosty in the freezer? As far as craft beers are concerned, just say no. Why? It has to do with serving temperature.

Serving Temperature

Unlike those lamentable fizzy yellow beer-like substances, craft beer should not be served in the taste-numbing 35 to 38°F range. I prefer a starting temperature between 40 and 50°F, depending on the style. Flavors and aromas are muted in colder foods and beverages. If you don't believe me, let some ice cream melt and come to room temperature, then give it a taste. You'll see that it's noticeably sweeter and more strongly flavored than it was when frozen. The same holds true for brews, so when you want to have a beer that's super ice-cold, reach for that can or bottle with the color-changing label. They don't want you drinking that swill until it tastes as close to nothing as possible!

With craft beers, where flavor and quality is of greater importance than quantity or "drinkability" (a marketing euphemism for mediocrity, predictability, and bland conformity), you'll notice that the flavor becomes more pronounced as your beverage warms a

bit. And by savoring your beer slowly and righteously, as those who carefully and artfully brewed it would wish you to, you can actually take the time to appreciate and enjoy the subtle changes of aroma and flavor that develop.

Think of it as analogous to the wine experience. Heavier, more robust reds are best served a few degrees warmer than, say, a delicate Pinot Noir. Moving further down the ideal serving temperature scale, you'll find rosés and white and sparkling wines that are served chilled (but still not ice-cold!) to aid in appreciation of their crisp character and refreshing zing. But this isn't a book on wine, now is it? Let's get on with beer. . . . Much of the heft that a beer with a huge, rich flavor profile, such as an imperial Russian stout, might bring to the table would be lost if it were served right out of the fridge into a frostbitten mug excavated from the barren depths of your freezer. If a bottle is too cold when you pull it out of the refrigerator, pour it into a room-temperature glass and let it sit for ten minutes. Your patience will be well rewarded.

Producing a Proper Pour

We've all poured a glass of pure foam before. It happens to the best of us. To minimize the risk and avoid waiting what seems like an eternity for your overly effervescent pint to subside, pour slowly and carefully. Tilt the glass at a 45-degree angle and pour the beer gently down the side. Turn the glass upright when it's half to two-thirds full, directing the flow down the

middle of glass to create a beautiful pour with a large, billowy head.

If you're enjoying a bottle-conditioned or unfiltered beer, there might be a small collection of yeast sediment at the bottom of the bottle. Choosing whether or not to drink this sediment (also called the lees) is strictly a matter of personal preference. It is quite rich in B vitamins, but contributes a somewhat earthy—and, well, yeasty—flavor to the beer. If you don't wish to leave the sediment behind, pour a majority of the beer into your glass, pausing to gently swirl the bottle when only a few ounces remain, mixing in the yeast before pouring it all into your glass. If drinking it isn't your thing, simply pour the beer slowly, so as to minimally disturb the layer of sediment, and stop the pour just shy of emptying the bottle.

Taking It All In

Beer should be an experience for several of your senses, not just taste. Take a close look at it. Hold the glass up to the light and admire the color and clarity (or lack thereof, depending on style).

Swirl the glass to kick up the volatile aromas, then stick your nose right in the glass and take a big whiff. Breathe in a few short breaths followed by a longer inhalation. Aroma is an important part of fully enjoying beer, especially because smell can account for up to 90 percent of what you taste.

The list of scents you may encounter is seemingly endless. Take note of any you recognize. Is the malt striking you with any bready, toasty, or roasty hints? Maybe caramel? Perhaps it's a darker beer and the malt is brimming with an air of chocolate or coffee. Are the hops redolent of citrus, pine, or maybe fresh-cut grass? Is the yeast chiming in with fruity esters? Spicy phenols? How about the alcohol? Is it making its presence known? Can you pick out any special ingredients the brewery mentions using?

And if the beer has been barrel aged, has it adopted any characteristics of either the barrel or the beverage that was previously aged within it? If the barrel was used to age bourbon or whiskey prior to your current libation, does that come through? Maybe the barrel held wine in another life, which can add vinous qualities to your suds.

The combinations are nearly unlimited, which is what makes our noble industry so grand—and what keeps the end result so ultimately enjoyable.

Taste. Enjoy. Repeat.

Now, after all the grandeur, you finally get to take a sip of the beer. Gently swish it around your mouth before swallowing. This will help cleanse your palate and wash away the flavors of any food you recently ate, gum you chewed, and so on. Take another sip, then part your lips and pull air over your palate to aerate the beer and move it over all of your taste buds. Finally, take a third drink from the glass and enjoy that beer as the brewer intended it to taste.

And while it's easy to get lost in the ceremony I've described here, it's important to understand that, in the end, beer is something that's meant to be enjoyed. There can be a fine line between beer appreciation and beer snobbery. Don't allow yourself to get so caught up in the pomp and circumstance of it all that you flat out forget how to just allow yourself to enjoy a good friggin' beer without completely overthinking it.

"DR." BILL'S GUIDE TO CELLARING BEER

Just as there are certain styles of wine that lend themselves well to extended aging and others that are meant to be consumed fresh, the same is true for particular styles of beer. And while setting a case of beer or wine in your garage next to the water heater for a few years is *technically* considered aging (though I guarantee you won't like the results), following some simple guidelines will help you create a stellar cellar for your prized potable possessions.

Picking a Spot

Select an area where the temperature doesn't fluctuate from one extreme to another. A great area to start storing beer is a closet, preferably in the middle of your home or office, without an external wall to help minimize temperature fluctuations. Heat is one of the major enemies of beer. It can produce all sorts of off flavors and will quickly degrade the glory and splendor of the hops. Ideally, the temperature of your cellaring area should be around 55°F, but anywhere that stays between 50 and 68°F will work. Extended aging at temperatures below that range can also be problematic, in that they inactivate or unnecessarily slow many of the changes that we are looking for in the yeast. Cold temperatures also tend to dry and shrink corks, which will allow oxygen into the bottle, which as you know by know, is bad juju.

Now that we have temperature under control, let's look at the issue of light. Beer is photosensitive, so you want to avoid exposure to light. Glass bottles let in UV rays from the sun and even fluorescent lights, which cause isohumulones (compounds naturally present in hops that contribute to bittering) to break down into mercaptans, sulfurous compounds that are very similar (both in chemical structure and odor) to a skunk's fetid spray. If you've ever heard that a beer tastes "skunky," it has most likely been exposed to light for extended periods of time (sometimes referred to as a light-struck beer). While brown beer bottles are better at keeping out UV rays than clear or green bottles, they still don't filter out all of the rays, so be sure to limit the amount of light as much as possible.

Stocking Up

Once you've identified an appropriate cellaring space, it's time to fill it. It's important to note that certain beer styles age better than others. While many craft beers are meant to be consumed fresh, there are quite a few styles that can transform and even improve with age. Generally speaking, there are a few simple guidelines for selecting beers that are likely to fare well over time, under the proper conditions.

Higher-Alcohol Beers

Alcohol acts as a natural preservative, and beers at 8% ABV or stronger tend to have a good chance of weathering the sands of time. Also of interest is that if a higher-alcohol beer tastes a little "hot" when fresh, that element of its flavor profile will typically subside over time, becoming smoother, mellower, and better integrated with overall flavor.

Sweet and Sour

Sour beers such as lambics and Flemish reds are practically made for aging. The lactic and acetic acids responsible for the pucker actually aid with preservation. Their sour notes also become more subtle and less punchy as the years progress.

These beers are also often brewed with hops that have been aged. Although this removes just about all traces of the hop flavor and aroma that IPA lovers go ga-ga over, it leaves intact the natural preservative compounds found in hops that help the beer age more gracefully.

The residual sugars left in some styles of beer, running the gamut from light to dark, also soften with age. Beers that may initially come off as cloyingly sweet often lose that edge and develop more of an aromatic hint of sweetness.

The Hops Dilemma

It's true that hops have a preservative quality, and this may tempt you to think of all the crazy IPAs you can set aside for future consumption. While you could do that, don't expect them to taste like IPAs in the end. The natural compounds that help the beer keep over time are extracted through the long boil. The flavor and aroma components that distinguish an IPA are largely released from hops added late in the boil, and they are very volatile. They deteriorate and fade away quickly, even under ideal conditions. To truly appreciate an IPA as an IPA, consume it fresh to get all of the hoppy goodness. That's not to say an IPA won't age well. It can and almost certainly will, but it will be a much different animal than the hop bomb it once was. There is a difference between "fresh tasting" and "not spoiled"—hops help preserve the latter, not the former.

Typical Styles to Age

Given the previous criteria, here's a list of beer styles that I have found to be conducive to cellaring, but feel free to experiment. Given the many variables that come into play, there's no way to be sure what will happen over time. There's always a chance that a beer you thought would age beautifully will become utterly undrinkable. Conversely, you also may find that a beer of a style *not* well known for aging becomes an amazing superbeer after you patiently waited (or forgot) to

drink it for ten years. It's a bit of a crapshoot, but that's what keeps it fun and interesting.

That said, allow me to offer a list based on my own experience. Generally speaking, I've found these styles to be particularly well suited to aging for at least three to five years:

- Barleywine
- Belgian strong ale
- Dubbel, tripel, and quadrupel ales
- Eisbock
- Flemish red
- Gueuze
- Imperial stout
- Lambic
- Old ale
- Oud bruin
- Rauchbier
- Scotch ale
- Trappist or abbey ale
- Wee heavy
- Wheatwine

Some can go on to develop for upwards of ten, twenty, or maybe even thirty years, but again, there's no telling.

Upright or Sideways?

Whether cellared beers should be stored upright or on their side is an excellent question—and one that causes much controversy among beer aficionados. And, truth be told, there's no definitive answer. Many wine drinkers and holdovers from the old school maintain that corked bottles especially should be laid on their side to prevent the cork from drying out and so on. Personally, I disagree. In my thirty-ish years of cellaring beers, I've chosen to store them upright and have yet to encounter any such problems. (Knock on wood.) The choice is entirely yours, and I recommend whichever system works best for maximizing your storage space.

Flavor Development

As beers age, they can take on many different flavors, primarily depending on the style. Actual flavor changes may not be noticeable early on; rather, you'll sense a general smoothing out of the rough edges and a rounding out of all the flavors. As months become years, oxidation will start having its way with your beer. Assuming you've created an ideal cellar environment, there is a good chance that this process will have a desirable effect on your brew, becoming a complementary part of the overall taste experience, rather than dominating or overwhelming it.

The resulting aromas and flavors are often redolent of aged sherry, port, or Madeira, fortified wines that undergo similar oxidative aging. Other descriptors are nutty, musty, and fruity, the latter running the gamut from fresh ripe red fruit and berries all the way to intense dried fruit like raisins and prunes. Caramel or toffee notes can evolve as well. On the less attractive side of the oxidation equation, medicinal or solvent-type notes, and characteristics of cardboard or wet dog are signs that your beer is a touch past its prime.

GREG: Wine pairing is so yesterday. Beer truly is food's best friend. In fact, we proved it. We participated in a series of three beer vs. wine dinners at Rancho Bernardo Inn's famed El Bizcocho restaurant. Since we were up against sommelier and certified wine educator Barry Wiss, of Napa's Trinchero Family Estates, we knew we had to come on strong.

The premise was simple: A six-course fine-dining experience with both a specially selected wine and a specially selected beer to go with each course. (And note that neither Barry nor I had any say in the creation of the menu.) All the attendees got a ballot to mark their preference for each course—either the beer or the wine. At the end of the dinner, the results were tallied and the winner announced.

When Team Beer won at the initial matchup in 2007, Team Wine demanded a rematch. I don't think they could believe it! We gladly took their challenge and even let 'em win Round Two the following year. (Barry's a great guy, and we didn't want to make him feel *too* bad! Plus, a best-two-out-of-three is much more suspenseful than a one-two knockout punch. . . . we had to keep 'em in the game!) But we came back even stronger for Round Three in 2009 and took home the championship trophy. Barry, never once wavering from his stature as a genuine gentleman, was kind enough to sincerely congratulate us—and even admit that the experience had really opened his eyes to the depth and complexity of great beer.

Ultimately, I learned something as well. When artfully selected and poured by an educated professional, yes, even I must admit, there can occasionally be a place for great wine at the dinner table. At least sometimes.

"DR." BILL'S GUIDE TO FOOD AND BEER PAIRING

Of all the different beverages I've paired with food over the years, beer is easily the most versatile. And even beyond its versatility, beer has several unique characteristics that make it not only a suitable pairing for food, but a *perfect* pairing. Let's take a look at why that may be the case.

Carbonation

The carbonation in beer gives it an edge over spirits and most wines, since carbonation acts as a palate cleanser. Between bites, the bubbles help wipe away any fat or heavy flavors that may be coating your tongue, allowing you to enjoy each bite as if it were the first. The effervescence also helps lift foods up, carrying their rich flavors all over your palate.

Malt

The malted grains used in brewing often contribute flavors to beer that are similar or complementary to flavors you find in roasted or grilled meats and vegetables. Perhaps the beer is a touch grainy, nutty, or bready. It might exhibit characteristics of caramel, biscuits, or toast. Darker roasts boast shades of coffee, chocolate, and earth. These flavors develop during the roasting of the grain, as well as during the boil. The fact that the same chemical processes, namely caramelization and the Maillard reaction, take place during high-temperature cooking, such as roasting and grilling, helps explain why beer and foods prepared in such a fashion have such a natural affinity for one another.

Hops

The sharp, bitter edge of the hops helps balance out heavier, fatty dishes while also working in unison with the bubbles to spread the unctuous goodness like no wine ever could. The floral, citrusy qualities of hops also play unbelievably well with spicy food, helping take a

BEER	RECOMMENDED FOOD PAIRINGS
Stone Pale Ale	Hamburgers, Parmesan cheese, fried chicken, bananas Foster
Stone Smoked Porter	Barbecue, roast beef, garlic mashed potatoes, Gruyère cheese, peanut butter cookies
Stone IPA	Curries, Thai food, Cheddar cheese, citrus dishes, carrot cake
Arrogant Bastard Ale	Pork chops, aged sheep's milk cheeses, duck tacos, spice cake
Stone Old Guardian Barley Wine	Beef carbonnade, lamb, Stilton cheese, caramel toffee
Double Bastard Ale	Venison, figs, Shropshire blue cheese, crème brûlée
Stone Imperial Russian Stout	Coffee-crusted pork tenderloin, foie gras, Gorgonzola cheese, chocolate
Stone Ruination IPA	Indian food, carne asada tacos, Maytag blue cheese, tapioca
Stone Levitation Ale	Pizza, tomato sauces, ratatouille, Gouda cheese, pumpkin pie
OAKED Arrogant Bastard Ale	Smoked turkey, grilled salmon, mushroom ragoût, washed rind cheeses, rum cake
Stone Cali-Belgique IPA	Calamari, roasted chicken, Bucherondin (French bloomy rind goat's milk cheese), persimmon tart
Stone Sublimely Self-Righteous Ale	Oaxacan mole, chili con carne, Piave vecchio (aged Italian cow's milk cheese), tiramisu
Stone Sawyer's Triple Ale	Lobster risotto, crab cakes, Brillat-Savarin (French bloomy rind, triple crème cow's milk cheese), baklava
Lukcy Basartd Ale	Rib eye steak, Cajun food, Noord Hollander Gouda cheese, oatmeal raisin cookies

little edge off of the heat while accentuating the underlying flavors present in chile pepper–tinged foods.

Herbs and Spices

Beers have long been brewed with herbs and spices. Historically, these ingredients were often incorporated so the beer could be used as a health tonic, or to help extend the life of the beer, predating hops as the favored preservative. However, it wasn't entirely a case of function before form, as there is no doubt that spices and various herbs were also added to impart their flavors to the brew.

Rosemary, basil, lavender, peppercorns, ginger, coriander, anise, nutmeg, and juniper berries are among the many spices and herbs that have been making their way into craft beers. They might be added as a subtle nuance, or they may play a dominant role in the beer's overall flavor and aroma. Either way, this creates a world of opportunity for food pairings, since these infused beers can accentuate, complement, or contrast seasonings used in the food, becoming an extension of the meal and an integrated component of the dish.

Yeast

Yeast strains can also contribute flavors redolent of particular spices. Typical Bavarian weissbier yeast strains are known for producing phenols that resemble cloves. Belgian yeast strains can contribute spice notes as well, but they tend to be a little more subtle. They're better known for providing fruity esters to the beer, adding complexity and depth of character.

Pairing Guidelines

When pairing food and beer, the whole will ideally be greater than the sum of the parts. The food should taste good on its own and the beer should taste good on its own, but when the pairing is done right, it should sing. The food should bring out something in the beer that you hadn't noticed before—and vice versa—or both should combine to create an entirely new flavor that didn't exist in either of them on their own. Here are some guidelines that can help you achieve these lofty goals:

- When pairing beer with food, look for either complementary or contrasting flavors. Whichever way you lean, always try to achieve a balance.
- Match the beer and food in terms of intensity of flavor. Subtle dishes deserve a subtle beer, while more flavorful foods require more robust flavors from the beer.
- Working with contrasting ingredients can produce some incredible flavor combinations. For example, bright citrusy IPAs pique slippery sweet caramelized onions in a tuna melt or veggie fajitas; and roasty, malty stouts accentuate a ripe, creamy blue cheese while rounding out its pleasantly pungent funk.

- Look for comparable flavors. The notes of coffee and smoke in darker beers like imperial stouts match amazingly well with all things chocolate. However, you must be careful when pairing like with like. For example, a pairing of beer brewed with orange peel and an orange-flavored dessert could lack pizzazz. Instead, perhaps try a lemon dessert or carrot cake to complement the orange flavor, rather than simply matching it.
- Think seasonally. Spiced winter brews are a wonderful match for robust soups and stews, whereas German hefeweizens and Belgian gueuzes are perfect for the heat of summer and go great with a refreshing salad.
- If preparing multiple courses, start with lighter beer and food and work your way up to heavier, more robust, or hoppier beers.
- Have fun! Experiment with your pairings. Not everything will work; keep track of what does and build from there.

Also, use reference tools. There are many great books and online websites that cover basic food pairing principles. *The Brewmaster's Table: Discovering the Pleasures of Real Beer with Real Food*, by Garrett Oliver, remains the ultimate guide on the subject. Our good friend Sam Calagione, from Dogfish Head Craft Brewery, also put out an excellent book on the subject, entitled *He Said Beer, She Said Wine*. Sam worked with sommelier Marnie Old to bring a unique perspective, offering up both beer and wine pairings for a great variety of dishes. Andrew Dornenburg and Karen Page also penned two helpful titles, albeit not quite as beer focused. Regardless, they're excellent guides for understanding flavors and pairing: *What to Drink with What You Eat*. Find even more info at www.craftbeer.com

To help you get into the swing of pairings, I've provided Recommended Beer notes throughout the recipe section. Enjoy!

RECIPES FROM THE STONE BREWING

Hey! Greg here again, ready to share the culinary treasures of Stone Brewing World Bistro & Gardens! Steve and I worked with Chef Alex and our kitchen team to select some of our favorite recipes and scale them down so you can make them right in the comfort of your own home. We even threw in a few new ones, well, just because we could—and because we thought you'd like them. If you've ever been to our bistro, you know that we've got some pretty amazing dishes, and we specialize in a rather eclectic range of choices. Moreover, you may have guessed that some of our recipes use beer. Bonus! It's especially nice when a recipe only uses a few ounces, because then you've got plenty of beer left, and you're left with a very important responsibility, or perhaps even obligation: to see that the remainder is properly consumed and enjoyed! *Honey, it's 10:30 a.m. Are you drinking beer?* No way, baby. I'm making mysel . . . er, us . . . I'm making *us* a . . . a romantic brunch! *Aww, that's so nice! Wait, so what's that in your glass?* Oh, it's just what was left in the bottle. It will go flat if I put it back in the fridge. I mean, this Stone stuff is kinda awesome, you know. You don't want me to waste it . . . do you?

Anyway, so where were we? Ah, yes! Cooking. Well, do yourself a favor. In fact, do us *all* a favor: cook smart. Our food stands for something, and even if we are Arrogant Bastards, we realize that the world doesn't revolve around us and that we should make conscious choices with our food and cooking. We use local ingredients whenever possible and seek out purveyors who are responsible stewards of the land, using organic and sustainable practices so that we can all live to enjoy another day here on this beautiful blue orb.

So don't be a numskull; put down that pesticide-laden, genetically modified Frankenfood flown in from halfway around the globe! We like to think of our approach to food as an extension of our philosophy on beer. And just as we eschew the boring, mass-market fizzy yellow stuff in place of delicious, flavorful craft beer, we lean toward high-quality, sustainable ingredients. They may cost a bit more, but we're furthering a grassroots movement. And they taste a helluva lot better. So shop local. Shop organic. Shop sustainable. Bring your own damn bags to the store. Cook. Eat. Crack a beer. Live. Love. Laugh. Repeat. Daily.

BREWER'S BARLEY CRACKER BREAD

We're a little spoiled here at the bistro. Besides having access to extremely local beer (i.e. made in the same building), we also get fun stuff to play around with, like hops and cracked barley. If you venture in to your friendly neighborhood homebrew supply shop, pick up some lightly toasted barley and run it through the grain mill there to make your own cracked barley for this recipe. If that isn't a viable option, you can substitute $^1/_2$ cup of pearl barley, pulsed lightly in a food processor, or $^1/_3$ cup barley grits, available at many natural food stores.

$1^3/_4$ cups plus 2 tablespoons ($8^1/_4$ ounces) all-purpose flour, or as needed

$^1/_2$ cup (2 ounces) cracked barley

2 teaspoons lightly packed light brown sugar

$^1/_4$ teaspoon instant yeast (also known as quick or rapid rise yeast)

$^1/_8$ teaspoon kosher salt, plus more for sprinkling

$^1/_2$ cup water, or more as needed

2 tablespoons olive oil, plus more for brushing

TIP: In lieu of using a stand mixer, you can knead the dough by hand for about 10 minutes, or pulse it in a food processor fitted with the dough blade for 45 seconds to 1 minute. Allow the dough to rest for 5 minutes, as in the instructions, then use the windowpane test to determine whether more kneading or processing is required. Be careful not to overwork the dough, especially if using a food processor.

Combine all of the ingredients in the bowl of a stand mixer fitted with the dough hook (see Tip). Mix at low speed until a shaggy dough has formed. Stop the mixer, cover the bowl with plastic wrap, and let the dough rest for 5 minutes.

Uncover the bowl and mix the dough at medium-low speed for about 8 minutes, until tacky but not sticky. Go by feel. Stop the mixer periodically to touch the dough. Tacky? Good. Sticky? Bad. You want it to slightly peel away from your hand, without actually sticking to it. Add more water or flour in small increments, if necessary. However, resist the urge to use excessive flour at any point in working with the dough; a wet dough is far preferable to a dry dough that has been overworked.

Cover the bowl again and let the dough rest for another 5 minutes. Take a small chunk of dough and stretch it to form a thin membrane. If you can stretch it thin enough that the dough is translucent, the gluten has been sufficiently developed. (This is known as the windowpane test.) If the dough tears before getting that thin, continue to knead it in the mixer until it passes the windowpane test.

Transfer the dough to a lightly floured work surface and divide into 12 relatively equal pieces. Work with one piece of dough at a time, keeping the rest covered with plastic wrap or a slightly damp kitchen towel to keep them from drying out. Flatten the piece of dough with the palm of your hand, then run it through a pasta machine several times, starting with the thickest setting and working down to setting #5, getting thinner with each successive pass. Alternatively, you can also roll each piece out as thin as possible with a rolling pin.

Preheat the oven to 350°F. Line several baking sheets with parchment paper or wax paper.

Lay 2 pieces of rolled-out dough on one of the prepared baking sheets, side-by-side. Brush a light layer of olive oil over the dough and sprinkle with a bit of kosher salt. Use a pizza cutter or knife to divide the dough into smaller rectangles, roughly 2 by 3 inches in size.

Bake for 8 to 12 minutes, until nicely browned and dry, crispy, and not at all soft when tapped with a fingernail. Keep a watchful eye toward the end of the baking time; the cracker bread is so thin that it can turn from tasty to burnt in about 30 seconds. Transfer to a wire rack and let cool completely, breaking up any pieces that fused together while baking.

Repeat with the remaining dough. Stored in a dry, airtight container, the cracker bread will keep for up to 2 weeks.

OUR PHILOSOPHY ON FOOD

At Stone Brewing World Bistro & Gardens, we use in-season, locally, regionally, and organically grown produce. We do this not just for the simple principles of freshness and sustainability, but also because fresh, local, and organic tastes better. It's also better for you and the world in which we live. It shouldn't be surprising to hear that we also use 100 percent naturally raised meats. The same fresh / artisanal / natural standard goes for all our food. It does cost more, and our prices reflect some of that reality. However, we also feel it is the much, much better way to go. Greg Koch and Steve Wagner, cofounders of Stone Brewing, have been involved in the international Slow Food movement since 2000. Slow Food promotes getting "back to the table" and celebrates artisanal, natural, and old-world approaches to food. At Stone, we celebrate our love of all things culinary by drawing freely from cultures and dishes from all over the world. We also celebrate all things local, and have an amazing selection of regional beers, wines, produce, meats, breads, and cheeses. Finally, we have sworn off all things mediocre, NO MATTER HOW POPULAR. We do not serve any industrial adjunct beers (aka "fizzy yellow beers") as they do not represent the best in beers in our opinion. Instead of generic orange-colored cheese varieties, we select flavorful artisanal cheeses. We are 100 percent high-fructose corn syrup free, as we don't think that ANYTHING that uses cheap sold-by-the-drum sweetener tastes as good as food and drink that's made with actual real, natural sugar. No, we're not health nuts, we're quality nuts! The fact that actual real food is better for you than the "food-like" substances that folks commonly eat is beside the point. Or is it?

FRESH COLUMBUS HOP VINAIGRETTE

We love this vinaigrette drizzled over our Stone Brewing World Bistro & Gardens Salad, where its bitter bite works perfectly with local organic baby greens, sunflower seeds, cucumbers, carrots, and rich, Rogue Creamery Smoky Blue Cheese. It's also great as a dressing for cold pasta salads or as a marinade for grilled chicken, salmon, or shrimp.

1 head Roasted Garlic (page 134)

2 medium shallots, minced

²/₃ cup balsamic vinegar

¹/₃ cup red wine vinegar

¹/₄ cup whole Columbus hop cones (see Tip)

1 tablespoon honey

¹/₂ teaspoon kosher salt

¹/₄ teaspoon freshly ground black pepper

5 tablespoons extra-virgin olive oil

Put the garlic, shallots, vinegars, hops, honey, salt, and pepper in a food processor or blender. Process until almost smooth. With the processor or blender running, slowly drizzle in the olive oil and continue processing until the oil is completely incorporated and the vinaigrette thickens a bit. Stored in an airtight container in the refrigerator, the vinaigrette will keep for up to 1 week.

TIP: Fresh hop cones are available for purchase at homebrew supply stores or from online homebrewing retailers. If Columbus hops are not available, by all means feel free to substitute another variety. If you can't find whole hop cones, use 2 heaping tablespoons of pelletized hops instead.

OAKED ARROGANT BASTARD ALE STEAK SAUCE

Calling this a steak sauce seems kind of limiting. Make no mistake: this is exactly what the steak doctor ordered for your giant caveman slab of grilled meat, but it also works great in marinades and countless other applications. Try adding a healthy dose of it to your next veggie stir-fry, pot of chili, or meatloaf.

2 tablespoons vegetable oil

$1/2$ cup chopped red onion

$1/2$ cup chopped red bell pepper

9 cloves garlic, minced

$3/4$ cup red wine vinegar

$3/4$ cup balsamic vinegar

3 leaves basil, very thinly sliced

$1/4$ to $1/2$ teaspoon crushed red pepper flakes

2 teaspoons granulated garlic

$1 1/2$ teaspoons granulated onion

$1 1/2$ teaspoons kosher salt

$1 1/2$ teaspoons freshly ground black pepper

2 anchovy fillets

$1 1/2$ tablespoons Dijon mustard

$2 1/2$ tablespoons Worcestershire sauce

$3/4$ cup (6 fluid ounces) OAKED Arrogant Bastard Ale

Heat the oil in a large saucepan over medium heat until the oil begins to shimmer. Add the onion and bell pepper and cook, stirring occasionally, until they begin to become translucent, 5 to 7 minutes. Stir in the garlic and cook just until it is aromatic, about 1 minute. Stir in the vinegars and bring to a simmer. Stir in the basil and crushed red pepper.

Lower the heat and continue to simmer until the liquid has mostly evaporated and the ingredients have a reflective sheen. Remove from the heat and stir in the granulated garlic, granulated onion, salt, pepper, anchovies, mustard, Worcestershire sauce, and ale. Puree until smooth with an immersion blender or in a regular blender.

Strain the sauce through a fine-mesh sieve, then let it cool completely. Stored in an airtight container in the refrigerator, it will keep for 1 month.

OAKED ARROGANT BASTARD ALE BEEF JERKY

MAKES ABOUT 1 POUND

If you just made a batch of OAKED Arrogant Bastard Ale Steak Sauce and are wondering just how many steaks you're going to have to "force down" to use all of it up, we've got an alternative use for it that we think you'll love: beef jerky made with steak sauce made with beer. Can you get much manlier than that? We think not.

3/4 cup OAKED Arrogant Bastard Ale Steak Sauce (page 123)

1/4 cup soy sauce

2 tablespoons light brown sugar

1 teaspoon garlic powder

1 teaspoon crushed red pepper flakes

1 teaspoon freshly ground black pepper

2 pounds boneless top- or bottom-sirloin roast, thinly sliced (see Tip)

TIP: Make friends with your neighborhood butcher and tell them what you're up to. Mention that you're making jerky, and they should be able to select a good cut of meat for you. You want a nice, lean roast, trimmed of excess fat, and you need it sliced about 1/8 inch thick, against the grain. If you're a do-it-yourselfer, stick the roast in the freezer for 30 to 45 minutes, until it has firmed up but isn't quite hard. Then, using a very sharp knife (and lots of extra caution), slice the meat as thinly as possible.

Whisk the steak sauce, soy sauce, brown sugar, garlic powder, crushed red pepper, and black pepper together until thoroughly combined. Put the meat and marinade in a large resealable plastic bag and seal, pressing out excess air. Refrigerate for at least 6 hours or overnight, turning occasionally to ensure even distribution of the marinade.

Preheat the oven to 200°F. Line 3 baking sheets with aluminum foil and put a wire rack on top of each. Lift the strips of beef out of the bag, shaking off any excess marinade, and lay them out flat on the racks, leaving a small space between the pieces to allow for sufficient air circulation.

Bake for about 4 hours, rotating the pans and moving each to a different rack in the oven every hour to ensure even cooking. It shouldn't be soft or moist to the touch when adequately baked. It will shrink significantly and should crack slightly when bent. Continue baking as long as needed, rotating the pans and checking doneness at least once an hour.

Remove from the oven and cool on the racks for 2 hours. Stored in an airtight container in a cool, dry place (not in your refrigerator or freezer), the jerky will keep for up to 3 months.

ARROGANT BASTARD ALE WILD MUSHROOMS

The bold, bitter Bastard is a perfect counterpart to the woodsy and earthy character of sautéed wild mushrooms. Cremini and portobello are widely available and work quite well, but if you're a more adventurous mycophagist, gather up a variety. Look around for fresh shiitake, king trumpet, chanterelle, porcini, maitake, or oyster mushrooms at your local farmers' market or green grocer. Whatever you do, don't use button mushrooms. Lame.

1¹/₂ pounds mixed wild mushrooms

¹/₄ cup grapeseed or vegetable oil

2 large shallots, minced

Salt

1 clove garlic, minced

³/₄ cup (6 fluid ounces) Arrogant Bastard Ale

Freshly ground black pepper

Clean the mushrooms, gently rubbing them with a clean, damp towel or mushroom brush to remove excess dirt. Avoid soaking or directly rinsing them with water, as they will absorb the water and get slimy. Slice the mushrooms ¹/₄ inch thick.

Heat the oil in a large cast-iron skillet or wok over very high heat until it begins to shimmer. Toss in the shallots and cook, stirring occasionally, for 30 seconds. Add the mushrooms along with a sprinkling of salt. Cook, stirring often, until the mushrooms have given off much of their moisture, shrunken in size, and begun to brown, 4 to 5 minutes. Stir in the garlic and cook just until it is aromatic, about 30 seconds.

Deglaze the pan by adding the Arrogant Bastard Ale, stirring and scraping up any browned bits that may be affixed to the pan. Continue cooking until the mushrooms are nearly dry. Season with salt and pepper to taste. Serve immediately.

THOSE DAMN ARROGANT BASTARD ALE ONION RINGS

"Back in the late nineties, Greg, Steve, and I were playing poker one night with a group of guys. We were talking about the anniversary party and putting together something for the guests to snack on. I suggested onion rings. Not only are they great with beer, they also wouldn't cost a lot to make. And then it came to us: Arrogant Bastard Ale Onion Rings, with thick-cut onions and a tempura beer batter.

They were immensely popular. Even though we kept making more and more every year, it was always hard to keep up with demand. At the 14th Anniversary Celebration, we used 1,300 pounds of onions and enough batter to fill two giant 120-quart coolers.

They're notoriously messy, and by the end of an anniversary party the deep fryers look like those Chianti bottles covered with candle wax that you sometimes see in corny Italian restaurants. One year at the old brewery, my feet looked like waffles, just completely covered in batter. Another year we'd set up on some newly planted grass, and the batter got mixed in with the dirt and turned into a slushy tempura mud. It was a mess. Over the years, I've gotten a little better at managing the mess, but it's just the nature of the beast." — VINCE MARSAGLIA, lord of the onion rings

As we planned the Stone World Bistro & Gardens, we knew that the ardently sought Arrogant Bastard Ale Onion Rings were a must on the menu. And that's when the real trouble started. I sent Vince an email asking if he'd be cool with us using his recipe, but I actually felt a bit guilty. He'd selflessly been working his butt off prepping, cooking, and serving onion rings at our events for years and had never gotten a thing in return other than accolades and innumerable words of thanks. And now I had the gall, the audacity, to casually email him and say "Hey Vince, would you be willing to share the recipe?"

Of course, he responded in typical Vince style, saying something like "Wow, I'd be honored if you served 'em at your new place. Really, I was hoping you'd ask!" What a prince of a man (and not just because of some onion ring recipe).

Turns out, though, there were complications due to our commitment to using natural ingredients. Vince had been using Krusteaz tempura mix to make the batter. And when we looked at the ingredient list on the Krusteaz package, we realized it didn't fit into the parameters that we'd set for our restaurant. So we experimented and eventually came up with our own recipe for an all-natural batter (well, as "natural" as anything can be that's intended for deep-frying).

Fast forward to early 2009. Arrogant Bastard Ale Onion Rings were one of the most popular items on our menu. Folks waxed poetically about them, made special trips to the bistro for them . . . and never stopped complaining about them.

They were people's favorite thing to love *and* to hate on our menu. True, the Mac 'n Beer Cheese and the Grilled Buffalo Burger were contenders, but the onion rings didn't just edge them out, they had a clear margin. Some people—maybe a lot of people—really *hated* them.

I didn't get it.

For some reason, among a certain sector of diners, the onion rings brought out not just a tepid response, but flowing and unrestrained vitriol. Expletives flew freely on restaurant review websites. What could there possibly be about an *onion ring* that caused such unbridled bile?

I think it was partially because they were one of the most . . . how to put it . . . "normal" things on our menu. So folks who were looking for 'normal' ordered them and were disappointed to find that they weren't—normal that is. (Probably precisely the issue with the Mac 'n Beer Cheese and the Grilled Buffalo Burger, as well).

And yet at the same time, we sold tons of them—and believe it or not, we actually weren't that thrilled about it. The problem wasn't profitability, where they ranked a solid "okay." It was making them.

When things got busy, the onion rings were usually what put us in the weeds. Four minutes frying time per batch. Period. If the person working that station was absolutely on it like clockwork, the two deep fryers we'd squeezed into the too-small kitchen could actually produce two batches every five minutes. So if we got thirty orders over a short period, which often happened when it was busy,

well, you can do the math. But just in case: that meant the thirtieth order came out an unacceptable 75 minutes later. Ugh. That was just plain ugly. Our guests were, and let's put it politely here, decidedly not stoked when they found out they were at the tail end of that chain. Can't say I blamed 'em.

After a little deliberation, we ended up scrapping them. But we still have Vince breaking 'em out for special occasions, like our anniversary parties or San Diego Beer Week. There's always a chance that we might work out the kinks in the production system sometime in the future and consider offering them. But for now, we'll just have to do the next best thing: give you the secret recipe.

ARROGANT BASTARD ALE ONION RINGS

After all of that (see preamble on page 126), do you really need some pithy, clever text with more information here? Just make them already! Geez!

4 very large yellow onions

1 recipe Arrogant Bastard Ale Batter (recipe follows)

Vegetable oil, for frying

Kosher salt

Stone Smoked Porter BBQ Sauce, for dipping

Cut off the ends of each onion, cut in half crosswise (around the equator), and remove the papery skin and thin outer membrane. Soak in a bowl of ice water for 10 minutes.

Drain the onions, separate the concentric rings, and spread them on a kitchen towel to dry.

Preheat the oven to 200°F. Prepare a deep fryer, filling it with oil to the manufacturer's suggested fill level. Alternately, use a wide cast-iron or other heavy-duty pan that's at least 4 inches deep, pouring in oil to a depth of 2 to 3 inches, and no more than halfway up the side of the pan. Heat the oil to 360°F.

Dunk the onion rings in the batter and fry in batches until crispy and deep reddish brown, 4 to 6 minutes. Be careful not to overcrowd the pan, as this will lower the temperature of the oil significantly and result in soggy onion rings. Transfer cooked onion rings to a wire rack set over a baking sheet (or directly on a parchment paper–lined baking sheet). Season with a sprinkling of salt and keep them in the oven until the entire batch has been fried.

Serve hot, with a side of Stone Smoked Porter BBQ Sauce for dipping. (NO ketchup!)

"DR." BILL'S RECOMMENDED BEER: STONE PALE ALE

Pale ales are wonderful with burgers and onion rings. Their clean, crisp flavor cuts right through these guilty little pleasures.

ARROGANT BASTARD ALE BATTER

MAKES 2 CUPS, ENOUGH FOR 1 BATCH OF CONTROVERSIAL ONION RINGS

Publicans the world round know what great affinity fried food and beer have for each other. And while we stay away from the standard jalapeño popper, buffalo wing, and mozzarella stick sampler platter of caloric/culinary doom, we do have a deep fryer in our kitchen and we do make some tasty stuff in it, like our Spud Buds (page 135). It certainly helps to have an awesome beer batter to dunk stuff in, and we really have the best around. You could probably fry an old shoe in this stuff and it would taste delicious. Don't—but take solace in knowing that you probably could.

2 cups (16 fluid ounces) cold Arrogant Bastard Ale

Heaping 3/4 teaspoon Cajun spice blend

Heaping 1/2 teaspoon kosher salt

1/2 teaspoon ground dried chipotle chiles

1/2 teaspoon smoked paprika

1/2 teaspoon granulated garlic

About 1 cup (4 ounces) all-purpose flour

1 teaspoon baking powder

Pour the Arrogant Bastard Ale into a high-sided narrow container. Stir in the Cajun spice blend, salt, chipotle, smoked paprika, and garlic. Sift the flour and baking powder together, then add them to the beer mixture slowly, whisking well until they're evenly and thoroughly incorporated. You may need a bit more or less flour to reach the ideal consistency for a tempura-style batter. It should be just thick enough to coat whatever you're frying.

TOASTED BARLEY AND QUINOA TABOULEH

SERVES 6 TO 8

Tabouleh, that familiar Middle Eastern salad, is typically made with bulgur wheat along with veggies, lemon juice, olive oil, and a healthy dose of parsley. Our version uses barley (we're at a friggin' brewery, after all) and quinoa in place of the bulgur. We like to serve it alongside our Spicy Almond-Crusted Tilapia (page 144), but you'll no doubt find about a million other dishes it complements just as well.

1/2 cup pearled barley

3 1/2 cups water

1 cup quinoa

3/4 cup freshly squeezed lemon juice

1/4 cup extra-virgin olive oil

1 tablespoon red wine vinegar

2 cups minced tomato

1 cup chopped parsley

3 cloves garlic, minced

1 tablespoon chopped mint

Salt

Freshly ground black pepper

In a large, dry saucepan, toast the barley over low heat, swirling the pan to toast it evenly. Cook until it's slightly browned and smells a little nutty, about 5 minutes. Stir in 1 1/2 cups of the water, raise the heat to high, and bring to a simmer. Turn the heat back down to low, cover, and cook until the barley is tender and most of the liquid has been absorbed, about 45 minutes. Remove from the heat and let sit for 5 minutes. Drain off any excess liquid, then fluff the grains with a fork.

While the barley is cooking, rinse the quinoa several times, using a fine-mesh strainer to drain off the water. Transfer the quinoa to a medium saucepan. Add the remaining 2 cups water and bring to a simmer over high heat. Turn the heat down to low, cover, and simmer until the quinoa is somewhat translucent and a white ring is clearly visible around the center of the grain, about 15 minutes. Remove from the heat and let sit for 5 minutes. Drain off any excess liquid and fluff with a fork.

Let the barley and quinoa cool to room temperature. Transfer to a large bowl and add the lemon juice, olive oil, vinegar, tomatoes, parsley, garlic, and mint. Stir until thoroughly combined. Season with salt and pepper to taste. Cover and refrigerate for at least 30 minutes to allow the flavors to mingle. Serve chilled. Stored in an airtight container in the refrigerator, any leftovers will keep for up to 5 days.

STONE PALE ALE AND GARLIC STIR-FRIED BRUSSELS SPROUTS

Did your folks used to force you to finish your brussels sprouts before excusing yourself from the table? Or maybe they threatened to withhold dessert until you gagged the last one down? Turns out all they needed to do was cook 'em in beer and we would have eaten 'em right up! After reaching this brilliant culinary epiphany, we've come to love brussels sprouts so much, we're even licking our plates clean! Ma and Pa would be proud.

1 pound brussels sprouts (about 4 cups)

¹/₄ cup canola or vegetable oil

¹/₄ pound pancetta, diced

6 cloves garlic, minced

1¹/₂ cups (12 fluid ounces) Stone Pale Ale

¹/₄ cup vegetable stock

Salt

Freshly ground black pepper

Finely diced tomato, for garnish

Shaved or grated Parmigiano-Reggiano cheese, for garnish

Set up a steamer with 1 to 2 inches of salted water and bring the water to a rolling boil. Put the brussels sprouts in the steamer, cover, and cook until slightly tender, about 4 minutes. Drain and immediately transfer the brussels sprouts to a large bowl of ice water to halt the cooking and preserve their bright green color. Let them cool in the ice water for about 1 minute, then drain. Lay them on a clean dish towel and pat dry. Cut them in half vertically, right through the core.

DID YOU KNOW?

Stone Pale Ale and Garlic Stir-Fried Brussels Sprouts was the first dish to be cooked in the bistro kitchen—like, first *ever*. It was on June 6, 2006—close to five months before the restaurant opened—and we decided to fire up a test batch to see what our little kitchen could do.

In a large wok or cast-iron skillet, heat the oil over high heat until it begins to shimmer. Turn the heat down to medium. Add the pancetta and cook, stirring occasionally, until it begins to brown. Stir in the garlic and cook until fragrant, about 30 seconds. Turn the heat up to high, add the brussels sprouts, and cook, stirring occasionally, until lightly browned, 4 to 5 minutes.

Add the beer and continue to cook over high heat until the liquid is mostly evaporated. Deglaze the pan by adding the vegetable stock, stirring and scraping up any browned bits that may be affixed to the pan.

Season with salt and pepper to taste. Garnish with the tomato and Parmigiano-Reggiano. Serve immediately.

"DR." BILL'S RECOMMENDED BEER: STONE SMOKED PORTER

I recommend Stone Smoked Porter with this dish, though Oktoberfest beers from Paulaner, Spaten, or Hacker-Pschorr are also winners. The caramelization of the brussels sprouts and the pancetta perfectly complements the roasty sweetness of the beer.

STONE IPA GARLICKY MASHED POTATOES

SERVES 4 TO 6

These vampire-fighting vegan mashed 'taters can serve multiple purposes. In addition to scooping them out as a tasty side dish, you can also batter and fry them to make Spud Buds (see sidebar) or use them to top Tempeh Shepherd's Pie (page 147).

1   head Roasted Garlic (recipe follows)

2   pounds Yukon Gold potatoes, quartered

2   tablespoons garlic-infused oil

1/4   cup (2 fluid ounces) Stone IPA, or more as needed

1/4   teaspoon brewer's yeast (see Tip)

1   teaspoon chopped parsley

Salt

Freshly ground black pepper

Put the potatoes in a saucepan and cover with cold salted water. Set the pan over high heat and bring the water to a boil. Lower the heat to medium, cover, and cook until the potatoes are tender and easily pierced with a knife, 15 to 20 minutes after the water started boiling.

Drain the potatoes and add the garlic oil, IPA, brewer's yeast, and parsley. Use a potato masher or ricer to work the potatoes to the desired consistency. If they're too stiff, adjust with more IPA. Season with salt and pepper to taste.

TIP: Brewer's yeast is available at most grocery stores and natural food stores, often located near the supplements or with the bulk foods. It's a good source of essential fatty acids and B vitamins, and has a nutty, slightly cheesy flavor, making it a great dairy-free addition to vegan recipes.

ROASTED GARLIC

MAKES ENOUGH TO KEEP YOUR AVERAGE VAMPIRE AT BAY

It's kind of ridiculous how much garlic we go through here at the Stone Brewing World Bistro & Gardens. But besides being insanely good for all sorts of things that ail you, it also just tastes really damn good. Poppin' whole cloves of the stuff raw is a bit strong for most, and, frankly, some members of society frown upon the havoc it unleashes on your breath. However, nice, slow roast solves that problem, yielding spreadably soft, buttery cloves without all the bite.

1   head garlic

1   tablespoon extra-virgin olive oil

Salt

Freshly ground black pepper

Preheat the oven to 350°F.

Cut the top 1/4 inch off of the head of garlic, leaving the head intact but exposing the individual cloves of garlic. Place it cut side up on a large sheet of aluminum foil. Drizzle the olive oil over the garlic and season with a sprinkling of salt and pepper. Gather the foil up around the garlic, folding or twisting the top to seal.

Roast for 1 hour, then let the garlic cool completely. Use a fork to pull the roasted cloves out from their papery skin. Alternatively, you can squeeze the cloves out from the bottom up using your hands.

SPUD BUDS

SERVES 4 TO 6 SNACKERS

Spud Buds are a favorite appetizer at the bistro, and they're easy to make. The mashed potatoes are portioned out ahead of time and stored in the freezer until you're ready to batter, fry, and enjoy them. Spud Buds can be ready for you and your buds' taste buds in mere minutes. Rad!

1 batch Stone IPA Garlicky Mashed Potatoes (page 134)

1 batch Arrogant Bastard Ale Batter (page 129)

Oil for frying

Salt

Start by letting the mashed potatoes cool down. Then portion out scoops of potatoes slightly larger than a golf ball. Roll into balls, then lay them out in a single layer on a baking sheet lined with parchment paper or wax paper.

Freeze for 3 to 4 hours, until firm and completely frozen. (At this point, you can transfer them to a ziplock bag and store in the freezer for up to 6 months.)

When you're ready to cook, prepare a batch of batter. Fill a deep fryer with oil to the manufacturer's suggested fill level. (Alternatively, you can use a wide cast-iron or other heavy-duty pan filled with oil to a depth of 2 to 3 inches, and no more than halfway up the side of the pan.) Heat the oil to 360°F.

Remove as many Spud Buds from the freezer as you'd like to cook. Dunk the frozen Spud Buds in the Arrogant Bastard Ale Batter, shaking off any excess, and carefully lower the taters into the oil. Fry until crispy and deep reddish brown, 6 to 8 minutes. Be careful not to overcrowd the pan, as this will lower the temperature of the oil significantly and result in soggy spuds. Season them with a sprinkling of kosher salt as they come out of the oil.

Serve hot with a side of Stone Smoked Porter BBQ Sauce. (NO ketchup!)

TIP: If you're making a large number and want to serve them all at once, preheat the oven to 200°F before you begin. When each batch of Spud Buds is fried, transfer them to a wire rack set over a baking sheet (or directly on a parchment paper–lined baking sheet) and hold them in the oven until all have all been fried.

GARLIC, CHEDDAR, AND STONE RUINATION IPA SOUP

SERVES 8

A healthy pour of Stone Ruination IPA imparts a bold dose of bitterness that perfectly complements the sticky sweet flavor of roasted garlic permeating every gooey spoonful of this hearty soup. We like to garnish this soup with broccoli tempura, but you can also serve it with the Brewer's Barley Cracker Bread (page 120).

1	cup unsalted butter
1¹/3	cups all-purpose flour

1 cup unsalted butter

1¹/₃ cups all-purpose flour

1 large yellow onion, diced

8 cloves garlic, minced

4 cups vegetable stock

1 cup (8 fluid ounces) Stone Ruination IPA

1 cup whole milk

3 heads Roasted Garlic (page 134)

1 tablespoon smoked paprika

¹/₂ teaspoon ground cumin

2¹/₄ pounds sharp white Cheddar cheese, grated

Salt

Freshly ground white pepper

Chopped fresh chives, for garnish

Melt ³/₄ cup of the butter in a small saucepan over medium heat. Add the flour, whisking briskly to avoid lumps. Cook, stirring frequently, until the flour takes on a light blond color, about 5 minutes. Remove from the heat.

Melt the remaining ¹/₄ cup butter in a large soup pot over medium heat. Stir in the onion and minced garlic and cook just until the garlic is aromatic, 30 seconds to 1 minute. Add the vegetable stock and IPA. When the liquid begins to simmer, stir in the garlic, paprika, and cumin. Using a handheld immersion blender or in a regular blender, puree until smooth. Whisk in the flour mixture. Add the cheese a handful at a time, whisking after each addition, until melted and smooth.

Season with salt and pepper to taste. Serve immediately, garnishing each serving with some of the chives.

"DR." BILL'S RECOMMENDED BEER: STONE RUINATION IPA

The perfect pairing is right in the title of the soup. Stone Ruination IPA all the way.

STONE BLT

We're supposed to put something clever or informative here, but does a BLT really need an introduction? Then again, we could tell you why ours is special. Perhaps it's the aroma of the basil or the fact that we use ciabatta rolls. (Seriously, how awesome is ciabatta?) And truth be told, it isn't (precisely speaking) a BLT at all, since we eschew lettuce in favor of peppery arugula. But somehow BAT doesn't have the same ring, so BLT it is.

4 Roma tomatoes

6 leaves fresh basil, very thinly sliced

1/4 cup diced red onion

1 clove garlic, minced

3 tablespoons balsamic vinegar

1 1/2 tablespoons extra-virgin olive oil

Salt

Freshly ground black pepper

4 ciabatta rolls

1/2 cup Roasted Garlic and Lemon Mayo (recipe follows)

1/2 cup whole-grain mustard

2 cups arugula

12 strips cooked bacon, preferably applewood-smoked

Cut the tomatoes in half lengthwise and discard the seeds. Slice the tomatoes 1/4 inch thick. Combine the tomatoes, basil, onion, garlic, vinegar, and olive oil in a nonreactive bowl and gently toss to combine. Season with salt and pepper to taste. (This mixture can be made up to 2 days in advance and kept in a covered container in the refrigerator.)

Split and lightly toast the ciabatta halves. For each sandwich, spread 2 tablespoons of mayo inside the top half and 2 tablespoons of mustard inside the bottom half. Layer one-fourth of the arugula on the bottom, then one-fourth of the tomato mixture, and then 3 slices of the bacon.

Replace the top half of the roll and cut the sandwich in half diagonally.

ROASTED GARLIC AND LEMON MAYO

MAKES ABOUT 1 1/2 CUPS

This creamy condiment is a great spread for sandwiches (including, of course, a BLT), and also makes a tasty dip for french fries and grilled artichokes.

6 egg yolks

2 tablespoons freshly squeezed lemon juice

1 cup canola or vegetable oil

1 head Roasted Garlic (page 134)

Salt

Put the egg yolks and lemon juice in a food processor or blender. Process for 10 seconds to combine. With the motor running, slowly drizzle in the oil and continue to process until completely emulsified. Add the roasted garlic and pulse until well incorporated. Season with salt to taste. Stored in an airtight container in the refrigerator, the mayo will keep for up to 2 weeks.

"DR." BILL'S RECOMMENDED BEER: OAKED ARROGANT BASTARD ALE

OAKED Arrogant Bastard Ale balances the flavors of this BLT wonderfully. You can also try a Belgian dubbel or German rauchbier to really let the bacon shine.

TEMPEH FUEGO BURGER

MAKES 4 BURGERS

This is our house veggie burger, seared and crispified in a pan and topped with hot chiles and melted white Cheddar. We serve it up on ciabatta with our Roasted Garlic and Lemon Mayo and a small salad on the side. Besides being a favorite on our traditional menu, it sells like crazy on our Meatless Monday nights!

4 tablespoons olive oil

1 cup yellow onion, finely chopped

1 cup king trumpet or portobello mushrooms (see sidebar at right), finely chopped

1 pound tempeh (see sidebar at right), crumbled

3 cloves garlic, minced

2 medium Yukon gold potatoes, baked and mashed

4 teaspoons Bragg Liquid Aminos (see Tip)

1 tablespoon brewer's yeast (see Tip)

1 1/2 teaspoons freshly ground black pepper

1 tablespoon arrowroot powder (see Tip)

1 tablespoon water

4 ciabatta rolls

Roasted Garlic and Lemon Mayo (page 139)

Fresh or pickled jalapeño or serrano peppers, sliced

4 slices white Cheddar cheese

Heat 3 tablespoons of the olive oil in a large saucepan over medium-high heat until the oil begins to shimmer. Add the onion and mushrooms and sauté until translucent, about 7 minutes. Add the tempeh and garlic. Cook, stirring occasionally, for 10 minutes. Add the potatoes, liquid aminos, brewer's yeast, and pepper. Continue to cook, stirring occasionally, for 5 minutes.

Combine the arrowroot powder and water, mixing to form a slurry. Add it to the tempeh mixture and stir until well combined. Cook for 1 more minute to allow the arrowroot to thicken the mixture.

Remove from the heat and let stand until cool enough to handle. Divide the mixture, which will be somewhat moist, into 4 equal portions and, as best you can, shape each to resemble a traditional hamburger patty.

Heat the remaining tablespoon of oil in a large cast-iron skillet over medium-high heat until the oil begins to shimmer. Carefully transfer the patties to the pan using a wide spatula and cook until seared and nicely crispy, 4 to 5 minutes. Flip the patties over and cook until a nice crust has developed on the other side and the patty is heated through, 3 to 4 minutes.

Split and lightly toast the ciabatta rolls. Spread a thin layer of the mayo on both split surfaces. Adorn the bottom half of each roll with a patty, add jalapeño slices to taste (*fuego* means fire, so don't wuss out on us now!), drape a slice of Cheddar over each, and crown with their matching ciabatta tops. Serve immediately.

"DR." BILL'S RECOMMENDED BEER: STONE IPA

This baby is hot! A big, hoppy West Coast IPA would be my beer of choice for this dish. It will soothe the spice at the front of your palate, but still allow a good bit of heat to linger on the finish.

HIPPIE INGREDIENTS EXPLAINED

King trumpet mushrooms, also known as king oyster, french horn, or eryngii mushrooms, are prized for their texture and meaty flavor. Matsutake or portobello mushrooms can be substituted.

Tempeh is a popular vegetarian protein source made from fermented soybeans. It differs from tofu in that it uses whole soybeans, and retains more protein, fiber, and nutrients. It is firmer than tofu, and has a stronger flavor. It is available in natural food stores and some supermarkets, in the refrigerated section with the tofu and other vegetarian proteins.

Bragg Liquid Aminos, a liquid protein concentrate made from soybeans and water, is readily available at natural food stores. Low-sodium soy sauce or tamari can be substituted.

Brewer's yeast is available at most grocery stores and natural food stores, often located near the supplements or with the bulk foods. It's a good source of essential fatty acids and B vitamins, and has a nutty, slightly cheesy flavor, making it a great dairy-free addition to vegan recipes.

Arrowroot powder is a natural starch used for its thickening properties. It's preferred by some chefs because it thickens well without imparting any real flavor of its own. Cornstarch is an acceptable substitution.

CHOOSING CLAMS

It's important to start with healthy, high-quality clams, and freshness is key. Look for a reputable vendor with a high turnover rate and a clean-looking establishment. You want clams that are tightly closed. If they don't close up when you tap 'em, you don't want 'em. That's a whole world of serious food poisoning waiting to happen. And when you tap them, they should sound firm and not hollow. Avoid chipped, broken, or otherwise questionable-looking shells.

Once you get your little mollusks home, store them in a colander on the bottom shelf of your refrigerator and use them within 24 to 48 hours, tops!

CLEANING CLAMS

There's nothing worse than a filthy clam. But you gotta remember, they spend their lives filtering sand and mud, so they're bound to be a little on the dirty side. Steamer clams are especially gritty since, unlike most other varieties, they never really close up all the way.

Here's a great technique for purging them of all that grit: soak them in fresh cold water for a good 30 minutes just before cooking time. Also, sprinkle a few tablespoons of cornmeal into the water. The clams eat it and then spit it out, along with sand, grit, and other impurities they may have been holding on to.

After the 30-minute soak, lift the clams out of the water and place them on a clean dish towel. (Don't pour them into a strainer or colander; that will just dump all the dirty sediment right back on top of them!) Give the shells a nice rubdown so they're just as clean on the outside as they are on the inside. Now they are ready to cook!

PANCETTA AND CLAMS

We like to take local bivalves and cook them Portuguese-style, kicked up with some Italian influence. Littleneck or Manila clams are great choices for this opulent and hedonistic treat. You can also use steamer clams, but be sure to clean them well, getting out all that nitty-gritty sand they like to keep inside. And while we use wine for this recipe in the bistro, feel free to sub in beer.

1 tablespoon extra-virgin olive oil

1/2 cup diced pancetta (about 1/4 pound)

1 cup dry white wine or Stone Levitation Ale

2 medium yellow onions, sliced

4 Roma tomatoes, seeded and chopped

1 1/2 teaspoons smoked paprika

1/2 teaspoon crushed red pepper flakes, or more to taste

Salt

Freshly ground black pepper

2 pounds clams in their shells, cleaned and scrubbed (see Tip)

2 tablespoons cold unsalted butter, cubed

1 1/2 tablespoons chopped fresh cilantro

1 lemon, quartered

Sliced baguette or crostini

Heat the oil in a large saucepan or cast-iron skillet over medium-high heat until the oil begins to shimmer. Add the pancetta and cook, stirring occasionally, until slightly crispy, 7 to 8 minutes. Deglaze the pan by adding the white wine, stirring and scraping up any browned bits that may be affixed to the pan. Add the onions, tomatoes, paprika, and crushed red pepper and cook, stirring occasionally, until the onions are soft, about 5 minutes. Add salt and pepper to taste, along with more crushed red pepper if you like more heat.

Add the clams. Dot with the butter, cover, and turn the heat up to high. Cook until all the clams have opened, about 5 minutes. Uncover, and cook for 1 more minute. Divide the clams and onion mixture between 4 bowls and garnish with some of the cilantro and a lemon wedge. Serve immediately with the sliced baguette or crostini, which are perfect for mopping up the sauce.

"DR." BILL'S RECOMMENDED BEER: STONE LEVITATION ALE

Amber ales go well with the unctuousness of this dish, allowing the flavors of the food to come through perfectly.

SPICY ALMOND-CRUSTED TILAPIA WITH HONEY BUTTER SAUCE

SERVES 4

This dainty fish dish is among the most popular on the bistro's menu. The light and wonderfully flaky fillets serve as a flavorful canvas for the lush honey butter sauce. We like to plate it up atop a comfy bed of our Toasted Barley and Quinoa Tabouleh (page 130), with a helping of sautéed green beans on the side.

1¹/₄ cups blanched slivered almonds

1 cup panko (Japanese bread crumbs)

1 serrano pepper, seeded and minced

1 teaspoon crushed red pepper flakes

¹/₄ cup all-purpose flour

¹/₂ teaspoon kosher salt

4 tilapia fillets

1 lime, quartered

2 tablespoons extra-virgin olive oil

Honey Butter Sauce (recipe follows)

Preheat the oven to 400°F.

Spread ¹/₄ cup of the slivered almonds in a single layer on a baking sheet. Roast the almonds for 4 minutes, then stir and turn them over and continue roasting until golden brown, an additional 4 to 5 minutes. Leave the oven on and set the almonds aside to cool.

Put the remaining 1 cup almonds in a food processor, along with the panko, serrano, crushed red pepper, flour, and salt. Pulse until the mixture is finely ground.

Coat the tilapia fillets with the mixture and squeeze a lime wedge over each fillet.

Heat the oil in an ovenproof pan or cast-iron skillet over high heat until the oil begins to shimmer. Sear the tilapia fillets until the crust is browned and crispy, 1 to 2 minutes per side. Set the pan in the oven and bake the fish until the flesh is opaque, 4 to 5 minutes. Serve immediately, topping each serving with a few tablespoons of Honey Butter Sauce. Garnish each serving with a sprinkling of the roasted almond slivers.

"DR." BILL'S RECOMMENDED BEER: STONE CALI-BELGIQUE IPA

A masterful pairing with this dish would be a Belgian IPA or a farmhouse-style saison. Pro tip: A saison is a marvelous go-to for lots of dishes; it's perhaps the most versatile beer style in the world when it comes to food pairing.

HONEY BUTTER SAUCE

MAKES ABOUT ¹/₂ CUP

Mastering this sauce takes a little bit of skill. Not because it's difficult, but be sure you read through the instructions once or twice before setting out to conquer it. We believe in you though. You can do it!

¹/₂ cup dry white wine

2 tablespoons white wine vinegar

¹/₂ teaspoon cracked black peppercorns

1 teaspoon minced shallot

1 small bay leaf

¹/₄ cup heavy cream

1¹/₂ teaspoons honey

¹/₂ cup very cold unsalted butter, cubed (see Tip)

Salt

Combine the wine, vinegar, peppercorns, shallots, and bay leaf in a medium saucepan over medium-high heat. Once the mixture is simmering, adjust the heat to

TIP: Stone Levitation Ale BBQ Sauce is made for us by our good friends at Carlsbad Gourmet using the potent Mexican chile de árbol. It's available at the Stone Company Store as well as online at StoneCompanyStore.com (hint hint).

CULINARY GOLD

You weren't going to actually throw away that duck fat, were you? Because you can do all sorts of awesome things with it. Store it in your fridge and use it along with lard or butter in pie and tart doughs. Roast or fry potato wedges in it. Smear some on the skin of a whole chicken or turkey instead of butter before roasting. Send your fried eggs to stratospheric new heights with it. Or try making a warm duck fat vinaigrette with apple cider vinegar, Dijon mustard, shallots, and thyme. Biscuits, Yorkshire pudding, popcorn, roasted vegetables, fried chicken, and more—all can be enhanced by duck fat. The possibilities are endless. Whatever you do, don't throw it away!

SALSA FRESCA

MAKES ABOUT 2 CUPS

This is a straight-up, no-frills, honest pico de gallo that's equally at home on top of a tortilla chip as it is adorning these BBQ Duck Tacos.

1$1/2$ cups diced seeded Roma tomatoes

$1/4$ cup diced yellow onion

$1/4$ cup finely diced seeded jalapeño peppers

$1/4$ cup freshly squeezed lime juice

2 tablespoons chopped fresh cilantro

Salt

Freshly ground black pepper

Put the tomatoes, onion, jalapeños, lime juice, and cilantro in a nonreactive bowl and stir to combine. Season with salt and pepper to taste. Cover and refrigerate for at least 30 minutes to allow flavors to mingle. It will keep, covered and refrigerated, for up to 3 days.

PINEAPPLE HABANERO SALSA

MAKES ABOUT 2 CUPS

Habanero peppers are wickedly hot, so be careful when working with them—be sure to wear gloves when handling. Above all, don't rub your eyes, avoid any skin contact with the habanero juices, and wash your hands thoroughly after working with the peppers.

1$3/4$ cups diced fresh pineapple

$1/4$ cup diced red onion

1 tablespoon finely minced seeded habanero pepper

2 tablespoons freshly squeezed lime juice

2 tablespoons chopped fresh cilantro

Salt

Freshly ground black pepper

Put the pineapple, onion, habanero, lime juice, and cilantro in a nonreactive bowl and stir to combine. Season with the salt and pepper to taste. Cover and refrigerate for at least 30 minutes to allow flavors to mingle. It will keep, covered and refrigerated, for up to 3 days.

"DR." BILL'S RECOMMENDED BEER: ARROGANT BASTARD ALE

Imperial amber ales pair perfectly with these beauties. The hop bitterness balances the richness of the duck and counters the sweetness of the barbeque sauce. Arrogant Bastard Ale is the beer I always recommend as a pairing in the bistro.

STONE IMPERIAL RUSSIAN STOUT BEERAMISU

SERVES 10 TO 12

Beeramisu is a gift from the gods. Trust. This is co-author Randy's own creation, so we'll turn the introduction over to him: "This is a recipe I love to make. I just want to clarify that it isn't on the menu at the bistro, so you don't march in there some day and confidently ask for the beeramisu only to have them give you a funny look. They aren't serving it there . . . yet. Until I manage to convince them, just make it yourself at home. It's pretty easy, and it's ridiculously good."

3/4 cup cold heavy cream

2 eggs

Pinch of salt

1 cup confectioners' sugar

1 1/2 tablespoons pure vanilla extract

2 (8-ounce) tubs mascarpone cheese, at room temperature

1/2 cup plus 2 tablespoons (5 fluid ounces) Stone Imperial Russian Stout

1/2 cup (4 fluid ounces, or 2 shots) brewed espresso (see Tip)

40 ladyfinger cookies

About 1/2 cup unsweetened cocoa powder

TIP: No go on the espresso? You can substitute 2 teaspoons of instant espresso powder dissolved in 1/2 cup of hot water for the brewed espresso, or use 1/2 cup of coffee brewed at double strength.

In a chilled mixing bowl, whip the cream until stiff peaks form, making sure not to overbeat. Gently transfer to a bowl, cover, and set aside in the refrigerator.

Rinse the bowl, then use it to beat the eggs and salt until the volume of the eggs doubles and their color lightens. Add the sugar, vanilla, and mascarpone and mix gently just until thoroughly combined. Fold in the whipped cream, then cover and set aside in the refrigerator.

In a shallow dish, stir together the stout and espresso. *Quickly* dunk both sides of the ladyfingers into the mixture, literally for about 1 second on each side. Arrange the ladyfingers in a single layer in an 8-inch square dish. (You can also build these as individual portions using small ramekins or interesting glassware.) Spread a layer of the mascarpone mixture over the ladyfingers. Sprinkle on a liberal amount of cocoa using a fine-mesh sieve. Repeat the layers, using all of the ladyfingers and mascarpone mixture, and generously dusting with cocoa once again. Cover and refrigerate for at least 2 hours before serving. Beeramisu will keep, covered and refrigerated, for up to 2 days.

RECIPES FROM THE STONE BREWING WORLD BISTRO & GARDENS

BLUE CHEESE JALAPEÑO CHEESECAKE

ONE 8-INCH CHEESECAKE

This is a weird one, but if you're a fan of blue cheese, you'll love it. The jalapeño doesn't add much heat, but it does contribute flavor. It took quite a bit of experimenting to get this one right, but we think pastry chef Andrew Higgins nailed it.

1 pound cream cheese, at room temperature

1/4 cup plus 2 tablespoons granulated sugar

12 ounces Rogue Creamery Smokey Blue Cheese, at room temperature

4 large eggs

2 ounces heavy cream

1 large jalapeño, ribs and seeds removed, finely diced

Non-stick cooking spray

1 pint fresh whole blueberries or quartered and hulled strawberries

2 tablespoons granulated sugar

Preheat the oven to 200°F. Combine the cream cheese and sugar in the bowl of a stand mixer fitted with the paddle attachment. Mix on a low speed for 10 minutes, stopping the mixer to scrape down the sides occasionally.

While the mixer is running, set a fine-mesh sieve over a medium mixing bowl. Press the blue cheese through the sieve using a rubber spatula. Set aside.

Once the cream cheese and sugar have finished their spin, add the eggs one at a time. After each egg is incorporated, add in one tablespoon of cream. After all the eggs and cream have been added, stop the mixer. Fold in the reserved blue cheese and jalapeño.

Prepare an 8-inch springform pan with a generous coating of non-stick cooking spray. Pour the batter into the pan. Bake until the cheesecake is set in the center and reaches an internal temperature of 170°F, 3 to 4 hours. Let cool completely on a wire rack, cover, then refrigerate for at least 4 hours.

While the cheesecake is cooling, combine the berries and sugar in a medium mixing bowl, tossing gently with a rubber spatula. Cover and refrigerate with the cheesecake. Just before serving, top the cheesecake with the macerated fruit. The cheesecake will keep, covered and refrigerated, for 3 days or frozen for 1 month.

CASTING YOUR FIRST STONE

"I'm done talking. Shocking, I know. But this is Steve's turf anyway. I hope you enjoyed my ramblings as much as I did. Steve, it's all yours now. Take it away!" — GREG

Homebrew demigod and dear friend Charlie Papazian says it best: 'Relax. Don't worry. Have a homebrew.' Here at Stone, we couldn't agree more. We've been strong proponents of homebrewing since, well, since we started homebrewing. The fact is, all the great brewers out there today no doubt got their start making small, 5-gallon batches in their kitchen, backyard, garage, or wherever. And if you've actually been reading this book, not just looking at the pretty pictures, you know that Greg and I put in a lot of homebrewing time before we opened Stone.

In the continued interest of promoting homebrewing, we host an annual membership rally for the American Homebrewers Association alongside our March Madness homebrew competition. But if for some reason you feel we've lost our way and forgotten about our own humble origins as homebrewers, allow me to dispel that myth here and now . . . by giving you our recipes to play with at home. Okay, so maybe not all of them (something has to be sacred in this day and age!), but those we chose include a good representation of some of our favorites we've crafted over the years, including the beer that started it all for us: Stone Pale Ale.

CLONE STONE

I hear what you're thinking: "You're saying I can go out and buy some simple equipment, malt, yeast, and hops, and make exact replicas of your beer?!"

In theory, yes. In reality, probably not. The fact is, there's a lot of variation inherent in the brewing process. Every homebrew setup is unique. Water profile varies from region to region. Different maltsters produce products with different characteristics, even when the name of the malt is the same, acid percentages fluctuate between hops growers, and from season to season. You'll hear brewers talk about other factors using technical-sounding phrases like "brewhouse efficiency" and "extraction rates." What I'm trying to say is, results will vary . . . and that's okay.

These are formulas that work for us, including the varieties of malt and hops we buy. But keep in mind that we use our proprietary yeast strain, our unique water, and our equipment. Regarding the yeast, our strain is kept for us by our friends over at White Labs. And as much as I like you, dear reader, you just can't have any of that. It isn't for sale. However, White Labs WLP007 Dry English Ale Yeast and WLP002 English Ale Yeast are pretty darn close substitutes, so that's what most of the recipes call for.

Regarding water, as you'll recall from early in the book (page 11), different sources of water have vastly different compositions and mineral profiles, and that plays a huge part in the final beer. At Stone, we shoot for fairly soft water. If you'd like a simple way to partially replicate our water, Mitch recommends a 50/50 blend of distilled water and carbon-filtered tap water. (And if you have some testing equipment and familiarity with water salts and really want to match our profile, who are we to stop you? We average about 30 ppm calcium, 85 ppm sulfate, 12 ppm magnesium, and 40 ppm sodium, and a pH of 7.1.)

We've made a few minor adjustments to our recipes for your homebrewing convenience, like calling for Irish moss to help clarify the beer. We don't use it at the brewery (we've got fancy filters to take care of that), but it's a great, all-natural product that does the trick nicely for homebrewing. Also, we're recommending that you use a little dose of dried malt extract at bottling time to facilitate carbonation—again, not something we do here because we have other ways of achieving that, but for homebrew we think it's best.

Also, take note that the recipes we present here are referred to as "all-grain" rather than "extract" since they don't use malt extract as a base. Brewing with malt extract is an easier approach for beginners and requires a little less equipment, but you do sacrifice some flavor—and a touch of the novelty involved in brewing, in my opinion. (And if you're already pro at this homebrewing stuff and you think these 5-gallon batches are for beginners, you're absolutely right! How

astute of you to notice. Worry not, we've got you covered, because we've included percentages and ratios that you can scale easily and adapt to your system.)

Most importantly, you should view these recipes as guidelines. And even if your batch of, say, Stone Old Guardian Barley Wine doesn't come out exactly like ours, it should be in the ballpark or, at the very least, turn out to be a tasty beer. If you're less than thrilled with the results, keep working at it. Take notes. Tweak amounts. Make it work for your setup. Heck, make something you like even better! Just remember that it's a learning process, and that's half the fun of it. Don't go out and buy a bunch of equipment, brew your first batch of beer, and hate it because it doesn't taste exactly like you thought it would. (And please don't then run off to tell your friends and everybody on BeerAdvocate.com how crappy this book is and how Stone sold out.) Just try again. Join a homebrew club. Ask questions. There's an amazing open exchange of ideas and information out there. We're all in this together, and all of us want to make and drink good beer.

And while it is our hope to equip you with enough information to successfully brew up a batch of beer by yourself (or better yet, with a friend or two), please know that this is not the be-all, end-all homebrew guide. Hardly. We couldn't write that if we wanted to, if only because it's already been done. *The Complete*

Joy of Homebrewing, penned by aforementioned home-brew guru Charlie Papazian, was published way back in 1984 and still stands as the ultimate resource for anyone serious about homebrew. Read it. Learn it. Brew it. Love it. Live it.

BASIC EQUIPMENT YOU'LL NEED

Track down your nearest homebrew supply store or find one online. Sporting goods and outdoorsman-type stores often carry homebrew equipment as well, but a dedicated homebrew store is far preferred if available, especially for ingredients, since the turnover rate is typically much greater, so the raw materials tend to be fresher.

The homebrew recipes in this section are written to be used with a 10-gallon insulated cooler as a mash tun and a 10-gallon brew kettle over an outdoor propane burner (think turkey fryer) for the boil. Some of the bigger beers that require more malt and longer boils also use the brew kettle as the mash tun, and the instructions will indicate that.

If your equipment varies or if you'd like to scale the recipes to yield a different amount, we've provided a formula for each beer after the recipe. There are also some great software programs that can help with this,

including BeerSmith, BeerAlchemy, BeerTools Pro, and ProMash.

Here's a list of basic equipment you'll need, and any homebrew store will also know exactly what you need to get started. There are plenty of other nifty bells and whistles out there that you will no doubt be tempted to buy—some that work, some that don't—but these are the bare-bones basics:

- 10-gallon insulated cooler
- 10-gallon stainless steel brew kettle with lid
- Propane burner
- Lauter tun with spigot
- 6 to 8 feet of vinyl tubing, plus a plastic crimp
- Floating thermometer
- Hops bags
- Hydrometer
- Wort chiller
- 6-gallon plastic primary fermentation bucket
- 5-gallon glass carboy
- Airlock
- #7 drilled rubber stopper
- Racking cane
- Bottles (around fifty-four 12-ounce bottles or thirty 22-ounce bottles)
- Bottling wand
- Crown caps
- Bottle capper

Perhaps the best tool in your arsenal is a friend who has homebrewed before. While not necessary, it's nice to have someone to help lead the way a bit. And you can give brewing a few tries on their system to see what kind of equipment you're comfortable with. Another great friend to make is the clerk at your local homebrewing store. They can guide you to the right set-up and answer just about any question you might come up with.

BREW DAY

Set aside a good 8 hours for your brew day. It might take less time, and, especially at first, there's a good chance it may take more time. What I'm saying is, don't make too many other plans. Before you begin, make sure your brewing environment is clean and all of your equipment is properly sanitized. This is essential, as it helps minimize the chances of rogue yeast or bacteria taking over and spoiling your fermentation. There are several sanitizer options: Star San, various iodophor products, and household bleach being among the most common. Whichever you choose, make sure you use it according to the manufacturer's directions.

After all of your equipment is cleaned and sanitized, read through the recipe several times. Measure out everything you can in advance. Have your water divided into separate pots, and think ahead so you bring each to the designated temperature in advance of when you need it.

There are a few procedures that don't change much or at all no matter what the brew, and in the interest of saving paper, I'm going to outline them in detail here once as a reference rather than including them in every single recipe. I hope you understand and applaud my ~~laziness~~ commitment to the environment.

Mashing

You always want to crush the malt before use. If you don't happen to have a grain mill lying around, any good homebrew store will have one available for use, or you can purchase your grains freshly crushed via online retailers.

As you'll see in the recipes, the temperatures in the mash stage are pretty particular. Small temperature changes can make a big difference in brewing, so it's best to keep as close to the prescribed mercury readings as possible. Maintaining a constant mash temperature is best achieved in an insulated cooler. However, if you're using your brew kettle as a mash tun, you can wrap it with blankets or foil-backed bubble wrap insulation to help maintain a steady temperature over the long mash time.

And, while we're dealing with temperature, it's important to never let your grain exceed 170°F, as that will extract undesirable tannins and off flavors.

Lautering and Sparging

After mashing is complete, carefully transfer the mash to the lauter tun to separate the liquid (the wort) from the grains. Run a length of vinyl tubing from the lauter tun to the brew kettle. Let the first few quarts of liquid run through. It will be cloudy and contain some undesirable particulates. Once the liquid coming through is clear, stop the flow and pour the cloudy liquid back into the lauter tun, where the husks from the crushed grain will act as a natural filter and help remove the sediment.

Allow the remainder of the wort to drain into the brew kettle at a slow, steady rate, restricting the flow with a plastic crimp on the tube. Once the liquid is lower than the level of the grain bed, begin the sparge.

The sparge water, which should never exceed 170°F, is added to the grain and allowed to drain off at a slow rate (regulated by the plastic crimp), extracting the remaining sugars and maximizing yield. This is not a step to be rushed; be prepared to spend at least an hour on lautering and sparging. Once the last of the sparge water has filtered through the grains and the flow from the lauter tun stops, you're ready to begin the boil.

The Boil

The boil is a very important step for proper flavor development, regulating alpha acid extraction from the hops, and many other benefits that were laid out earlier (page 18). And it's a full, rolling boil that we're after here. Do exercise caution, as you are dealing with a hot flame and lots of very hot liquid. As tempting as it may

be to "set it and forget it," especially with longer boil times, *never* leave your brew kettle unattended. Foam can build and boil over (lower the heat and/or use a spray bottle filled with filtered water to tame rising foam) and the wort requires frequent stirring to prevent scorching, so grab a beer and a lawn chair. Stick around.

Don't just throw away the spent grains after sparging! You can use them in bread recipes, and they also make great mulch, compost, or livestock feed. If you choose to dispose of them, do so with yard wastes if your city collects those separately. (And if they don't, tell them they should.)

MAKING A YEAST STARTER

While commercial liquid yeast can be pitched directly into the wort, making a yeast starter a day or so before brewing day is a great way to promote healthy, hungry, happy yeast. And for beers with a starting gravity higher than 1.060 (14.5 Plato), it's almost necessary (read: *highly* recommended; just do it!).

Between 24 and 36 hours before the yeast will be pitched, get started on your starter. Combine 1 cup of dried malt extract, 1/4 teaspoon yeast nutrient, and 4 cups of water in a large saucepan over medium-high heat. Bring to a boil, then continue boiling for 20 minutes, stirring occasionally. Pour the mixture into a sterilized flask or small jar and cover with a loose lid or foil. Place the vessel in an ice bath to rapidly cool the starter to about 70°F. Shake well, then add the yeast. Replace the loose lid, gently shake or swirl to combine, and let ferment at room temperature until ready to use. And do give it an occasional swirl throughout the day while its fermenting.

Cooling

Sanitation is very important at every step of homebrewing, but particularly after the boil. The wort is a sugar- and protein-rich concoction practically begging microbes to come enjoy (and potentially spoil) it. Working with clean, sanitized equipment is crucial, as is cooling the wort quickly. Place the brew kettle in a large sink, bathtub, or cooler partially filled with ice water. Place your sanitized wort chiller in the wort and run cold water through it until the wort comes down to 72°F.

Pitching the Yeast and Fermentation

The yeast should be removed from the refrigerator about 2 hours before use so it acclimates to room temperature. Slowly pour the cooled wort into a sanitized primary fermentation bucket. Stir vigorously with a sanitized spoon or carefully shake the fermenter (sealed of course) for about 10 minutes to aerate the wort. Shake the container of yeast, add it directly to the wort, and stir vigorously to combine. Cover the bucket with the lid, fitted with the proper stopper and an airlock filled halfway with water. Place the bucket in a cool, dark place and keep it at 72°F unless otherwise noted.

Signs of primary fermentation should be evident after about 6 to 12 hours. Let the wort ferment until the bubbles coming from the airlock have slowed to a rate of about one per minute. This can take anywhere from 4 days to over 1 week.

Once this occurs, it's time to transfer the beer to a (sanitized) glass carboy for secondary fermentation. Attach a length of (sanitized) vinyl tubing to the (sanitized) racking cane, and carefully siphon the wort into the carboy, being careful to leave behind the sediment at the bottom of the plastic fermenter. The vinyl tubing should extend to the bottom of the carboy to prevent splashing. While oxygen is crucial for the yeast at the beginning of fermentation, after that you want to minimize the wort's exposure to it. If herbs, spices, or dry hops are called for in secondary fermentation, they should be added to the carboy at this time, according to each formula's instructions.

Seal the carboy with the drilled stopper and an airlock filled halfway with water. Allow the wort to continue fermenting until it reaches the target final gravity. Again, this may be anywhere from 4 days to over 1 week.

Bottling

When the wort reaches its target final gravity, it's time to bottle. Be sure to clean and sanitize the bottles, caps, bottling wand, racking cane, and tubing. Put the dried malt extract in a medium saucepan and stir in just enough water to dissolve it. Bring the mixture to a boil over high heat. Remove from the heat, cover, and let cool slightly. Pour this mixture into a clean, sanitized bucket with a spigot. Attach a length of vinyl tubing to the racking cane and carefully siphon the beer into the bucket, being careful to leave behind the sediment at the bottom of the carboy. The vinyl tubing should extend to the bottom of the bucket to prevent splashing.

Remove the racking cane and attach the bottling wand to one end of the vinyl tubing and the other to the spigot at the bottom of the bucket. Open the spigot and begin filling the bottles, leaving about 1 inch of headspace in each bottle. Once the bottles have been filled, cap them using a bottle capper (or simply close the tops if you're using swing-top style bottles). Store properly in a cool, dry place for 2 weeks so the beer can carbonate well. Cheers!

STONE PALE ALE

5 gallons (about fifty-four 12-ounce bottles or thirty 22-ounce bottles)

10 pounds, 7.0 ounces crushed North American two-row pale malt

1 pound, 4.2 ounces crushed 60L crystal malt

4.8 ounces crushed 75L crystal malt

About 9 gallons water

0.44 ounce Columbus hops (12.9% alpha acid)

1/2 teaspoon Irish moss

0.77 ounce Ahtanum hops (6.0% alpha acid)

1.19 ounces Ahtanum hops (6.0% alpha acid)

1 (35 ml) package White Labs WLP007 Dry English Ale Yeast or WLP002 English Ale Yeast

1 cup plus 3 tablespoons light dried malt extract

I can't stress it enough: clean and sanitize everything.

Mashing

In a 10-gallon insulated cooler, combine the crushed malts with 3 gallons plus 12 cups of 172°F water. The water should cool slightly when mixed with the grain. Hold the mash at 156°F for 20 minutes.

Add 2 gallons plus 2 cups of 184°F water. The mixture should come up to 165°F.

Lautering and Sparging

Lauter the mash according to the instructions on page 159. Once the liquid is lower than the level of the grain, begin to slowly sprinkle 3 gallons plus 1 cup of 168°F water over the grains to start the sparge. Continue sparging as instructed on page 159.

The Boil

For safety's sake, set up your propane burner outside. Set the brew kettle of wort on top and add water to bring the wort level up to about 6 gallons plus 12 cups, if needed. Bring the wort to a rapid, rolling boil. As it begins to come to a boil, a layer of foam and scum may develop at the surface. Skim it off and discard. Once the wort is at a full boil, put a hops bag containing the Columbus hops in the kettle and set a timer for 90 minutes. Stir the wort frequently during the boil, and be watchful to avoid boilovers.

At 15 minutes before the end of the boil, stir in the Irish moss. At 10 minutes before the end of the boil, put a hops bag containing the 0.77 ounce of Ahtanum hops in the kettle. When the boiling time is over, turn off the heat and put a hops bag containing the 1.19 ounces of Ahtanum hops in the kettle. Cover the kettle and immediately begin cooling the wort quickly (see page 160).

Pitching the Yeast and Fermentation

Once the wort has cooled to 72°F, discard the spent hops and check the specific gravity of the wort with a hydrometer. The target starting gravity is 1.057 (14 Plato).

Transfer the wort to the primary fermentation bucket according to the instructions on page 160. Pitch the yeast (or prepare a yeast starter) according to the instructions on page 160.

Allow the wort to ferment through primary and secondary fermentation (see page 160) at 72°F until it reaches a specific gravity of 1.014 (3.5 Plato).

Bottling

When you're ready to bottle, clean and sanitize the bottles, caps, and bottling equipment. Put the dried malt extract in a medium saucepan and stir in just enough water to dissolve it. Bring the mixture to a boil over high heat. Remove from the heat, cover, and let cool slightly. Proceed with bottling according to the instructions on page 161.

ADVANCED: STONE PALE ALE

87.0% crushed North American two-row pale malt

10.5% crushed 60L crystal malt

2.5% crushed 75L crystal malt

Conversion temperature 156°F [20 minutes]

Mash out 165°F

0.171 lb/bbl Columbus hops (12.9% alpha acid) [90 minutes]

0.30 lb/bbl Ahtanum hops (6.0% alpha acid) [10 minutes]

0.46 lb/bbl Ahtanum hops (6.0% alpha acid) [0 minutes]

White Labs WLP007 Dry English Ale Yeast or WLP002 English Ale Yeast

Pitch rate 16 to 18

Starting gravity 1.057 (14 Plato)

Final gravity 1.014 (3.5 Plato)

Ferment at 72°F

STONE SMOKED PORTER

5 gallons (about fifty-four 12-ounce bottles or thirty 22-ounce bottles)

10   pounds, 0.8 ounce crushed North American two-row pale malt

1   pound, 2.5 ounces crushed 75L crystal malt

10.7 ounces crushed chocolate malt

4.9 ounces crushed peat-smoked malt

     About 9 gallons plus 4 cups water

0.71 ounce Columbus hops (12.9% alpha acid)

1/2 teaspoon Irish moss

0.60 ounce Mt. Hood hops (6.0% alpha acid)

1   (35 ml) package White Labs WLP007 Dry English Ale Yeast or WLP002 English Ale Yeast

1   cup plus 3 tablespoons light dried malt extract

Clean and sanitize everything. Did I mention that already? Good, because I can't stress it enough: clean and sanitize everything.

Mashing

In a 10-gallon insulated cooler, combine the crushed malts with 3 gallons plus 13 cups of 173°F water. The water should cool slightly when mixed with the grain. Hold the mash at 157°F for 10 minutes.

Add 2 gallons plus 2 cups of 182°F water. The mixture should come up to 165°F.

Lautering and Sparging

Lauter the mash according to the instructions on page 159. Once the liquid is lower than the level of the grain, begin to slowly sprinkle 3 gallons plus 2 cups of 168°F water over the grains to start the sparge. Continue sparging as instructed on page 159.

The Boil

For safety's sake, set up your propane burner outside. Set the brew kettle of wort on top and add water to bring the wort level up to about 6 gallons plus 12 cups, if needed. Bring the wort to a rapid, rolling boil. As it begins to come to a boil, a layer of foam and scum may develop at the surface. Skim it off and discard. Once the wort is at a full boil, put a hops bag containing the Columbus hops in the kettle and set a timer for 90 minutes. Stir the wort frequently during the boil, and be watchful to avoid boilovers.

At 15 minutes before the end of the boil, stir in the Irish moss. When the boiling time is over, turn off the heat and put a hops bag containing the Mt. Hood hops in the kettle. Cover the kettle and immediately begin cooling the wort quickly (see page 160).

Pitching the Yeast and Fermentation

Once the wort has cooled to 72°F, discard the spent hops and check the specific gravity of the wort with a hydrometer. The target starting gravity is 1.065 (16 Plato).

Transfer the wort to the primary fermentation bucket according to the instructions on page 160. Pitch the yeast (or prepare a yeast starter) according to the instructions on page 160.

Allow the wort to ferment through primary and secondary fermentation (see page 160) at 72°F until it reaches a specific gravity of 1.018 (4.5 Plato).

Bottling

When you're ready to bottle, clean and sanitize the bottles, caps, and bottling equipment. Put the dried malt extract in a medium saucepan and stir in just enough water to dissolve it. Bring the mixture to a boil over high heat. Remove from the heat, cover, and let cool slightly. Proceed with bottling according to the instructions on page 161.

VARIATIONS ON A THEME

We've come up with a few slight changes to the Stone Smoked Porter that we like to make from time to time, just to keep things interesting.

Stone Smoked Porter with Chipotle: Put 0.42 ounce of chopped dried chipotle peppers in a hops bag, add it during secondary fermentation, and allow it to steep for 3 days (or more or less, depending on how spicy you'd like your brew to be).

Stone Smoked Porter with Vanilla Beans: Place 0.42 ounce of split, scraped, and chopped Madagascar vanilla beans in a hops bag, add it during secondary fermentation, and allow it to steep for 3 days (or more or less, as you wish).

ADVANCED: STONE SMOKED PORTER

82.5% crushed North American two-row pale malt

9.5% crushed 75L crystal malt

5.5% crushed chocolate malt

2.5% crushed peat-smoked malt

Conversion temperature 157°F [10 minutes]

Mash out 165°F

0.293 lb/bbl Columbus hops (12.9% alpha acid) [90 minutes]

0.23 lb/bbl Mt. Hood hops (6.0% alpha acid) [0 minutes]

White Labs WLP007 Dry English Ale Yeast or WLP002 English Ale Yeast

Pitch rate 16 to 18

Starting gravity 1.065 (16 Plato)

Final gravity 1.018 (4.5 Plato)

Ferment at 72°F

STONE LEVITATION ALE

5 gallons (about fifty-four 12-ounce bottles or thirty 22-ounce bottles)

8 pounds, 8.0 ounces crushed North American two-row pale malt

14.4 ounces crushed 75L crystal malt

8.3 ounces crushed 150L crystal malt

1.3 ounces crushed black malt

About 8 gallons plus 12 cups water

0.28 ounce Columbus hops (12.9% alpha acid)

$^1/_2$ teaspoon Irish moss

0.90 ounce Amarillo hops (8.5% alpha acid)

0.90 ounce Crystal hops (3.5% alpha acid)

0.26 ounce Simcoe hops (13.0% alpha acid)

1 (35 ml) package White Labs WLP007 Dry English Ale Yeast or WLP002 English Ale Yeast

0.77 ounce Amarillo hops (8.5% alpha acid)

1 cup plus 3 tablespoons light dried malt extract

I can't stress it enough: clean and sanitize everything.

Mashing

In a 10-gallon insulated cooler, combine the malts with 3 gallons plus 2 cups of 173°F water. The water should cool slightly when mixed with the grain. Hold the mash at 157°F for 10 minutes.

Add 1 gallon plus 12 cups of 182°F water. The mixture should come up to 165°F.

Lautering and Sparging

Lauter the mash according to the instructions on page 159. Once the liquid is lower than the level of the grain, begin to slowly sprinkle 3 gallons plus 14 cups of 168°F water over the grains to start the sparge. Continue sparging as instructed on page 159.

The Boil

For safety's sake, set up your propane burner outside. Set the brew kettle of wort on top and add water to bring the wort level up to about 6 gallons plus 12 cups, if needed. Bring the wort to a rapid, rolling boil. As it begins to come to a boil, a layer of foam and scum may develop at the surface. Skim it off and discard. Once the wort is at a full boil, put a hops bag containing the Columbus hops in the kettle and set a timer for 90 minutes. Stir the wort frequently during the boil, and be watchful to avoid boilovers.

At 15 minutes before the end of the boil, stir in the Irish moss. At 10 minutes before the end of the boil, put a hops bag containing the 0.90 ounce of Amarillo hops in the kettle. When the boiling time is over, turn off the heat and put a hops bag containing the Crystal and Simcoe hops in the kettle. Cover the kettle and immediately begin cooling the wort quickly (see page 160).

Pitching the Yeast and Fermentation

Once the wort has cooled to 72°F, discard the spent hops and check the specific gravity of the wort with a hydrometer. The target starting gravity is 1.048 (12 Plato).

Transfer the wort to the primary fermentation bucket according to the instructions on page 160. Pitch the yeast (or prepare a yeast starter) according to the instructions on page 160.

Allow the wort to ferment through primary fermentation (see page 160) at 72°F, then transfer the wort to a carboy for dry hopping and secondary fermentation (see page 160).

Dry Hopping

Put the 0.77 ounce of Amarillo hops in a hops bag and put it in the carboy. Seal the carboy with the drilled stopper and an airlock filled halfway with water and ferment at 72°F.

After 7 days, dry hopping is complete. Remove the hops bag and discard the hops. Check the specific gravity of the beer. If it's reached the target final gravity of 1.013 (3.2 Plato), it's ready to bottle. If not, allow it to continue fermenting at 72°F until it reaches the target.

Bottling

When you're ready to bottle, clean and sanitize the bottles, caps, and bottling equipment. Put the dried malt extract in a medium saucepan and stir in just enough water to dissolve it. Bring the mixture to a boil over high heat. Remove from the heat, cover, and let cool slightly. Proceed with bottling according to the instructions on page 161.

ADVANCED: STONE LEVITATION ALE

85.0% crushed North American two-row pale malt

9.0% crushed 75L crystal malt

5.2% crushed 150L crystal malt

0.8% crushed black malt

Conversion temperature 157°F [10 minutes]

Mash out 165°F

0.108 lb/bbl Columbus hops (12.9% alpha acid)
    [90 minutes]

0.35 lb/bbl Amarillo hops (8.5% alpha acid)
    [10 minutes]

0.35 lb/bbl Crystal hops (3.5% alpha acid)
    [0 minutes]

0.10 lb/bbl Simcoe hops (13.0% alpha acid)
    [0 minutes]

White Labs WLP007 Dry English Ale Yeast or
    WLP002 English Ale Yeast

Pitch rate 12

0.30 lb/bbl Amarillo hops (8.5% alpha acid)
    [Dry hop, 7 days]

Starting gravity 1.048 (12 Plato)

Final gravity 1.013 (3.2 Plato)

Ferment at 72°F

STONE 4TH ANNIVERSARY IPA

5 gallons (about fifty-four 12-ounce bottles or thirty 22-ounce bottles)

15 pounds, 13.4 ounces crushed North American two-row pale malt

1 pound, 2.6 ounces crushed 15L crystal malt

About 10 gallons plus 4 cups water

3.87 ounces Magnum hops (14.0% alpha acid)

1/2 teaspoon Irish moss

1.55 ounces Centennial hops (9.8% alpha acid)

1 (35 ml) package White Labs WLP007 Dry English Ale Yeast or WLP002 English Ale Yeast

1.94 ounces Centennial hops (10.0% alpha acid)

1 cup plus 3 tablespoons light dried malt extract

I can't stress it enough: clean and sanitize everything.

Mashing

In a 10-gallon insulated cooler, combine the crushed malts with 5 gallons plus 5 cups of 166°F water. The water should cool slightly when mixed with the grain. Hold the mash at 151°F for 60 minutes.

Lautering and Sparging

Lauter the mash according to the instructions on page 159. Once the liquid is lower than the level of the grain, begin to slowly sprinkle 4 gallons plus 12 cups of 168°F water over the grains to start the sparge. Continue sparging as instructed on page 159.

The Boil

For safety's sake, set up your propane burner outside. Set the brew kettle of wort on top and add water to bring the wort level up to about 7 gallons plus 4 cups, if needed. Bring the wort to a rapid, rolling boil. As it begins to come to a boil, a layer of foam and scum may develop at the surface. Skim it off and discard. Once the wort is at a full boil, put a hops bag containing the Magnum hops in the kettle and set a timer for 2 hours. Stir the wort frequently during the boil, and be watchful to avoid boilovers.

At 15 minutes before the end of the boil, stir in the Irish moss. When the boiling time is over, turn off the heat and put a hops bag containing the 1.55 ounces of Centennial hops in the kettle. Cover the kettle and immediately begin cooling the wort quickly (see page 160).

Pitching the Yeast and Fermentation

Once the wort has cooled to 72°F, discard the spent hops and check the specific gravity of the wort with a hydrometer. The target starting gravity is 1.079 (19 Plato).

Transfer the wort to the primary fermentation bucket according to the instructions on page 160. Pitch the yeast (or prepare a yeast starter) according to the instructions on page 160.

Allow the wort to ferment through primary fermentation (see page 160) at 72°F, then transfer the wort to a carboy for dry hopping and secondary fermentation.

Dry Hopping

Put the 1.94 ounces of Centennial hops in a hops bag and put it in the carboy. Seal the carboy with the drilled stopper and an airlock filled halfway with water and ferment at 72°F.

After 7 days, dry hopping is complete. Remove the hops bag and discard the hops. Check the specific gravity of the beer. If it's reached the target final gravity of 1.013 (3.2 Plato), it's ready to bottle. If not, allow it to continue fermenting at 72°F until it reaches the target.

Bottling

When you're ready to bottle, clean and sanitize the bottles, caps, and bottling equipment. Put the dried malt extract in a medium saucepan and stir in just enough water to dissolve it. Bring the mixture to a boil over high heat. Remove from the heat, cover, and let cool slightly. Proceed with bottling according to the instructions on page 161.

ADVANCED: STONE 4TH ANNIVERSARY IPA

93.2% crushed North American two-row pale malt

6.8% crushed 15L crystal malt

Conversion temperature 151°F [60 minutes]

Sparge, no mash out

1.50 lb/bbl Magnum hops (14.0% alpha acid) [120 minutes]

0.60 lb/bbl Centennial hops (10.0% alpha acid) [0 minutes]

White Labs WLP007 Dry English Ale Yeast or WLP002 English Ale Yeast

Pitch rate 20

0.75 lb/bbl Centennial hops (10.0% alpha acid) [Dry hop, 7 days]

Starting gravity 1.079 (19 Plato)

Final gravity 1.013 (3.2 Plato)

Ferment at 72°F

STONE 6TH ANNIVERSARY PORTER

5 gallons (about fifty-four 12-ounce bottles or thirty 22-ounce bottles)

15 pounds, 1.9 ounces crushed North American two-row pale malt

1 pound, 10.2 ounces crushed 75L crystal malt

13.3 ounces crushed chocolate malt

6.4 ounces crushed peat-smoked malt

About 9 gallons plus 12 cups water

1.55 ounces Tomahawk hops (15.5% alpha acid)

½ teaspoon Irish moss

0.77 ounce Tomahawk hops (15.5% alpha acid)

1.29 ounces Tomahawk hops (15.5% alpha acid)

1 (35 ml) package White Labs WLP007 Dry English Ale Yeast or WLP002 English Ale Yeast

1 cup plus 3 tablespoons light dried malt extract

I can't stress it enough: clean and sanitize everything.

Mashing

In a 10-gallon insulated cooler, combine the crushed malts with 5 gallons plus 10 cups of 166°F water. The water should cool slightly when mixed with the grain. Hold the mash at 151°F for 60 minutes.

Lautering and Sparging

Lauter the mash according to the instructions on page 159. Once the liquid is lower than the level of the grain, begin to slowly sprinkle 4 gallons plus 2 cups of 168°F water over the grains to start the sparge. Continue sparging as instructed on page 159.

The Boil

For safety's sake, set up your propane burner outside. Set the brew kettle of wort on top and add water to bring the wort level up to about 6 gallons plus 12 cups, if needed. Bring the wort to a rapid, rolling boil. As it begins to come to a boil, a layer of foam and scum may develop at the surface. Skim it off and discard. Once the wort is at a full boil, put a hops bag containing the 1.55 ounces of Tomahawk hops in the kettle and set a timer for 90 minutes. Stir the wort frequently during the boil, and be watchful to avoid boilovers.

At 15 minutes before the end of the boil, stir in the Irish moss. At 10 minutes before the end of the boil, put a hops bag containing the 0.77 ounce of Tomahawk hops in the kettle. When the boiling time is over, turn off the heat and put a hops bag containing the 1.29 ounces of Tomahawk hops in the kettle. Cover the kettle and immediately begin cooling the wort quickly (see page 160).

Pitching the Yeast and Fermentation

Once the wort has cooled to 72°F, discard the spent hops and check the specific gravity of the wort with a hydrometer. The target starting gravity is 1.083 (20 Plato).

Transfer the wort to the primary fermentation bucket according to the instructions on page 160. Pitch the yeast (or prepare a yeast starter) according to the instructions on page 160.

Allow the wort to ferment through primary and secondary fermentation (see page 160) at 72°F until it reaches a specific gravity of 1.020 (5 Plato).

Bottling

When you're ready to bottle, clean and sanitize the bottles, caps, and bottling equipment. Put the dried malt extract in a medium saucepan and stir in just enough water to dissolve it. Bring the mixture to a boil over high heat. Remove from the heat, cover, and let cool slightly. Proceed with bottling according to the instructions on page 161.

ADVANCED: STONE 6TH ANNIVERSARY PORTER

84.1% crushed North American two-row pale malt

9.1% crushed 75L crystal malt

4.6% crushed chocolate malt

2.2% crushed peat-smoked malt

Conversion temperature 151°F [60 minutes]

Sparge, no mash out

0.60 lb/bbl Tomahawk hops (15.5% alpha acid) [90 minutes]

0.30 lb/bbl Tomahawk hops (15.5% alpha acid) [10 minutes]

0.50 lb/bbl Tomahawk hops (15.5% alpha acid) [0 minutes]

White Labs WLP007 Dry English Ale Yeast or WLP002 English Ale Yeast

Pitch rate 20

Starting gravity 1.083 (20 Plato)

Final gravity 1.020 (5 Plato)

Ferment at 72°F

STONE 7TH ANNIVERSARY ALE

5 gallons (about fifty-four 12-ounce bottles or thirty 22-ounce bottles)

 15 pounds, 0.3 ounce crushed North American two-row pale malt

  1 pound, 2.6 ounces crushed 60L crystal malt

 12.5 ounces crushed victory malt

    About 10 gallons plus 12 cups water

 1.03 ounces Magnum hops (14.0% alpha acid)

  $^1/_2$ teaspoon Irish moss

 2.58 ounces Ahtanum hops (6.0% alpha acid)

 2.58 ounces Ahtanum hops (6.0% alpha acid)

  1 (35 ml) package White Labs WLP007 Dry English Ale Yeast or WLP002 English Ale Yeast

  1 cup plus 3 tablespoons light dried malt extract

I can't stress it enough: clean and sanitize everything.

Mashing

In a 10-gallon insulated cooler, combine the crushed malts with 5 gallons plus 5 cups of 166°F water. The water should cool slightly when mixed with the grain. Hold the mash at 151°F for 60 minutes.

Lautering and Sparging

Lauter the mash according to the instructions on page 159. Once the liquid is lower than the level of the grain, begin to slowly sprinkle 5 gallons plus 4 cups of 168°F water over the grains to start the sparge. Continue sparging as instructed on page 159.

The Boil

For safety's sake, set up your propane burner outside. Set the brew kettle of wort on top and add water to bring the wort level up to about 7 gallons plus 12 cups, if needed. Bring the wort to a rapid, rolling boil. As it begins to come to a boil, a layer of foam and scum may develop at the surface. Skim it off and discard. Once the wort is at a full boil, put a hops bag containing the Magnum hops in the kettle and set a timer for 2$^1/_2$ hours. Stir the wort frequently during the boil, and be watchful to avoid boilovers.

At 15 minutes before the end of the boil, stir in the Irish moss. At 10 minutes before the end of the boil, put a hops bag containing 2.58 ounces of Ahtanum hops in the kettle. When the boiling time is over, turn off the heat and put a hops bag containing the remaining 2.58 ounces of Ahtanum hops in the kettle. Cover the kettle and immediately begin cooling the wort quickly (see page 160).

Pitching the Yeast and Fermentation

Once the wort has cooled to 72°F, discard the spent hops and check the specific gravity of the wort with a hydrometer. The target starting gravity is 1.079 (19 Plato).

Transfer the wort to the primary fermentation bucket according to the instructions on page 160. Pitch the yeast (or prepare a yeast starter) according to the instructions on page 160.

Allow the wort to ferment through primary and secondary fermentation (see page 160) at 72°F until it reaches a specific gravity of 1.016 (4 Plato).

Bottling

When you're ready to bottle, clean and sanitize the bottles, caps, and bottling equipment. Put the dried malt extract in a medium saucepan and stir in just enough water to dissolve it. Bring the mixture to a boil over high heat. Remove from the heat, cover, and let cool slightly. Proceed with bottling according to the instructions on page 161.

ADVANCED:
STONE 7TH ANNIVERSARY ALE

88.6% crushed North American two-row pale malt

6.8% crushed 60L crystal malt

4.6% crushed victory malt

Conversion temperature 151°F [60 minutes]

Sparge, no mash out

0.40 lb/bbl Magnum hops (14.0% alpha acid)
[2 1/2 hours]

1.00 lb/bbl Ahtanum hops (6.0% alpha acid)
[10 minutes]

1.00 lb/bbl Ahtanum hops (6.0% alpha acid)
[0 minutes]

White Labs WLP007 Dry English Ale Yeast or
WLP002 English Ale Yeast

Pitch rate 20

Starting gravity 1.079 (19 Plato)

Final gravity 1.016 (4 Plato)

Ferment at 72°F

STONE 8TH ANNIVERSARY ALE

5 gallons (about fifty-four 12-ounce bottles or thirty 22-ounce bottles)

13 pounds, 10.9 ounces crushed North American two-row pale malt

1 pound, 4.0 ounces crushed brown malt

1 pound, 2.6 ounces crushed 150L crystal malt

6.6 ounces crushed pale chocolate malt

About 10 gallons plus 8 cups water

1.45 ounces Amarillo hops (8.5% alpha acid)

1/2 teaspoon Irish moss

0.36 ounce Amarillo hops (8.5% alpha acid)

1 (35 ml) package White Labs WLP007 Dry English Ale Yeast or WLP002 English Ale Yeast

1 cup plus 3 tablespoons light dried malt extract

I can't stress it enough: clean and sanitize everything.

Mashing

In a 10-gallon insulated cooler, combine the crushed malts with 5 gallons plus 2 cups of 173°F water. The water should cool slightly when mixed with the grain. Hold the mash at 157°F for 30 minutes.

Lautering and Sparging

Lauter the mash according to the instructions on page 159. Once the liquid is lower than the level of the grain, begin to slowly sprinkle 5 gallons plus 6 cups of 168°F water over the grains to start the sparge. Continue sparging as instructed on page 159.

The Boil

For safety's sake, set up your propane burner outside. Set the brew kettle of wort on top and add water to bring the wort level up to about 7 gallons plus 12 cups, if needed. Bring the wort to a rapid, rolling boil. As it begins to come to a boil, a layer of foam and scum may develop at the surface. Skim it off and discard. Once the wort is at a full boil, put a hops bag containing the 1.45 ounces of Amarillo hops in the kettle and set a timer for 2 1/2 hours. Stir the wort frequently during the boil, and be watchful to avoid boilovers.

At 15 minutes before the end of the boil, stir in the Irish moss. When the boiling time is over, turn off the heat and put a hops bag containing the remaining 0.36 ounce of Amarillo hops in the kettle. Cover the kettle and immediately begin cooling the wort quickly (see page 160).

Pitching the Yeast and Fermentation

Once the wort has cooled to 72°F, discard the spent hops and check the specific gravity of the wort with a hydrometer. The target starting gravity is 1.076 (18.5 Plato).

Transfer the wort to the primary fermentation bucket according to the instructions on page 160. Pitch the yeast (or prepare a yeast starter) according to the instructions on page 160.

Allow the wort to ferment through primary and secondary fermentation (see page 160) at 72°F until it reaches a specific gravity of 1.016 (4 Plato).

Bottling

When you're ready to bottle, clean and sanitize the bottles, caps, and bottling equipment. Put the dried malt extract in a medium saucepan and stir in just enough water to dissolve it. Bring the mixture to a boil over high heat. Remove from the heat, cover, and let cool slightly. Proceed with bottling according to the instructions on page 161.

ADVANCED: STONE 8TH ANNIVERSARY ALE

82.9% crushed North American two-row pale malt

7.6% crushed brown malt

7.0% crushed 150L crystal malt

2.5% crushed pale chocolate malt

Conversion temperature 157°F [30 minutes]

Sparge, no mash out

0.56 lb/bbl Amarillo hops (8.5% alpha acid)
[2$^{1}/_{2}$ hours]

0.14 lb/bbl Amarillo hops (8.5% alpha acid)
[0 minutes]

White Labs WLP007 Dry English Ale Yeast or
WLP002 English Ale Yeast

Pitch rate 20

Starting gravity 1.076 (18.5 Plato)

Final gravity 1.016 (4 Plato)

Ferment at 72°F

STONE 9TH ANNIVERSARY ALE

5 gallons (about fifty-four 12-ounce bottles or thirty 22-ounce bottles)

13 pounds, 8.5 ounces crushed North American two-row pale malt

3 pounds, 7.5 ounces crushed American wheat malt

About 10 gallons plus 12 cups water

0.71 ounce Warrior hops (17.0% alpha acid)

$^1/_2$ teaspoon Irish moss

0.52 ounce Centennial hops (10.0% alpha acid)

1.29 ounces Crystal hops (3.5% alpha acid)

1 (35 ml) package White Labs WLP007 Dry English Ale Yeast or WLP002 English Ale Yeast

0.90 ounce Amarillo hops (8.5% alpha acid)

0.65 ounce Crystal hops (3.5% alpha acid)

1 cup plus 3 tablespoons light dried malt extract

I can't stress it enough: clean and sanitize everything.

Mashing

In a 10-gallon insulated cooler, combine the crushed malts with 5 gallons plus 4 cups of 162°F water. The water should cool slightly when mixed with the grain. Hold the mash at 148°F for 30 minutes.

Lautering and Sparging

Lauter the mash according to the instructions on page 159. Once the liquid is lower than the level of the grain, begin to slowly sprinkle 5 gallons plus 4 cups of 168°F water over the grains to start the sparge. Continue sparging as instructed on page 159.

The Boil

For safety's sake, set up your propane burner outside. Set the brew kettle of wort on top and add water to bring the wort level up to about 7 gallons plus 12 cups, if needed. Bring the wort to a rapid, rolling boil. As it begins to come to a boil, a layer of foam and scum may develop at the surface. Skim it off and discard. Once the wort is at a full boil, put a hops bag containing the Warrior hops in the kettle and set a timer for 2$^1/_2$ hours. Stir the wort frequently during the boil, and be watchful to avoid boilovers.

At 15 minutes before the end of the boil, stir in the Irish moss. At 10 minutes before the end of the boil, put a hops bag containing the Centennial hops in the kettle. When the boiling time is over, turn off the heat and put a hops bag containing the 1.29 ounces of Crystal hops in the kettle. Cover the kettle and immediately begin cooling the wort quickly (see page 160).

Pitching the Yeast and Fermentation

Once the wort has cooled to 72°F, discard the spent hops and check the specific gravity of the wort with a hydrometer. The target starting gravity is 1.079 (19 Plato).

Transfer the wort to the primary fermentation bucket according to the instructions on page 160. Pitch the yeast (or prepare a yeast starter) according to the instructions on page 160.

Allow the wort to ferment through primary fermentation (see page 160) at 72°F, then transfer the wort to a carboy for dry hopping and secondary fermentation (see page 160).

Dry Hopping

Put the Amarillo hops and the remaining 0.65 ounce of Crystal hops in a hops bag and put it in the carboy. Seal the carboy with the drilled stopper and an airlock filled halfway with water and ferment at 72°F.

After 7 days, dry hopping is complete. Remove the hops bag and discard the hops. Check the specific gravity of the beer. If it's reached the target final gravity of 1.010 (2.5 Plato), it's ready to bottle. If not, allow it to continue fermenting at 72°F until it reaches the target.

Bottling

When you're ready to bottle, clean and sanitize the bottles, caps, and bottling equipment. Put the dried malt extract in a medium saucepan and stir in just enough water to dissolve it. Bring the mixture to a boil over high heat. Remove from the heat, cover, and let cool slightly. Proceed with bottling according to the instructions on page 161.

ADVANCED: STONE 9TH ANNIVERSARY ALE

79.6% crushed North American two-row pale malt

20.4% crushed American wheat malt

Conversion temperature 148°F [30 minutes]

Sparge, no mash out

0.275 lb/bbl Warrior hops (17.0% alpha acid) [2½ hours]

0.20 lb/bbl Centennial hops (10.0% alpha acid) [10 minutes]

0.50 lb/bbl Crystal hops (3.5% alpha acid) [0 minutes]

White Labs WLP007 Dry English Ale Yeast or WLP002 English Ale Yeast

Pitch rate 20

0.275 lb/bbl Warrior hops (17.0% alpha acid) [Dry hop, 7 days]

0.25 lb/bbl Crystal hops (3.5% alpha acid) [Dry hop, 7 days]

Starting gravity 1.079 (19 Plato)

Final gravity 1.010 (2.5 Plato)

Ferment at 72°F

STONE 12TH ANNIVERSARY BITTER CHOCOLATE OATMEAL STOUT

5 gallons (about fifty-four 12-ounce bottles or thirty 22-ounce bottles)

14 pounds, 6.9 ounces crushed North American two-row pale malt

1 pound, 15.9 ounces flaked oats

1 pound, 8.6 ounces crushed chocolate malt (U.K.)

14.9 ounces crushed 15L crystal malt

14.4 ounces crushed black malt

14.4 ounces crushed roasted barley

13.1 ounces crushed Carapils malt

About 10 gallons plus 4 cups water

1.01 ounces Galena hops (13.0% alpha acid)

0.85 ounce Ahtanum hops (6.0% alpha acid)

3.25 ounces crushed cacao nibs

1/2 teaspoon Irish moss

1 (35 ml) package White Labs WLP007 Dry English Ale Yeast or WLP002 English Ale Yeast

1 cup plus 3 tablespoons light dried malt extract

I can't stress it enough: clean and sanitize everything.

Mashing

In a 10-gallon brew kettle, combine the crushed malts, flaked oats, and roasted barley with 6 gallons plus 11 cups of 162°F water. The water should cool slightly when mixed with the grain. Cover and hold the mash at 148°F for 90 minutes. For safety's sake, set up your propane burner outside. Set the brew kettle of mash on top and heat to 160°F, stirring frequently to avoid scorching. Turn off the heat. The mash will continue to increase in temperature to about 165°F.

Lautering and Sparging

Lauter the mash according to the instructions on page 159. Once the liquid is lower than the level of the grain, begin to slowly sprinkle 3 gallons plus 8 cups of 168°F water over the grains to start the sparge. Continue sparging as instructed on page 159.

The Boil

Set the brew kettle of wort on your outdoor propane burner and add water to bring the wort level up to 6 gallons plus 12 cups, if needed. Bring the wort to a rapid, rolling boil. As it begins to come to a boil, a layer of foam and scum may develop at the surface. Skim it off and discard. Once the wort is at a full boil, put a hops bag containing the Galena and Ahtanum hops in the kettle and add the cacao nibs directly to the wort. Set a timer for 90 minutes. Stir the wort frequently during the boil, and be watchful to avoid boilovers.

At 15 minutes before the end of the boil, stir in the Irish moss. When the boiling time is over, turn off the heat. Cover the kettle and immediately begin cooling the wort quickly (see page 160).

Pitching the Yeast and Fermentation

Once the wort has cooled to 75°F, discard the spent hops and check the specific gravity of the wort with a hydrometer. The target starting gravity is 1.099 (23.5 Plato).

Transfer the wort to the primary fermentation bucket according to the instructions on page 160. Pitch the yeast (or prepare a yeast starter) according to the instructions on page 160.

Allow the wort to ferment through primary and secondary fermentation (see page 160) at 75°F until it reaches a specific gravity of 1.022 (5.7 Plato).

Bottling

When you're ready to bottle, clean and sanitize the bottles, caps, and bottling equipment. Put the dried malt extract in a medium saucepan and stir in just enough water to dissolve it. Bring the mixture to a boil over high heat. Remove from the heat, cover, and let cool slightly. Proceed with bottling according to the instructions on page 161.

ADVANCED: STONE 12TH ANNIVERSARY BITTER CHOCOLATE OATMEAL STOUT

67.1% crushed North American two-row pale malt

9.2% flaked oats

7.2% crushed chocolate malt (U.K.)

4.3% crushed 15L crystal malt

4.2% crushed black malt

4.2% crushed roasted barley

3.8% crushed Carapils malt

Conversion temperature 148°F [90 minutes]

Mash out 165°F

0.39 lb/bbl Galena hops (13.0% alpha acid) [90 minutes]

0.33 lb/bbl Ahtanum hops (6.0% alpha acid) [90 minutes]

1.25 lb/bbl crushed cacao nibs [90 minutes]

White Labs WLP007 Dry English Ale Yeast or WLP002 English Ale Yeast

Pitch rate 25

Starting gravity 1.099 (23.5 Plato)

Final gravity 1.022 (5.7 Plato)

Ferment at 75°F

STONE 13TH ANNIVERSARY ALE

5 gallons (about fifty-four 12-ounce bottles or thirty 22-ounce bottles)

16 pounds, 1.8 ounces crushed North American two-row pale malt

1 pound, 3.7 ounces crushed 60L crystal malt

1 pound, 0.5 ounce 150L crystal malt

14.4 ounces crushed CaraVienne malt

9.9 ounces crushed 75L crystal malt

7.2 ounces crushed amber malt

2.6 ounces crushed chocolate malt

About 10 gallons water

3.87 ounces Chinook hops (13.0% alpha acid)

1/2 teaspoon Irish moss

2.58 ounces Chinook hops (13.0% alpha acid)

1 (35 ml) package White Labs WLP007 Dry English Ale Yeast or WLP002 English Ale Yeast

1.94 ounces Centennial hops (10.0% alpha acid)

1.94 ounces Simcoe hops (13.0% alpha acid)

0.65 ounce Centennial hops (10.0% alpha acid)

0.65 ounce Simcoe hops (13.0% alpha acid)

1 cup plus 3 tablespoons light dried malt extract

I can't stress it enough: clean and sanitize everything.

Mashing

In a 10-gallon brew kettle, combine the crushed malts with 6 gallons plus 6 cups of 162°F water. The water should cool slightly when mixed with the grain. Cover and hold the mash at 148°F for 90 minutes.

For safety's sake, set up your propane burner outside. Set the brew kettle of mash on top and heat to 160°F, stirring frequently to avoid scorching. Turn off the heat. The mash will continue to increase in temperature to about 165°F.

Lautering and Sparging

Lauter the mash according to the instructions on page 159. Once the liquid is lower than the level of the grain, begin to slowly sprinkle 3 gallons plus 11 cups of 168°F water over the grains to start the sparge. Continue sparging as instructed on page 159.

The Boil

Set the brew kettle of wort on your outdoor propane burner and add water to bring the wort level up to about 6 gallons plus 12 cups, if needed. Bring the wort to a rapid, rolling boil. As it begins to come to a boil, a layer of foam and scum may develop at the surface. Skim it off and discard. Once the wort is at a full boil, put a hops bag containing the 3.87 ounces of Chinook hops in the kettle and set a timer for 90 minutes. Stir the wort frequently during the boil, and be watchful to avoid boilovers.

At 15 minutes before the end of the boil, stir in the Irish moss. When the boiling time is over, turn off the heat and put a hops bag containing the 2.58 ounces of Chinook hops in the kettle. Cover the kettle and immediately begin cooling the wort quickly (see page 160).

Pitching the Yeast and Fermentation

Once the wort has cooled to 72°F, discard the spent hops and check the specific gravity of the wort with a hydrometer. The target starting gravity is 1.094 (22.5 Plato).

Transfer the wort to the primary fermentation bucket according to the instructions on page 160. Pitch the yeast (or prepare a yeast starter) according to the instructions on page 160.

Allow the wort to ferment through primary fermentation (see page 160) at 72°F, then transfer the wort to a carboy for double dry hopping and secondary fermentation (see page 160).

Double Dry Hopping

Put the 1.94 ounces of Centennial and Simcoe hops in a hops bag and put it in the carboy. Seal the carboy with the drilled stopper and an airlock filled halfway with water and ferment at 72°F.

After 7 days, remove the hops bag and discard the hops. Put the 0.65 ounce of Centennial and Simcoe hops in a hops bag and put it in the carboy. Seal the carboy with the drilled stopper and an airlock filled halfway with water and ferment at 72°F.

After 7 more days, dry hopping is complete. Remove the hops bag and discard the hops. Check the specific gravity of the beer. If it's reached the target final gravity of 1.018 (4.5 Plato), it's ready to bottle. If not, allow it to continue fermenting at 72°F until it reaches the target.

Bottling

When you're ready to bottle, clean and sanitize the bottles, caps, and bottling equipment. Put the dried malt extract in a medium saucepan and stir in just enough water to dissolve it. Bring the mixture to a boil over high heat. Remove from the heat, cover, and let cool slightly. Proceed with bottling according to the instructions on page 161.

ADVANCED: STONE 13TH ANNIVERSARY ALE

78.6% crushed North American two-row pale malt

6.0% crushed 60L crystal malt

5.0% crushed 150L crystal malt

4.4% crushed CaraVienne malt

3.0% crushed 75L crystal malt

2.2% crushed amber malt

0.8% crushed chocolate malt

Conversion temperature 148°F [90 minutes]

Mash out 165°F

1.50 lb/bbl Chinook hops (13.0% alpha acid) [90 minutes]

1.00 lb/bbl Chinook hops (13.0% alpha acid) [0 minutes]

White Labs WLP007 Dry English Ale Yeast or WLP002 English Ale Yeast

Pitch rate 25

0.75 lb/bbl Centennial hops (10.0% alpha acid) [Dry hop, 7 days]

0.75 lb/bbl Simcoe hops (13.0% alpha acid) [Dry hop, 7 days]

Double dry hop: After 7 days, discard first dry hops and replace with:

0.25 lb/bbl Centennial hops (10.0% alpha acid) [Dry hop, 7 days]

0.25 lb/bbl Simcoe hops (13.0% alpha acid) [Dry hop, 7 days]

Starting gravity 1.094 (22.5 Plato)

Final gravity 1.018 (4.5 Plato)

Ferment at 72°F

LEE'S MILD

5 gallons (about fifty-four 12-ounce bottles or thirty 22-ounce bottles)

6 pounds, 10.1 ounces crushed North American two-row pale malt

9.8 ounces crushed brown malt

9.0 ounces crushed 150L crystal malt

3.2 ounces crushed pale chocolate malt

About 9 gallons water

0.75 ounce Northern Brewer hops (8.5% alpha acid)

1/2 teaspoon Irish moss

1 (35 ml) package White Labs WLP007 Dry English Ale Yeast or WLP002 English Ale Yeast

1 cup plus 3 tablespoons light dried malt extract

I can't stress it enough: clean and sanitize everything.

Mashing

In a 10-gallon insulated cooler, combine the crushed malts with 2 gallons plus 8 cups of 169°F water. The water should cool slightly when mixed with the grain. Hold the mash at 154°F for 60 minutes.

Lautering and Sparging

Lauter the mash according to the instructions on page 159. Once the liquid is lower than the level of the grain, begin to slowly sprinkle 6 gallons plus 8 cups of 168°F water over the grains to start the sparge. Continue sparging as instructed on page 159.

The Boil

For safety's sake, set up your propane burner outside. Set the brew kettle of wort on top and add water to bring the wort level up to about 7 gallons plus 4 cups, if needed. Bring the wort to a rapid, rolling boil. As it begins to come to a boil, a layer of foam and scum may develop at the surface. Skim it off and discard. Once the wort is at a full boil, put a hops bag containing the Northern Brewer hops in the kettle and set a timer for 2 hours. Stir the wort frequently during the boil, and be watchful to avoid boilovers.

At 15 minutes before the end of the boil, stir in the Irish moss. When the boiling time is over, turn off the heat. Cover the kettle and immediately begin cooling the wort quickly (see page 160).

Pitching the Yeast and Fermentation

Once the wort has cooled to 72°F, discard the spent hops and check the specific gravity of the wort with a hydrometer. The target starting gravity is 1.040 (10 Plato).

Transfer the wort to the primary fermentation bucket according to the instructions on page 160. Pitch the yeast (or prepare a yeast starter) according to the instructions on page 160.

Allow the wort to ferment through primary and secondary fermentation (see page 160) at 72°F until it reaches a specific gravity of 1.011 (2.9 Plato).

Bottling

When you're ready to bottle, clean and sanitize the bottles, caps, and bottling equipment. Put the dried malt extract in a medium saucepan and stir in just enough water to dissolve it. Bring the mixture to a boil over high heat. Remove from the heat, cover, and let cool slightly. Proceed with bottling according to the instructions on page 161.

ADVANCED: LEE'S MILD

82.9% crushed North American two-row pale malt

7.6% crushed brown malt

7.0% crushed 150L crystal malt

2.5% crushed pale chocolate malt

Conversion temperature 154°F [60 minutes]

Sparge, no mash out

0.29 lb/bbl Northern Brewer hops (8.5% alpha acid) [2 hours]

White Labs WLP007 Dry English Ale Yeast or WLP002 English Ale Yeast

Pitch rate 12

Starting gravity 1.040 (10 Plato)

Final gravity 1.011 (2.9 Plato)

Ferment at 72°F

HEAT SEEKING WHEAT

5 gallons (about fifty-four 12-ounce bottles or thirty 22-ounce bottles)

7   pounds, 3.2 ounces crushed North American two-row pale malt

2   pounds, 12.8 ounces crushed American wheat malt

About 8 gallons plus 12 cups water

0.65   ounce Northern Brewer hops (8.5% alpha acid)

1/2   teaspoon Irish moss

0.39   ounce Mt. Hood hops (6.0% alpha acid)

1   (35 ml) package White Labs WLP007 Dry English Ale Yeast or WLP002 English Ale Yeast

1   cup plus 3 tablespoons light dried malt extract

I can't stress it enough: clean and sanitize everything.

Mashing

In a 10-gallon insulated cooler, combine the crushed malts with 3 gallons plus 3 cups of 171°F water. The water should cool slightly when mixed with the grain. Hold the mash at 156°F for 60 minutes.

Lautering and Sparging

Lauter the mash according to the instructions on page 159. Once the liquid is lower than the level of the grain, begin to slowly sprinkle 5 gallons plus 9 cups of 168°F water over the grains to start the sparge. Continue sparging as instructed on page 159.

The Boil

For safety's sake, set up your propane burner outside. Set the brew kettle of wort on top and add water to bring the wort level up to about 6 gallons plus 12 cups, if needed. Bring the wort to a rapid, rolling boil. As it begins to come to a boil, a layer of foam and scum may develop at the surface. Skim it off and discard. Once the wort is at a full boil, put a hops bag containing the Northern Brewer hops in the kettle and set a timer for 90 minutes. Stir the wort frequently during the boil, and be watchful to avoid boilovers.

At 15 minutes before the end of the boil, stir in the Irish moss. When the boiling time is over, turn off the heat and put a hops bag containing the Mt. Hood hops in the kettle. Cover the kettle and immediately begin cooling the wort quickly (see page 160).

Pitching the Yeast and Fermentation

Once the wort has cooled to 70°F, discard the spent hops and check the specific gravity of the wort with a hydrometer. The target starting gravity is 1.048 (12 Plato).

Transfer the wort to the primary fermentation bucket according to the instructions on page 160. Pitch the yeast (or prepare a yeast starter) according to the instructions on page 160.

Allow the wort to ferment through primary and secondary fermentation (see page 160) at 70°F until it reaches a specific gravity of 1.010 (2.5 Plato).

Bottling

When you're ready to bottle, clean and sanitize the bottles, caps, and bottling equipment. Put the dried malt extract in a medium saucepan and stir in just enough water to dissolve it. Bring the mixture to a boil over high heat. Remove from the heat, cover, and let cool slightly. Proceed with bottling according to the instructions on page 161.

ADVANCED: HEAT SEEKING WHEAT

72.0% crushed North American two-row pale malt

28.0% crushed American wheat malt

Conversion temperature 156°F [60 minutes]

Sparge, no mash out

0.25 lb/bbl Northern Brewer hops (8.5% alpha acid) [90 minutes]

0.15 lb/bbl Mt. Hood hops (6.0% alpha acid) [0 minutes]

White Labs WLP007 Dry English Ale Yeast or WLP002 English Ale Yeast

Pitch rate 12

Starting gravity 1.048 (12 Plato)

Final gravity 1.010 (2.5 Plato)

Ferment at 70°F

STONE OLD GUARDIAN BARLEY WINE

5 gallons (about fifty-four 12-ounce bottles or thirty 22-ounce bottles)

21 pounds, 9.6 ounces crushed North American two-row pale malt

14.4 ounces crushed 60L crystal malt

About 10 gallons plus 8 cups water

1.69 ounces Warrior hops (15.0% alpha acid)

1/2 teaspoon Irish moss

1.94 ounces Crystal hops (3.5% alpha acid)

1 (35 ml) package White Labs WLP007 Dry English Ale Yeast or WLP002 English Ale Yeast

1 cup plus 3 tablespoons light dried malt extract

I can't stress it enough: clean and sanitize everything.

Mashing

In a 10-gallon brew kettle, combine the crushed malts with 7 gallons plus 1 cup of 161°F water. The water should cool slightly when mixed with the grain. Cover and hold the mash at 148°F for 90 minutes.

For safety's sake, set up your propane burner outside. Set the brew kettle of mash on top and heat to 160°F, stirring frequently to avoid scorching. Turn off the heat. The mash will continue to increase in temperature to about 165°F.

Lautering and Sparging

Lauter the mash according to the instructions on page 159. Once the liquid is lower than the level of the grain, begin to slowly sprinkle 3 gallons plus 7 cups of 168°F water over the grains to start the sparge. Continue sparging as instructed on page 159.

The Boil

Set the brew kettle of wort on your outdoor propane burner and add water to bring the wort level up to 7 gallons, if needed. Bring the wort to a rapid, rolling boil. As it begins to come to a boil, a layer of foam and scum may develop at the surface. Skim it off and discard. Once the wort is at a full boil, put a hops bag containing the Warrior hops in the kettle and set a timer for 1 hour and 45 minutes. Stir the wort frequently during the boil, and be watchful to avoid boilovers.

At 15 minutes before the end of the boil, stir in the Irish moss. When the boiling time is over, turn off the heat and put a hops bag containing the Crystal hops in the kettle. Cover the kettle and immediately begin cooling the wort quickly (see page 160).

Pitching the Yeast and Fermentation

Once the wort has cooled to 72°F, discard the spent hops and check the specific gravity of the wort with a hydrometer. The target starting gravity is 1.103 (24.5 Plato).

Transfer the wort to the primary fermentation bucket according to the instructions on page 160. Pitch the yeast (or prepare a yeast starter) according to the instructions on page 160.

Allow the wort to ferment through primary and secondary fermentation (see page 160) at 72°F until it reaches a specific gravity of 1.016 (4 Plato).

If you've been paying extra close attention, you no doubt know that the recipe for Stone Old Guardian Barley Wine changes slightly from year to year. So which version is this? Why, the recipe that took a silver medal at the Great American Beer Festival in 2000, of course!

Bottling

When you're ready to bottle, clean and sanitize the bottles, caps, and bottling equipment. Put the dried malt extract in a medium saucepan and stir in just enough water to dissolve it. Bring the mixture to a boil over high heat. Remove from the heat, cover, and let cool slightly. Proceed with bottling according to the instructions on page 161.

ADVANCED: STONE OLD GUARDIAN BARLEY WINE

96.0% crushed North American two-row pale malt

4.0% crushed 60L crystal malt

Conversion temperature 148°F [90 minutes]

Mash out 165°F

0.653 lb/bbl Warrior hops (15.0% alpha acid)
    [1 hour and 45 minutes]

0.75 lb/bbl Crystal hops (3.5% alpha acid)
    [0 minutes]

White Labs WLP007 Dry English Ale Yeast or
    WLP002 English Ale Yeast

Pitch rate 25 to 30

Starting gravity 1.103 (24.5 Plato)

Final gravity 1.016 (4 Plato)

Ferment at 72°F

JOLLY PUMPKIN / NØGNE-Ø / STONE
SPECIAL HOLIDAY ALE

5 gallons (about fifty-four 12-ounce bottles or thirty 22-ounce bottles)

9 pounds, 15.7 ounces crushed North American two-row pale malt

4 pounds, 12.3 ounces crushed rye malt

1 pound, 12.3 ounces crushed Munich malt

1 pound, 0.8 ounce 150L crystal malt

15.2 ounces flaked oats

4.6 ounces crushed Special B malt

3.0 ounces crushed chocolate malt

5.2 ounces dried chestnuts

About 9 gallons plus 12 cups water

0.49 ounce German Perle hops (10.0% alpha acid)

1/2 teaspoon Irish moss

1.73 ounces Columbus hops (12.9% alpha acid)

0.09 ounce white sage leaves

0.17 ounce whole juniper berries

0.24 ounce whole caraway seeds

1 (35 ml) package White Labs WLP007 Dry English Ale Yeast or WLP002 English Ale Yeast

1 cup plus 3 tablespoons light dried malt extract

I can't stress it enough: clean and sanitize everything.

Mashing

In a 10-gallon insulated cooler, combine the crushed malts, flaked oats, and chestnuts with 5 gallons plus 15 cups of 172°F water. The water should cool slightly when mixed with the grain. Hold the mash at 156°F for 30 minutes.

Add 2 gallons plus 6 cups of 204°F water. The mixture should come up to 165°F.

Lautering and Sparging

Lauter the mash according to the instructions on page 159. Once the liquid is lower than the level of the grain, begin to slowly sprinkle 1 gallon plus 8 cups of 168°F water over the grains to start the sparge. Continue sparging as instructed on page 159. (Rye is notoriously difficult to work with at this stage because it doesn't allow for drainage as well as barley, so prepare for what could be a very lengthy lauter and sparge. Your patience will be rewarded.)

The Boil

For safety's sake, set up your propane burner outside. Set the brew kettle of wort on top and add water to bring the wort level up to about 6 gallons plus 12 cups, if needed. Bring the wort to a rapid, rolling boil. As it begins to come to a boil, a layer of foam and scum may develop at the surface. Skim it off and discard. Once the wort is at a full boil, put a hops bag containing the German Perle hops in the kettle and set a timer for 90 minutes. Stir the wort frequently during the boil, and be watchful to avoid boilovers.

At 15 minutes before the end of the boil, stir in the Irish moss. When the boiling time is over, turn off the heat and put a hops bag containing the Columbus hops, white sage, juniper berries, and caraway seeds in the kettle. Cover the kettle and immediately begin cooling the wort quickly (see page 160).

Pitching the Yeast and Fermentation

Once the wort has cooled to 72°F, remove the hops bags and discard their content. Check the specific gravity of the wort with a hydrometer. The target starting gravity is 1.087 (21 Plato).

Transfer the wort to the primary fermentation bucket according to the instructions on page 160. Pitch the yeast (or prepare a yeast starter) according to the instructions on page 160.

Allow the wort to ferment through primary and secondary fermentation (see page 160) at 72°F until it reaches a specific gravity of 1.021 (5.4 Plato).

Bottling

When you're ready to bottle, clean and sanitize the bottles, caps, and bottling equipment. Put the dried malt extract in a medium saucepan and stir in just enough water to dissolve it. Bring the mixture to a boil over high heat. Remove from the heat, cover, and let cool slightly. Proceed with bottling according to the instructions on page 161.

ADVANCED:
JOLLY PUMPKIN / NØGNE-Ø / STONE
SPECIAL HOLIDAY ALE

52.5% crushed North American two-row pale malt

25.2% crushed rye malt

9.3% crushed Munich malt

5.5% crushed 150L crystal malt

5.0% flaked oats

1.5% crushed Special B malt

1.0% crushed chocolate malt

2.0 lb/bbl dried chestnuts

Conversion temperature 156°F [30 minutes]

Mash out 165°F

0.19 lb/bbl German Perle hops (10.0% alpha acid) [90 minutes]

0.67 lb/bbl Columbus hops (12.9% alpha acid) [0 minutes]

0.013 lb/bbl white sage [0 minutes]

0.066 lb/bbl juniper berries [0 minutes]

0.093 lb/bbl caraway seeds [0 minutes]

White Labs WLP007 Dry English Ale Yeast or WLP002 English Ale Yeast

Pitch rate 25

Starting gravity 1.087 (21 Plato)

Final gravity 1.021 (5.4 Plato)

Ferment at 72°F

BrewDog / Cambridge / Stone
JUXTAPOSITION BLACK PILSNER

5 gallons (about fifty-four 12-ounce bottles or thirty 22-ounce bottles)

18 pounds, 4.2 ounces crushed German pilsner malt

2 pounds, 10.2 ounces crushed Vienna malt

1 pound, 1.6 ounces crushed Carafa III malt

0.65 ounce Sorachi Ace hops (10.5% alpha acid)

About 10 gallons plus 4 cups water

0.65 ounce Sorachi Ace hops (10.5% alpha acid)

2.58 ounces Motueka hops (8.5% alpha acid)

2.58 ounces Sorachi Ace hops (10.5% alpha acid)

1/2 teaspoon Irish moss

2.58 ounces Saphir hops (4.0% alpha acid)

2.58 ounces Motueka hops (8.5% alpha acid)

1 (125 ml) package Wyeast Labs WY2206 Bavarian Lager Yeast

1.94 ounces Saphir hops (4.0% alpha acid)

0.65 ounce Sorachi Ace hops (10.5% alpha acid)

1 cup plus 3 tablespoons light dried malt extract

I can't stress it enough: clean and sanitize everything.

Mashing

In a 10-gallon brew kettle, combine the crushed malts and the first 0.65 ounce of Sorachi Ace hops with 6 gallons plus 14 cups of 162°F water. The water should cool slightly when mixed with the grain. Cover and hold the mash at 148°F for 60 minutes.

For safety's sake, set up your propane burner outside. Set the brew kettle of mash on top and heat to 160°F, stirring frequently to avoid scorching. Turn off the heat. The mash will continue to increase in temperature to about 165°F.

Lautering and Sparging

Lauter the mash according to the instructions on page 159. After recirculating the initial cloudy wort runoff over the grain, put a hops bag containing the second 0.65 ounce of Sorachi Ace hops in the brew kettle. (Adding hops at this stage is called first wort hopping.) Allow the wort to continue draining from the lauter tun into the brew kettle as usual. Once the liquid is lower than the level of the grain, begin to slowly sprinkle 3 gallons plus 4 cups of 168°F water over the grains to start the sparge. Continue sparging as instructed on page 159.

The Boil

Set the brew kettle of wort on your outdoor propane burner and add water to bring the wort level up to about 6 gallons plus 12 cups, if needed. Bring the wort to a rapid, rolling boil. As it begins to come to a boil, a layer of foam and scum may develop at the surface. Skim it off and discard. Divide the first 2.58 ounces of Saphir and Moteuka hops into 10 equal portions. Once the wort is at a full boil, add 1 portion of the hops to a large hops bag or a grain bag and add it to the kettle, tying it to one of the kettle handles so it's easily retrieved for further hop additions. (Or use 10 hops bags; your choice.) Set a timer for 90 minutes. Stir the wort frequently during the boil, and be watchful to avoid boilovers. Every 10 minutes, *carefully* lift the bag from the wort using tongs and insulated rubber electrical gloves and add an another portion of the Saphir and Motueka hops to it. (Or add each portion in its own bag if you're going that route.)

At 15 minutes before the end of the boil, stir in the Irish moss. When the boiling time is over, turn off the heat. Add the remaining 2.58 ounces of Saphir and Matueka hops to the hops bag or put them in another hops bag and add it to the kettle. Cover the kettle and immediately begin cooling the wort quickly (see page 160).

Pitching the Yeast and Fermentation

Once the wort has cooled to 50°F, discard the spent hops and check the specific gravity of the wort with a hydrometer. The target starting gravity is 1.101 (24 Plato).

Transfer the wort to the primary fermentation bucket according to the instructions on page 160. Pitch the yeast (or prepare a yeast starter) according to the instructions on page 160.

Ferment at 50°F. Because of the colder temperature, expect longer fermentation times. After primary fermentation has completed (about 14 to 18 days), transfer the wort to a carboy for dry hopping and secondary fermentation (see page 160).

Dry Hopping

Put the 1.94 ounces of Saphir hops and 0.65 ounce of Sorachi Ace hops in a hops bag and put it in the carboy. Seal the carboy with the drilled stopper and an airlock filled halfway with water. Let the beer ferment at 50°F for 60 days, removing and discarding the dry hops once 2 weeks have passed.

After 60 days, check the specific gravity. If it's reached the target final gravity of 1.021 (5.2 Plato), it's ready to bottle. If not, raise the fermenting temperature to 55°F and allow it to continue fermenting until it reaches the target.

Bottling

When you're ready to bottle, clean and sanitize the bottles, caps, and bottling equipment. Put the dried malt extract in a medium saucepan and stir in just enough water to dissolve it. Bring the mixture to a boil over high heat. Remove from the heat, cover, and let cool slightly. Proceed with bottling according to the instructions on page 161.

ADVANCED:
BrewDog/Cambridge/Stone
JUXTAPOSITION BLACK PILSNER

83.0% crushed German pilsner malt

12.0% crushed Vienna malt

5.0% crushed Carafa III malt

0.25 lb/bbl Sorachi Ace hops (10.5% alpha acid)

Conversion temperature 148°F [60 minutes]

Mash out 165°F

0.25 lb/bbl Sorachi Ace hops (10.5% alpha acid)
   [First wort hop]

For the boil, divide:

1.00 lb/bbl Motueka hops (8.5% alpha acid) and

1.00 lb/bbl Sorachi Ace hops (10.5% alpha acid)
   into 10 equal portions

Add 1 portion every 10 minutes for 90 minutes

1.00 lb/bbl Saphir hops (4.0% alpha acid)
   [0 minutes]

1.00 lb/bbl Motueka hops (8.5% alpha acid)
   [0 minutes]

Wyeast Labs WY2206 Bavarian Lager Yeast

Pitch rate 25 to 30

0.75 lb/bbl Saphir hops (4.0% alpha acid)
   [Dry hop, 14 days]

0.25 lb/bbl Sorachi Ace hops (10.5% alpha acid)
   [Dry hop, 14 days]

Starting gravity 1.101 (24 Plato)

Final gravity 1.021 (5.2 Plato)

Ferment at 50°F (primary: 14 to 18 days; secondary: about 60 days)

21ST AMENDMENT / FIRESTONE WALKER / STONE
EL CAMINO (UN)REAL BLACK ALE

5 gallons (about fifty-four 12-ounce bottles or thirty 22-ounce bottles)

15 pounds, 0.6 ounce crushed North American two-row pale malt

1 pound, 1.8 ounces crushed CaraMunich malt

1 pound, 0.2 ounce crushed Special B malt

14.1 ounces crushed Carafa III malt

12.8 ounces crushed roasted barley

8.0 ounces flaked oats

7.0 ounces crushed chocolate malt (U.K.)

About 10 gallons water

1 pound, 3.5 ounces Belgian dark candi sugar

2.06 ounces Challenger hops (6.5% alpha acid)

1/2 teaspoon Irish moss

1.29 ounces East Kent Goldings hops (4.5% alpha acid)

1.50 ounces Styrian Goldings hops (5.4% alpha acid)

0.46 ounce whole fennel seeds

0.46 ounce whole chia seeds

0.26 ounce whole pink peppercorns

1 (35 ml) package White Labs WLP001 California Ale Yeast

0.9 ounce dried black Mission figs, chopped and soaked in bourbon for 4 hours

1.70 ounces Styrian Goldings hops (5.4% alpha acid)

8.0 ounces oak chips

1 cup plus 3 tablespoons light dried malt extract

I can't stress it enough: clean and sanitize everything.

Mashing

In a 10-gallon brew kettle, combine the crushed malts roasted barley, and flaked oats with 6 gallons plus 3 cups of 163°F water. The water should cool slightly when mixed with the grain. Cover and hold the mash at 149°F for 60 minutes.

For safety's sake, set up your propane burner outside. Set the brew kettle of mash on top and heat to 160°F, stirring frequently to avoid scorching. Turn off the heat. The mash will continue to increase in temperature to about 165°F.

Lautering and Sparging

Lauter the mash according to the instructions on page 159. Once the liquid is lower than the level of the grain, begin to slowly sprinkle 3 gallons plus 12 cups of 168°F water over the grains to start the sparge. Continue sparging as instructed on page 159.

The Boil

Set the brew kettle of wort on your outdoor propane burner and add the Belgian dark candi sugar to the wort and stir to combine. Add water to bring the wort level up to about 6 gallons plus 12 cups, if needed. Bring the wort to a rapid, rolling boil. As it begins to come to a boil, a layer of foam and scum may develop at the surface. Skim it off and discard. Once the wort is at a full boil, put a hops bag containing the Challenger hops in the kettle and set a timer for 90 minutes. Stir the wort frequently during the boil, and be watchful to avoid boilovers.

At 15 minutes before the end of the boil, stir in the Irish moss. At 10 minutes before the end of the boil, put a hops bag containing the East Kent Goldings hops in the kettle. When the boiling time is over, turn off the heat and put a hops bag containing the 1.50 ounces Styrian Goldings hops, fennel seeds, chia seeds, and pink peppercorns in the kettle. Cover the kettle and immediately begin cooling the wort quickly (see page 160).

Pitching the Yeast and Fermentation

Once the wort has cooled to 68°F, discard the spent hops and check the specific gravity of the wort with a hydrometer. The target starting gravity is 1.096 (23 Plato).

Transfer the wort to the primary fermentation bucket according to the instructions on page 160. Pitch the yeast (or prepare a yeast starter) according to the instructions on page 160.

Allow the wort to ferment through primary fermentation (see page 160) at 68 to 70°F, then transfer the wort to a carboy for dry hopping, oaking, and secondary fermentation (see page 160).

Dry Hopping

Put the 1.70 ounces of Styrian Goldings hops and the figs in a hops bag. (Use that fig-infused bourbon to make yourself a righteous figgy Manhattan.) Put the oak chips in a separate hops bag. Put both bags in the carboy. Seal the carboy with the drilled stopper and an airlock filled halfway with water, and ferment at 68 to 70°F.

After 3 days, remove the bag with the oak chips and discard the oak chips. After 4 more days, remove the bag with the dry hops and figs and discard its contents. Check the specific gravity of the beer. If it's reached the target final gravity of 1.021 (5.2 Plato), it's ready to bottle. If not, allow it to continue fermenting at 68 to 70°F until it reaches the target.

Bottling

When you're ready to bottle, clean and sanitize the bottles, caps, and bottling equipment. Put the dried malt extract in a medium saucepan and stir in just enough water to dissolve it. Bring the mixture to a boil over high heat. Remove from the heat, cover, and let cool slightly. Proceed with bottling according to the instructions on page 161.

ADVANCED:
21ST AMENDMENT/FIRESTONE WALKER/STONE EL CAMINO (UN)REAL BLACK ALE

71.6% crushed North American two-row pale malt

5.3% crushed CaraMunich malt

4.8% crushed Special B malt

4.2% crushed Carafa III malt

3.8% crushed roasted barley

2.4% flaked oats

2.1% crushed chocolate malt (U.K.)

Conversion temperature 149°F [60 minutes]

Mash out 165°F

5.8% Belgian dark candi sugar [90 minutes]

0.80 lb/bbl Challenger hops (6.5% alpha acid) [90 minutes]

0.50 lb/bbl East Kent Goldings hops (4.5% alpha acid) [10 minutes]

0.58 lb/bbl Styrian Goldings hops (5.4% alpha acid) [0 minutes]

0.18 lb/bbl fennel seeds [0 minutes]

0.18 lb/bbl chia seeds [0 minutes]

0.10 lb/bbl pink peppercorns [0 minutes]

White Labs WLP001 California Ale Yeast

Pitch rate 25

0.66 lb/bbl Styrian Goldings hops (5.4% alpha acid) [Dry hop, 7 days]

0.35 lb/bbl dried black Mission figs, chopped and soaked in bourbon for 4 hours [Secondary fermentation, steep 7 days]

3.1 lb/bbl oak chips [Secondary fermentation, steep 3 days]

Starting gravity 1.096 (23 Plato)

Final gravity 1.021 (5.2 Plato)

Ferment at 68 to 70°F

Dogfish Head / Victory / Stone
SAISON DU BUFF

5 gallons (about fifty-four 12-ounce bottles or thirty 22-ounce bottles)

4 pounds, 15.8 ounces crushed German pilsner malt

4 pounds, 15.4 ounces crushed North American two-row pale malt

1 pound, 14.6 ounces crushed wheat malt

10.2 ounces flaked rye

About 9 gallons plus 4 cups water

0.58 ounce Centennial hops (9.8% alpha acid)

1/2 teaspoon Irish moss

2.58 ounces Amarillo hops (8.5% alpha acid)

0.24 ounce fresh parsley

0.09 ounce fresh rosemary

0.09 ounce fresh lemon thyme

0.04 ounce fresh white sage

1 (125 ml) package Wyeast Labs WY3711 French Saison Yeast

0.77 ounce Citra hops (11.0% alpha acid)

1 cup plus 3 tablespoons light dried malt extract

I can't stress it enough: clean and sanitize everything.

Mashing

In a 10-gallon brew kettle, combine the crushed malts and flaked rye with 4 gallons of 163°F water. The water should cool slightly when mixed with the grain. Cover and hold the mash at 149°F for 2 hours.

For safety's sake, set up your propane burner outside. Set the brew kettle of mash on top and heat to 160°F, stirring frequently to avoid scorching. Turn off the heat. The mash will continue to increase in temperature to about 165°F.

Lautering and Sparging

Lauter the mash according to the instructions on page 159. Once the liquid is lower than the level of the grain, begin to slowly sprinkle 5 gallons plus 1 cup of 168°F water over the grains to start the sparge. Continue sparging as instructed on page 159.

The Boil

Set the brew kettle of wort on your outdoor propane burner and add water to bring the wort level up to about 6 gallons plus 12 cups, if needed. Bring the wort to a rapid, rolling boil. As it begins to come to a boil, a layer of foam and scum may develop at the surface. Skim it off and discard. Once the wort is at a full boil, put a hops bag containing the Centennial hops in the kettle and set a timer for 90 minutes. Stir the wort frequently during the boil, and be watchful to avoid boilovers.

At 15 minutes before the end of the boil, stir in the Irish moss. When the boiling time is over, turn off the heat and put a hops bag containing the Amarillo hops, parsley, rosemary, lemon thyme, and white sage in the kettle. Cover the kettle and immediately begin cooling the wort quickly (see page 160).

Pitching the Yeast and Fermentation

Once the wort has cooled to 70°F, discard the spent hops and herbs and check the specific gravity of the wort with a hydrometer. The target starting gravity is 1.059 (14.5 Plato).

Transfer the wort to the primary fermentation bucket according to the instructions on page 160. Pitch the yeast (or prepare a yeast starter) according to the instructions on page 160.

Allow the wort to ferment through primary fermentation (see page 160) at 70°F, then transfer the wort to a carboy for dry hopping and secondary fermentation (see page 160).

Dry Hopping

Put the Citra hops in a hops bag and put it in the carboy. Seal the carboy with the drilled stopper and an airlock filled halfway with water and ferment at 70°F.

After 7 days, dry hopping is complete. Remove the hops bag and discard the hops. Check the specific gravity of the beer. If it's reached the target final gravity of 1.007 (1.8 Plato), it's ready to bottle. If not, allow it to continue fermenting at 70°F until it reaches the target.

Bottling

When you're ready to bottle, clean and sanitize the bottles, caps, and bottling equipment. Put the dried malt extract in a medium saucepan and stir in just enough water to dissolve it. Bring the mixture to a boil over high heat. Remove from the heat, cover, and let cool slightly. Proceed with bottling according to the instructions on page 160.

ADVANCED:
Dogfish Head/Victory/Stone
SAISON DU BUFF

39.9% crushed German pilsner malt

39.7% crushed North American two-row pale malt

15.3% crushed American wheat malt

5.1% flaked rye

Conversion temperature 149°F [2 hours]

Mash out 165°F

0.224 lb/bbl Centennial hops (9.8% alpha acid) [90 minutes]

1.00 lb/bbl Amarillo hops (8.5% alpha acid) [0 minutes]

0.093 lb/bbl fresh parsley [0 minutes]

0.033 lb/bbl fresh rosemary [0 minutes]

0.033 lb/bbl fresh lemon thyme [0 minutes]

0.013 lb/bbl fresh white sage [0 minutes]

1 (125 ml) package Wyeast Labs WY3711 French Saison Yeast

Pitch rate 25

0.30 lb/bbl Citra hops (11.0% alpha acid) [Dry hop, 7 days]

Starting gravity 1.059 (14.5 Plato)

Final gravity 1.007 (1.8 Plato)

Ferment at 70°F

Ballast Point / Kelsey McNair / Stone
SAN DIEGO COUNTY SESSION ALE

5 gallons (about fifty-four 12-ounce bottles or thirty 22-ounce bottles)

1¼ teaspoons gypsum (calcium sulfate, a natural water salt)

   About 8 gallons plus 12 cups water

7 pounds, 7.7 ounces crushed North American two-row pale malt

6.7 ounces crushed Carapils malt

6.7 ounces crushed 60L crystal malt

1.4 ounces crushed CaraVienne malt

1.4 ounces crushed honey malt

0.31 ounce Warrior hops (17.0% alpha acid)

1.55 ounces Columbus hops (12.9% alpha acid)

½ teaspoon Irish moss

1.55 ounces Amarillo hops (8.5% alpha acid)

1.55 ounces Simcoe hops (13.0% alpha acid)

0.72 ounce Amarillo hops (8.5% alpha acid)

0.72 ounce Centennial hops (10.0% alpha acid)

0.72 ounce Citra hops (11.0% alpha acid)

0.72 ounce Columbus hops (12.9% alpha acid)

0.72 ounce Simcoe hops (13.0% alpha acid)

1 (35 ml) package White Labs WLP001 California Ale Yeast

0.72 ounce Amarillo hops (8.5% alpha acid)

0.72 ounce Centennial hops (10.0% alpha acid)

0.72 ounce Citra hops (11.0% alpha acid)

0.72 ounce Columbus hops (12.9% alpha acid)

0.72 ounce Simcoe hops (13.0% alpha acid)

1 cup plus 3 tablespoons light dried malt extract

I can't stress it enough: clean and sanitize everything.

Mashing

Mix the gypsum with 4 gallons plus 3 cups of water. Heat 2 gallons plus 11 cups of the treated water to 172°F. In a separate pot, heat the remaining 1 gallon plus 8 cups to 184°F. In a 10-gallon insulated cooler, combine the crushed malts with the 2 gallons plus 11 cups of 172°F water. The water should cool slightly when mixed with the grain. Hold the mash at 157°F for 20 minutes.

Add the 1 gallon plus 8 cups of 184°F water. The mixture should come up to 165°F.

Lautering and Sparging

Lauter the mash according to the instructions on page 159. Once the liquid is lower than the level of the grain, begin to slowly sprinkle 4 gallons plus 7 cups of 168°F water over the grains to start the sparge. Continue sparging as instructed on page 159.

The Boil

For safety's sake, set up your propane burner outside. Set the brew kettle of wort on top and add water to bring the wort level up to about 6 gallons plus 12 cups, if needed. Bring the wort to a rapid, rolling boil. As it begins to come to a boil, a layer of foam and scum may develop at the surface. Skim it off and discard. Once the wort is at a full boil, put a hops bag containing the 0.31 ounce Warrior hops in the kettle and set a timer for 90 minutes. Stir the wort frequently during the boil, and be watchful to avoid boilovers.

At 30 minutes before the end of the boil, put a hops bag containing the 1.55 ounces of Columbus hops in the kettle. At 15 minutes before the end of the boil, stir in the Irish moss, then add a hops bag containing the 1.55 ounces each of Amarillo and Simcoe hops. When the boiling time is over, turn off the heat. Put the first 0.72 ounce each of Amarillo, Centennial, Citra, Columbus, and Simcoe hops in a hops bag and add it to the wort. Cover the kettle and immediately begin cooling the wort quickly (see page 160).

Pitching the Yeast and Fermentation

Once the wort has cooled to 70°F, discard the spent hops and check the specific gravity of the wort with a hydrometer. The target starting gravity is 1.042 (10.5 Plato).

Transfer the wort to the primary fermentation bucket according to the instructions on page 160. Pitch the yeast (or prepare a yeast starter) according to the instructions on page 160.

Allow the wort to ferment through primary fermentation (see page 160) at 72°F, then transfer the wort to a carboy for dry hopping and secondary fermentation (see page 160).

Dry Hopping

Put the second 0.72 ounce each of Amarillo, Centennial, Citra, Columbus, and Simcoe hops in a hops bag and put it in the carboy. Seal the carboy with the drilled stopper and an airlock filled halfway with water and ferment at 72°F.

After 7 days, dry hopping is complete. Remove the hops bag and discard the hops. Check the specific gravity of the beer. If it's reached the target final gravity of 1.009 (2.3 Plato), it's ready to bottle. If not, allow it to continue fermenting at 72°F until it reaches the target.

Bottling

When you're ready to bottle, clean and sanitize the bottles, caps, and bottling equipment. Put the dried malt extract in a medium saucepan and stir in just enough water to dissolve it. Bring the mixture to a boil over high heat. Remove from the heat, cover, and let cool slightly. Proceed with bottling according to the instructions on page 161.

ADVANCED:
Bᴀʟʟᴀsᴛ Pᴏɪɴᴛ/Kᴇʟsᴇʏ McNᴀɪʀ/Sᴛᴏɴᴇ
SAN DIEGO COUNTY SESSION ALE

Mash water adjusted to about 250 ppm sulfate

88.0% crushed North American two-row pale malt

5.0% crushed Carapils malt

5.0% crushed 60L crystal malt

1.0% crushed CaraVienne malt

1.0% crushed honey malt

Conversion temperature 157°F [20 minutes]

Mash out 165°F

0.12 lb/bbl Warrior hops (17.0 % alpha acid)
   [90 minutes]

0.60 lb/bbl Columbus hops (12.9% alpha acid)
   [30 minutes]

0.60 lb/bbl Amarillo hops (8.5% alpha acid)
   [15 minutes]

0.60 lb/bbl Simcoe hops (13.0% alpha acid)
   [15 minutes]

0.28 lb/bbl Amarillo hops (8.5% alpha acid)
   [0 minutes]

0.28 lb/bbl Centennial hops (10.0% alpha acid)
   [0 minutes]

0.28 lb/bbl Citra hops (11.0% alpha acid)
   [0 minutes]

0.28 lb/bbl Columbus hops (12.9% alpha acid)
   [0 minutes]

0.28 lb/bbl Simcoe hops (13.0% alpha acid)
   [0 minutes]

White Labs WLP001 California Ale Yeast

Pitch rate 12 to 14

0.28 lb/bbl Amarillo hops (8.5% alpha acid)
   [Dry hop, 7 days]

0.28 lb/bbl Centennial hops (10.0% alpha acid)
   [Dry hop, 7 days]

0.28 lb/bbl Citra hops (11.0% alpha acid)
   [Dry hop, 7 days]

0.28 lb/bbl Columbus hops (12.9% alpha acid)
   [Dry hop, 7 days]

0.28 lb/bbl Simcoe hops (13.0% alpha acid)
   [Dry hop, 7 days]

Starting gravity 1.042 (10.5 Plato)

Final gravity 1.009 (2.3 Plato)

Ferment at 72°F

INDEX

Ten Speed Press and the Ten Speed Press colophon are registered trademarks of Random House, Inc.
Photographs copyright © 1997–2011 by John Schulz Photography, www.studioschulz.com
Photographs pages 6, 11, 30, 34, 36, 37, 38, 41, 45, 46, 49, 50, 51, 57, 63, 65, 68, 74, 79, 81, 82, 86, 93, 98, 99, 101, 102, 103, 122, 126, 127, 155 courtesy Stone Brewing Co.
Photograph page 24 courtesy Anchor Brewing Company
Photograph page 25 courtesy Charlie Papazian
Photographs page 62 courtesy Belgian Brewers
Photograph pages 118–119 courtesy Darren Bradley
Illustration page 84 courtesy Arne Frantzell

Library of Congress Cataloging-in-Publication Data is on file with the publisher.

ISBN 978-1-60774-055-1

Printed in China on paper sourced in accordance with sustainable forest management and recycled content

Design by Julie White and Colleen Cain

10 9 8 7 6 5 4 3 2

First Edition